# Self-Improvement for Men

*Accelerate Your Career and Optimize Your Relationships by applying Emotional Intelligence, Thinking Models and Memory Techniques Used by the Rich for High Productivity*

**By**

*John Adams*

# © Copyright 2019 - All rights reserved.

The content contained within this book may not be reproduced, duplicated or transmitted without direct written permission from the author or the publisher.

Under no circumstances will any blame or legal responsibility be held against the publisher, or author, for any damages, reparation, or monetary loss due to the information contained within this book. Either directly or indirectly.

Legal Notice:

This book is copyright protected. This book is only for personal use. You cannot amend, distribute, sell, use, quote or paraphrase any part, or the content within this book, without the consent of the author or publisher.

Disclaimer Notice:

Please note the information contained within this document is for educational and entertainment purposes only. All effort has been executed to present accurate, up to date, and reliable, complete information. No warranties of any kind are declared or implied. Readers acknowledge that the author is not engaging in the rendering of legal, financial, medical or professional advice. The content within this book has been derived from various sources. Please consult a licensed professional before attempting any techniques outlined in this book.

By reading this document, the reader agrees that under no circumstances is the author responsible for any losses, direct or indirect, which are incurred as a result of the use of the information contained within this document, including, but not limited to, — errors, omissions, or inaccuracies.

# Table Of Contents

**Part 1: Practical Thought Models for Men**   9

  Introduction   11

  Chapter 1: I Don't Use Models, Or Do I?   19

  Chapter 2: I Know It Better... Or Not?   35

  Chapter 3: Let's Do It Like This... Or Wait... Maybe...   57

  Chapter 4: This Can Be Done Faster...   83

  Chapter 5: Getting Want You Want... Like This   115

**Part 2: Memory Improvement, Accelerated Learning and Brain Training**   **141**

  Introduction – Know Your Brain   143

  Chapter 1: Memory: An Evidence Of Your Existence   151

  Chapter 2: Memory Types and Their Need   161

  Chapter 3: Memory Preferences and Brain Waves: Accelerating Your Learning Channels   171

  Chapter 4: Visual Mnemonics: Tools & Techniques   187

  Chapter 5: Verbal Mnemonics: Tools & Techniques   207

  Chapter 6: Food for Your Memory   213

  Chapter 7: Physical Fitness for Improved Memory and Brain Function   225

  Chapter 8: The Importance and Influence of Sleep   235

  Chapter 9: Studying Hard Is Old School, Study Smart for Exams   245

  Chapter 10: Bring Your A-game at Work   253

  Chapter 11: Mistakes and Learning: How to Get Fastest Results   265

  Chapter 12: What You May Not Be Aware Of   277

**Part 3: Masculine Emotional Intelligence**   **291**

  Introduction   293

Chapter 1: Human Emotions . . . 299
Chapter 2: The EQ Models . . . 331
Chapter 3: Be Aware of Yourself . . . 339
Chapter 4: Regulate Yourself . . . 351
Chapter 5: Recognizing Emotions . . . 363
Chapter 6: Social Skills . . . 379
Chapter 7: 30 Day Emotional Intelligence Booster Program . . . 389
Conclusion . . . 409

**References** . . . **415**

**Hello,**

As an independent author,
 and one-man operation
 - my marketing budget is next to zero.

As such, the only way
 I can get my books in front of valued customers
 is with reviews.

Unfortunately, I'm competing against authors and
 giant publishing companies
 with multi-million-dollar marketing teams.

These behemoths can afford
 to give away hundreds of free books
 to boost their ranking and success.

Which as much as I'd love to –
 I simply can't afford to do.

That's why your honest review
 will not only be invaluable to me,
 but also to other readers.

Happy reading,

**John Adams**

# Part 1: Practical Thought Models for Men

*Use mental techniques of the world´s greatest leaders to make better decisions, conquer any obstacle, build self-confidence and make lasting progress in life and work*

# Introduction

It feels great to set definite goals, work towards them, and achieve them. Although this may not happen 100% of the time, it is still a great morale booster. On the flip side, it is frustrating to have most of your best efforts truncated because of poor decisions, wrong choices, and error in judgment. The experience of continuous failure can be demoralizing and can lead to throwing in the towel. This unpleasant experience seems to be the lot of the average modern man (and woman too!) who are continually faced with several challenges, which they must overcome or risk feeling insignificant.

As a man, your challenges may appear peculiar to you depending on what you are trying to accomplish, your priorities in life, and what is most important to you, but the truth is that you are in the same boat with more people than you realize. You may be trying to:

- Overcome procrastination and get things done at the right time.
- Manage your anger which tends to be destroying a lot of your personal and professional relationships.
- Improve the communication that you've found to be ineffective and lead to frequent misunderstandings and unsaid intentions.
- Cope with the stress of a demanding job or career.
- Raise your teenagers in the best way possible without losing your mind.
- Manage your lean finances – a feat for which many people seem to lack the very fundamentals.

- Improve your time management by strictly keeping family and work completely separate or figuring out how best to share your time between your team and your primary schedule.
- Work on improving your failing self-confidence, poor self-esteem, and a general poor self-image.
- Overcoming lust and pornography – two factors that are negatively affecting your relationship with the opposite sex.
- Improve your failing marriage or struggling to fix intimacy issues.
- Overcome addiction to alcohol or other unhealthy substances.
- Reduce weight and stay true to a diet program.
- Overcome pride that can lead to living in denial or refusing to admit that you even have issues with these challenges to begin with.

Whatever your particular situation is, you are not alone. Every single adult, regardless of race, belief, gender, financial status, and so on, has one or more challenging situations that they are working to overcome. The difference is that while successful people have internalized certain principles that help them learn faster, think better, and decide smarter, the majority of the other "struggling" people are groping in the darkness of erroneous thinking patterns.

It doesn't matter how well-intentioned you are, if you live your life based on a false premise or based on faulty thinking, your results will most likely be short of what you truly desire. This brings to mind the picture of a bird smashing into a glass window in the hope of getting to the vegetation reflected on the glass or in the hope of flying through it as it reflects the sky. Although the bird can see the glass, its limited or faulty thinking pattern (its mental model) does not permit it to see the error in its interpretation of reality. Forcefully, it hits the glass and dies on the spot or gets stunned and gradually recovers to try again using the same pattern of thinking!

Repeating the same thing can only guarantee one outcome: the same result! This can be tiring and frustrating (not for the birds; I'm talking about us humans!) It is the frustration that comes from repeated failure that often leads to some ridiculous conclusions about cause and effect. The worst kind of thinking would be to attribute your repeated failures to some spiritual forces which are meddling in your personal affairs. As much as that could be a plausible argument, your best bet to making failure a less-occurring feature in your life is to change your thought patterns.

We are all on a journey of seeking the truth (about different aspects of our lives), problem-solving, and decision making. Every single day, and for more times than we care to note, we make decisions. It seems our lives are a string of decisions and choices. This means that the more wrong choices we make, the unhappier our lives will be. And the righter choices or decisions we make, the happier and more fulfilled our lives will be. Therefore, we must devote our time to learning methods that can help us make sense of our daily challenging situations, help us generate better ideas, and also help us in our decision-making process. In other words, we must give our undivided attention to developing ways that can help us approach challenging situations in more innovative and novel ways. This can only be possible if we are willing to be malleable and give up the thinking patterns that are no longer useful to us, irrespective of how dear they are to us.

You do not need to have a desire to be the next Albert Einstein or Jeff Bezos for you to find this book useful. As a matter of fact, this book was primarily written for those who simply want to make sense of their day-to-day challenges and live a more fulfilled life, even if that means simplifying their decision-making process. Whether you are a parent seeking better ways to handle the upbringing of your children, a team leader at work trying to cope with the stress of leadership, a budding business owner who is in search of better ways to make more profit, or an employee who just wants to improve his career, this book will guide you on how to make quality decisions to improve your quality of thinking. When you make more good decisions than you make bad ones, you improve your chances of getting promoted at work, attracting opportunities in business, gaining more respect from family, friends, and colleagues, and becoming a better person on the whole.

The concepts and ideas that are shared in this book are capable of challenging your assumptions and tightly held beliefs about life. But beyond challenging your suppositions, beliefs, and specific ways of thinking, this book will feed your mind and help you to become wiser and more discerning of situations. The goal of this book is to help men the world over live a more fulfilled and meaningful life by sharing thought-provoking mental models that will nudge them towards making fewer wrong choices.

Although this book, Mental Model for Men, tends to be gender-biased, women too can benefit immensely from it because the mental models work based on principles that are not gender-based.

Society tends to put the responsibility for living successful lives more on the shoulders of men. We have come to accept that the man should fend for his family (wife and children) and that is not a light burden. The pressure from the home front and that from work can make the average man cringe in pain. But with the right mental model, he can leverage time-tested principles and succeed faster than his peers.

This book will present several short stories of successful men in many areas of life, great leaders, and captains of industry, all of whom have had cause to face challenges similar to the ones you are facing today and overcame. Nevertheless, the focus of this book is not successful people; instead, the focus is on the methods that brought about their success. Often, it can be annoying to read about business moguls and their huge financial empires when you can barely stop yourself from losing money on your tiny investments. I do not intend to wow you with the impressive achievements of famous people. No. Those are not the types of stories I intend to share with you. To begin with, you may not even be interested in becoming a captain of any industry or a leader in your company. My goal for presenting you with some of these inspiring stories is to demonstrate the practicability of these mental models in everyday life.

This book shall take you through some of your biases and prejudices that are preventing you from objectively considering your situations and the many challenging issues that confront your almost daily. We shall take a somewhat rollercoaster ride across several mental models to help you see your live events from different perspectives because the more you can master multiple mental models, the more options and approaches you can apply to different situations in your life.

But beyond different mental models, this book will help you to understand how to apply these models in your life. I have downplayed the theories and academic works relating to mental models and presented only the facts and details you need to make high-quality decisions, simply your decision-making process, and reduce your biases. Therefore, expect to get information that can:

- Help you make faster decisions.
- Work more efficiently as you apply simple but effective principles.
- Help you gain new insights on how to overcome the challenges that are making you feel stuck in your professional and personal life.

As much as I would like for you to quickly devour the contents of this book, I encourage you to take your time to comprehend the information contained in this book. Keep in mind that, as with many other things in life, consistent practice is what leads to mastery. You're not going to magically transform your thought processes or thinking pattern by merely reading this book or any other for that matter! A lot of effort is required on your part – the practical application of what you have learned.

I urge you to begin with baby steps. Apply these mental models consistently and see how they positively impact one simple area of your life where you do not have serious challenges. Little by little, you will gain more confidence to take on more challenging areas of your life. In all likelihood, the positive changes you seek will not happen overnight, but it will definitely happen if you remain consistent.

Here is to a happy and more fulfilled you as you learn and apply the mental models of the ultra-successful of our world.

# Chapter 1: I Don't Use Models, Or Do I?

Picture in your mind's eye for a minute, a drunk frantically looking for his house keys at night, but he is only searching under the streetlight because his hazed mind tells him that's where the light is. He can only see where there is light, so he doesn't bother to look for his keys where there is no light. Perhaps, if he were sober, he could have figured out that his keys could be anywhere whether there was light or not.

Analogies are hardly perfect, but the above scenario captures the essence of mental models. You can only figure out things to the extent your mental model permits. If you have a mental model of the drunk, your search for success, more money, efficiency, time management, love, and so on, will be limited to where there is light. You will not bother to look where the beam of the streetlight can't reach because your model doesn't support it. Your life can only be as great as your mental models.

To assess whether your mental models are good and useful, you should evaluate the results you have in every aspect of your life. For many people, this assessment has driven them to search for better ways to approach their life's challenges. And that search has resulted in reading this book. They understand that to effectively change their approach, there is a need to adjust their internal picture of how the world works.

But what if you don't use a mental model? Or do we all use one?

Well, to answer that, let's first see what mental models are.

## Mental Models Explained

According to the Business Dictionary website, mental models are "Beliefs, ideas, images, and verbal descriptions that we consciously or unconsciously form from our experiences and which (when formed) guide our thoughts and actions within narrow channels" (BusinessDictionary.com, n.d.). In simple English, a mental model is a mental representation of your world's view. It is your perception of what reality is (and isn't) and it plays a major role in how you behave and respond to the situations you encounter daily.

When you picture a challenging situation your mind predicts or figures out an outcome using a set of ideas and assumptions you have built over time, that is your mental model at work. We all use mental models in our daily lives. It doesn't matter whether you are aware of it or not; it certainly doesn't matter if you took the time to build or formulate one for yourself or not. The fact is that all of us use mental models, and by the way, that's a good thing! Your thought processes about how something works is a mental model for that thing. Your conception of a thing, your expected results and consequences of specific actions, your interpretation of events, and your problem-solving approach are all as a reflection of your mental model.

Here's a simplified example of how mental models work. Let us assume that you are playing a game with a young child of about 7 years old using a scale model of the house you currently live in. The model house is complete with furnishing. You hide a miniature book in the closet of the model house while the child carefully observes the location of the hidden book. Now you ask the child to locate the real book in the real house. Guess where he or she will look first? In the closet! A younger child of 2 or 3 years old may look in several locations before going to the closet. But at 7, the child is wise enough to analogize the house in his head. That is how we all have the world in our heads – as little maps that help use "locate" (figure out) solutions.

In general, we tend to unconsciously develop several mental models from when we were little toddlers. Events that shape our world when we were children tend to shape our perspective for a lifetime unless of course, we deliberately make the effort to change such mental models. For example, if a child grows up in a dysfunctional family where he is exposed to incessant fights, violence, and physical abuse (either on him or between his parents), it wouldn't be surprising for such a child to grow up into thinking and behaving in ways that can result in a series of dysfunctional relationships in his adult years. This is because, over time, he has developed an unhealthy mental model about relationships.

Equally, a boy that grows up in a home where both parents work outside the home tends to build a mental model where both parents need to work to take care of the family. He will likely grow up to prefer women who work outside the home. His choice of a life partner is most likely to be influenced by the mental model he developed while growing up.

You may not realize it, but almost every decisive choice you make and the important action you take in your life passed through the filter of the models you carry around in your head. Just like the 7-year-old who searched first in the closet, your choices and actions, even though they may appear random to you, are dictated by your mental models. Perhaps you need to pause and ask yourself why your default behavior in certain situations is not the same as the next person's default behavior. The answer lies in the behavior of the 7-year-old after observing the model house! Looking first in the closet can be described as a default behavior. When you have observed different models life has exposed you to for a long time, your default behavior will result from such mental models.

So, if your life's results are not too satisfactory or you have been struggling for a while to break free from a streak of failure and struggles, you need to start taking a look at other models that have worked for other people.

## Mental Models: The Good

On one hand, mental models create a sense of internal stability in the individual. This is particularly useful if you consider that the world we live in is constantly changing. I mean, imagine what it will look like if you were to wake up each morning and begin to learn afresh how to approach every single thing in your life all over again (like a 2-year-old kid searching for the hidden book!) There is a need for a certain level of stability to prevent you from being swept by every wind of change. This makes it possible for you to approach challenging situations with time-tested ideologies that worked over and again without wasting time, energy, and resources. If you are losing money or missing out on great opportunities in life, it is an indication that you are working with mental models that are no longer serving you. This means you need to unlearn what you knew previously and learn a new set of mental models.

Periodically, organizations analyze the mental models of their customers (using surveys) to find out what their customers' biases and preferences are and then tailor their products and services towards those biases. Does that not make you want to have a second thought about how important mental models are? I mean, think about it for a minute. Why would multinational corporations go through all the trouble of analyzing mental models of their customers? Here are a few reasons they do that:

- To understand the minds of their customers.
- To gather real-world perspectives about their services.
- To use the information they gathered to improve their customers' experience.
- To guide them to think strategically about the solutions for their customers' problems.
- To expose areas where they are making wrong assumptions about customer's needs.
- To recognize new opportunities.
- To recognize faults in current solutions and seek ways to fix them.

All these translate into more profits, more opportunities, and more customer satisfaction. But we are not talking about companies or customers; our focus is on you – the struggling individual who wants to seize more of his opportunities, make more money, increase his chances of getting promoted, minimize his chances of failure in his investments, managing his time more effectively, get his family life in order, or create more happiness in his life. These can only be achieved by a shift in your thinking processes because your actions result from your thoughts. So, if we can dig down to the faulty thought processes and install a new set of mental models that work, your actions and subsequent results will reflect the new change you seek.

## Mental Models: The Bad

On the other hand, there are some huge drawbacks to mental models. If these drawbacks are not recognized, it can lead the individual into very myopic and incorrect worldviews. As you may have deduced by now, maps are not 100% the same as the real world. What you have in your head as mental models are mere maps; they do not contain every single detail of the real world, nor should they. Overdependence on an analogy, as you know, is like staking your hard-earned money on a leaky bucket; one moment it is full; the next, it is completely empty!

We have to be careful not to be fixated on one mental model. There is no one mental model that is suitable for all situations. As a matter of fact, a mental model that worked for one situation may fail when applied to another situation because, as earlier stated, we live in a constantly changing world. Becoming set in your mental model and refusing to change even when there is glaring evidence that suggests the need for a different approach can lead to unnecessary suffering, loss of time and energy.

This is why many men – good men, I must add – who are working hard on their dreams never seem to achieve those dreams. They put in a lot of effort, but the rewards in terms of money, time, freedom, love, ease, promotion, building teams and systems, and so on, seem to constantly elude them. Reaching your desired goals is not just about being good, nor is it about having noble intentions. It is one thing to want to be a great father, for example, but if your mental model about family and relationship is faulty, then your best intentions will always meet a Waterloo. To correct this, there is a need to properly scrutinize your thought processes with a view to finding out where the error in thinking lies. It is like taking apart the various sections of a faulty computer program to isolate which section is encoded wrongly and causing the error in the entire program – a process known as debugging.

But, just as it happens in effective debugging, you need to think things through before delving into the program code and changing things. Usually, when you shift commands around in the code, that section of the program may work well because you have isolated and fixed the local issue. But another problem will soon arise that will make you start the debugging process all over again. However, when you take the time to think about how the bug (fault or problem) began, you will most likely discover how to improve the entire program design and put a stop to more bugs.

This book is designed to offer you debugging options that will help you dig deep into your ideologies and fish out exactly what has been preventing you from hitting your target in spite of your best intentions. But beyond isolating bugs and faults in thinking and beyond looking at your life's program code line after line to trace where the bugs could be, we shall see how to consider the entire program for each aspect of your life and see what models work best for them. We shall go into various mental models that can be very useful, but first, you need to understand that, like many other things in life, mental models can be fallible.

## Mental Models: A Better Approach

Change is constant! Have I said that enough times yet? Well, there is a reason I keep repeating that. Humans tend to stick to something if it works a few times. We are quick to declare, "I have discovered the truth! This is my secret formula for success!" We then go ahead to overuse that one formula or approach for every problem we face. But the fact that something worked for a particular situation doesn't automatically mean it will work for every situation. We must keep in mind that what we regard as truth is subjective and can become obsolete with time.

Consider, as an example, the approach of Niels Bohr, one of the pioneers of quantum physics, when he was trying to understand the dual nature of matter. (Don't worry; I'm not going to bore you with any physics jargon!) For nearly two decades, Bohr tried to understand why photons show up as waves in an experiment, yet the same photons show up as particles if the experiment is set up another way. It simply doesn't make any sense, nor does it agree with any of the laws of our physical universe known to man at that time. But the real problem Bohr had was in his mental model. He was using an outmoded model to figure out a solution for a phenomenon that is on a higher level of understanding. Niels Bohr finally came to understand that quantum physics was on a higher level of truth than the Newtonian physics the world was used to at that time (Scientific Thought: In Context, 2009).

There were several truths that were displaced by higher truths, not because the lower truths were false, but because they were no longer applicable given the current circumstances. Higher truths, must out of necessity, build on lower truths. For example, Newtonian physics displaced the Aristotelian worldview by building on what was previously true in the Aristotelian era. Einstein's physics displaced the lower truths presented by Newtonian physics, and quantum physics displaced some of the lower truths in Einstein's physics. None of these previously held ideologies were wrong; they only presented solutions based on the level of understanding they were exposed to at that time.

Here's how all this applies to you. When situations change, it will be almost impossible to approach the new change with lower truths or understanding. In other words, having a static mental model is simply a precursor for failure. Remember the analogy in the introduction of the bird flying into the glass window? That's exactly what it looks like when you keep approaching situations with lower truths or outmoded mental models. They may have worked for some situations in the past, but in the light of current events, they are no longer useful. The approach that worked for the successful man in the Stone Age must be discarded in the Iron Age if a man must experience any semblance of success. Equally, the mental model of the Iron Age must give way in the Industrial Age, if a man must make significant progress. You must be open and willing to embrace change that displaces your previously held mental models if you must keep up with changing times and situations.

## *Forget Perfection, Focus on Applicability*

I strongly suggest that you approach the use of mental models from an angle that considers how useful they are in the daily application instead of how perfect the models are. As the famous British statistician, George Box, puts it, "All models are approximations. Essentially, all models are wrong, but some are useful. However, the approximate nature of the model must always be borne in mind" (Box, 1987, p. 424).

In other words, give up the search for one particular "secret" to success! There is no such thing as one mental model that is perfect for all situations. What you should concern yourself with is thinking about the utility of a model rather than its accuracy in all situations. The more a mental model can help you to figure out how to tackle everyday challenges, the better and more useful it is.

However, given the fact that no one mental model is suitable for every situation, your best bet is to be open to developing a collection of mental models that you can use collectively to approach problems and decision making. This makes good sense because the more mental models you can access, the better your chances of making better decisions or fewer wrong decisions. Someone with only a handful of mental models is limited to think from the few models he has. He can't see beyond his limited models; therefore, his choices and subsequent outcomes are limited.

Imagine for a minute that you are a carpenter with only a hammer and a bunch of nails in your tool belt. Hammering nails and banging things into place is about all the options you have. But that is pretty limiting to accomplish any meaning task. This brings to mind the saying, "To the man with only a hammer, every problem looks like a nail!" Now imagine what it would be like to have your tool belt packed and ready with screws, utility knife, hammer, pliers, pencil, nail sets, electrical tape, and a screwdriver. That gives you a whole lot of options and choices. You can fix and invent several things because your creative juices have been given a boost!

That is exactly how having access to several useful mental models work. The more mental models you can apply to different areas of your life, the more you call forth your ingenuity to handle everyday situations.

Here's an example that illustrates how to combine different mental models for boosting creativity in your life. I'll use three different mental models for a fictitious character called Sam.

Lately, Sam has been worried about his productivity level which seems to be consistently going down in recent times. He is a struggling blogger who is trying to break even. He battles with procrastination and a general lack of time management. He feels overwhelmed at the number of things he has to do every day just to stay afloat and not be drowned by his family responsibilities and job demands. He spends more time on his phone chatting with friends because that seems to be the only time he has some sense of happiness, but that habit robs him of his time. Although he is reluctant about giving it up, he realizes that he needs to go to social media cold turkey if he must increase his productivity both at home and at work.

Sam stumbles on a great book that explains the use of different mental models. He identified three mental models that can help him with his current challenge, namely; the Ivy Lee method, the 2-minute rule, and the Seinfeld strategy. He understands that none of these models are perfect on their own, but he found a way to combine them to help him get over his procrastination and addiction to social media.

First, Sam began deliberately planning his day from the previous night by creating a to-do list of the most important things he would like to achieve the next day. But he didn't just write out one long list; he went over his list pruning it down to only six items and prioritizing them according to their order of importance and urgency. By doing this, he was utilizing the Ivy Lee method.

Next, he committed to taking action immediately. He began to consider the time it took to accomplish certain tasks and discovered a whole lot of tasks could be accomplished in two minutes or less as suggested by the 2-minute rule. So, Sam began getting many of his tasks done more effectively. Tasks like sending a quick email, cleaning up clutter, taking out the garbage, and so on were handled immediately. Sometimes, he still had the urge to put some things off, especially when they take more than two minutes to accomplish, but he took that as his cue to work on them immediately. When he identified tasks that took more than two minutes to accomplish, Sam simply started the process of accomplishing them in two minutes or less. So, when he has a big task like writing a blog, he started with just a sentence but later finds he has written for more than an hour! When he was feeling lazy about reading a whole book, he simply read a couple of paragraphs and before he knows it, he was neck-deep in the book.

Keeping this habit up was a bit of a challenge. But thanks to the Seinfeld strategy, Sam was able to remain consistent about his new habit. He made a commitment to spend only one hour a day on social media, write for two hours a day, and then place a checkmark on his calendar to indicate that he has successfully accomplished his goals for the day. Sam wasn't too focused on his results as he was concerned about sticking to his commitment and seeing the unbroken chain of marks on his calendar. Before long, Sam's productivity skyrocketed, and he was able to manage his time better. His struggle with procrastination is now a thing of the past and he is able to take action right away on things that are important to him.

But Sam's success isn't so much of a surprise because he was using the mental models of successful people. Take the Seinfeld strategy for example. The strategy was named after Jerry Seinfeld whose remarkable consistency led to incredible successes. In 1998, he became the highest annual earner ever for a TV actor, and he holds the Guinness World Record for that (Guinness World Record, 1999). Little wonder those who use this mental model like artists, CEOs, athletes, and so on (including Sam in our example) are likely to be more productive than their peers.

Let me bring this chapter to a close a brief story. This time it is a true story of one of the billionaires of our time – Charles "Charlie" Thomas Munger, the American investor, businessman, and philanthropist.

Many people think that attaining success is all about setting goals, having a vision, and working hard to achieve those goals. However, things usually go wrong no matter how great our visions are and how lofty our goals may be. When things do go wrong, we are quick to blame ourselves for not staying through to our visions and goals.

Charlie Munger trained as a lawyer at Harvard and a meteorologist in the days of World War II. He later committed to learning several disciplines like history, economics, biology, physics, psychology, and a few others. This gave him an edge in exploring several great mental models that helped him overcome complex problems.

One of his successful approaches to accomplishing great feats was being both optimistic and pessimistic at the same time. This may come as counterproductive to the mental model of being optimistic at all times and in all situations, but Munger's mental model worked and his results are very glaring (he is a billionaire for God's sake!)

Munger thought through what could possibly go wrong with his projects and investments. He looked at a situation backward, upside down, and inside out to figure out every possible thing that can go wrong. This is known as reverse thinking. In his words, "What happens if all our plans go wrong? Where don't we want to go, and how do you get there? Instead of looking for success, make a list of how to fail instead; through sloth, envy, resentment, self-pity, entitlement, all the mental habits of self-defeat. Avoid these qualities and you will succeed. Tell me where I'm going to die so I don't go there" (Munger, 2005).

This approach helped Munger to stay away from solutions that only looked good temporary and only worked with solutions that are long-lasting. The approach helped him to avoid pitfalls and roadblocks; and in the event that something goes wrong, Munger was more disposed to handling it. In essence, Muller combined both goal setting and invert thinking to achieve success.

While positive thinking can lead to success, envisioning obstacles and building your life's plan to avoid those obstacles can bring lasting success devoid of a constant need to debug and figure out what is wrong with your plan.

Munger's mental model that led to his success story can be summarized in one simple sentence: the most effective way to avert trouble is to steer clear of it altogether by discovering what works and what doesn't.

# Chapter 2: I Know It Better... Or Not?

You can only see what you want to see. If you think something is irrelevant your mind will filter it out and make only relevant things dominant in your perception. Your mind helps you to pick out only things you believe to be true or supports your belief. This is how your reality and life experience are shaped. Your mind helps you do all this to keep you sane! And I'll show you in a bit how all these happen. The downside to keeping you sane is that you tend to think in stereotypes or allow default thinking to run your decisions. In other words, you become biased to certain beliefs. This causes you to think that you know better unless you become deliberate and start forcing your brain to actually think! In this chapter, we shall take a close look at some of the mental biases that can greatly influence our decision-making process and ultimately our behaviors.

## Selective Perception

If you were to respond to the entire stimulus coming at you every single second, you would be worse than insane! In fact, it is practically impossible to think, feel, and see everything in your reality at the same time. This is why you can only see what you want to see. Here's an interesting piece of science fact: the human brain can only process only about 50 bits of information per second out of the 11 million bits sent to it every single second (Encyclopedia Britannica, n.d.).

If you find it difficult to accept this, I invite you to try this simple exercise. Get a pen and a piece of paper and begin to write down all the things that you can see, feel, taste, smell, and hear right now. After writing for about 5 minutes, you'll discover that you are ignoring to write down some stimulus. Why is that so? It's simple: you simply cannot keep up with the entire stimulus coming at you at the same time.

## What is Selective Perception?

Your brain helps you to focus only on things that you've consciously or subconsciously instructed it to focus on through a process known as selective perception. Selective perception is the process where your brain analyzes, categorizes, and selects stimuli from your environment that resonates with your belief or focus and discards or blocks out stimuli that are not in agreement with your belief or focus.

### *The Problem with Selective Perception?*

Getting us to focus on the task at hand is a good thing and helps us to concentrate. But as noble as selective perception may be, it has an inherent drawback. We are not always good at telling our brains what is relevant and what is not. And I am not just referring to minor errors in perception. For example, In *How Doctors Think*, Jerome Groopman, M.D. notes that 60% of trained radiologists failed to notice a missing collarbone in someone's chest x-ray due to an analysis that influenced their perception (Groopman, 2007, p. 179).

The implication of this is that even in serious situations or when faced with major life-altering decisions, you could be missing out on important pieces of information because of how your mind has been conditioned by your beliefs.

Your ability to focus on one thing means other things are automatically out of focus. Anyone who knows how to use a camera will tell you that! This is why a smoker can read an entire magazine and even make some purchases from the adverts in the magazine but completely fail to notice all the warnings against smoking in the same magazine. His selective perception blocks out those warnings because they don't agree with his set of beliefs.

Selective perception is the reason we tend to overestimate our capacity to make rational decisions and criticize others for being partial. But if you take the time to really scrutinize your decisions, you will discover that it is almost impossible to escape this naturally occurring bias. For example, in a soccer match, we can quickly point out acts of partiality when the referee appears to be deliberately favoring a team we don't support. However, we conveniently ignore it when the same referee awards the team we support an unjustified penalty.

If you take a little time to think about it, sexism, racism, and other types of discrimination stem from selective perception. Your prejudice can stop you from accepting useful information from a certain group of people because they don't fit into the category you deem useful or good. This is exactly why someone from a particular religion or political party can easily dismiss information from other groups because his filter doesn't favor their views. I am not suggesting that you should accept every data (stimuli from all sources) without scrutinizing it. However, when you begin to eliminate "inconvenient data," you are leaning more toward auto-pilot behavior instead of deliberate or conscious behavior.

# Perception and Decision-Making

Question: How do we make decisions that are not based on limited perception?

Short answer: You don't!

Long answer: Your perceptions will always be limited to some extent. The best you can do is to expand your perception to include a wider range of information that you'll ordinarily be closed off to. We'll see how to do just that in the next section. Attempting to critically analyze a problem or situation from all possible angles can lead to analysis paralysis – a situation where no forward movement in terms of decision or cause of action is reached. For now, let us see how you can use the rational decision-making model to sidestep negative and narrow perceptions.

## *The Rational Decision-Making Model*

I do not intend to go into any lengthy lecture about the theories of this mental model. I'll simply explain what it is and the steps involved in using it.

The rational decision-making model is a process involving a series of steps geared towards problem-solving beginning at defining the problem through selecting the best alternative given the available information. This model helps you look beyond your set of limiting beliefs to make logically sound decisions.

Below are the steps.

1. **Define the problem**: This involves stating exactly what the problem is and its cause (not the symptom). For example, you want to buy a bigger house because your family has outgrown the current one. The problem is not buying a new house; that is a symptom or an alternative solution. The real problem is inadequate space. Properly identifying the cause of the problem can help you think about your current state and the desired state in a proper light. In our example, defining space as the cause of the problem can lead to comparing alternatives such as buying a new house, expanding the current house, or getting rid of unnecessary stuff to free up space.
2. **Identify the decision criteria:** The next step is to consider the available criteria. Using our example above, the criteria could be time and cost. Ask exactly when you will need the extra space, how long will each alternative takes, and when would it become very crucial to solve that space problem. Consider how much each alternative will cost and how much money you have at hand or have access to.
3. **Assign weights to the criteria:** Next, weigh your options. You can compare your options to one another (relative comparison) to pick which one stands out as more important or use an absolute comparison method where you consider each alternative on its merit.
4. **List out alternatives:** Think up as many alternatives as possible that can solve the problem. It doesn't matter if an

alternative appears good or bad; simply list them and think about them in the next step. Again, from our example, your alternatives to solving the space problem could be discarding unnecessary stuff, placing some rarely used possessions in storage, building additional rooms, buying a new house, sending kids to a boarding house, and so on.

5. **Evaluate alternatives:** Use the criteria you have identified earlier in Step 2 to evaluate the alternatives you've listed to determine which option is more viable.
6. **Choose the optimal alternative:** From your evaluation, determine the best alternative and use that in making your decision.

This is just one model. There are several models you can use to reach logically sound and rational decisions. However, whichever model you wish to use in making your decisions, always keep in mind that models are logical and well organized only as ideas. In the real world, nothing is ever that way!

# Expanding Your Perception

Obviously, you cannot use the entire information available to you at the same time. Some of them must be filtered out. But how can you broaden your perception so that you leave out less information?

The first step is becoming aware that you are constantly filtering information, which this chapter has exposed you to. Being aware that there is a problem usually is the first step towards successfully tackling the problem.

Secondly, and very importantly, there must be a willingness to deliberately shift your paradigm. This may not be a walk in the park for many people; the process can be really difficult and requires a lot of practice. "Drop all your mental conditioning and biases" is easy advice to give, but difficult to put into practice. And by the way, I dare say that's bad advice! Mental conditionings play vital roles in keeping us sane and efficient. Rather than attempting to give up all of your mental conditioning and biases (which is impossible!), I'll strongly suggest the following ways to help you expand your perception as well as help you avoid narrowmindedness.

1. Isolate one belief and try to question it. Give your mind permission to allow authentic answers to come to you. Remember that when you ask genuine questions, you are inviting your mind to seek that which is broader than your current perspective.
2. Look for alternatives to that idea or belief. When you flip your belief over, you give the knowledge room to grow and expand beyond your current reality.
3. Ask yourself if what you are observing or perceiving is really true

or just one way to look at it. Remember that everything is perception! There is no such thing as absolute truth. Take time to probe your mind by asking questions such as "Am I missing something here?" "Is this information complete as it is?" "How else can I look at this?"

4. Learn how to withhold judgment or criticism until you gather enough facts. This is particularly useful during conversations with your spouse or a coworker. As I write this, I recall a story shared by Stephen Covey in his book, *7 Habits of Highly Effective People*. A man whose children were disturbing almost everyone in a subway did not bother one bit to control them. They were so loud and irksome, yet the man paid no attention to them. When asked to bring his children to order, he quietly responded, "Oh, you're right. I guess I should do something about it. We just came from the hospital where their mother died about an hour ago. I don't know what to think, and I guess they don't know how to handle it either" (Covey, 1989). That response changed everything! More information was brought to light and all judgments and criticisms gave way to empathy and compassion.

5. Ask clarifying and leading questions during conversations whether it is in a professional or social interaction. This will bring more information to light and help you get the right perspective. To be sure you are on the same page and seeing things from the same perspective as the person you are interacting with, give them feedback about your understanding. For example, "So, if get what you are saying correctly, you mean..." and state your understanding. Doing this can significantly reduce conflicts that can arise due to selective

perception. It is not necessary that you must agree with the other person. However, a clearer understanding of their position helps you to relate better with them with fewer chances of misunderstandings.

## Confirmation Bias

Very closely linked to selective perception is another cognitive bias known as the confirmation bias. This bias keeps you focused on gathering the information that supports your beliefs and disregards anything to the contrary. Many of us are genuinely convinced that our beliefs are very logical, rational, and impartial because we have experienced them for several years. However, many of us do not realize that our so-called impartial, logical, and rational beliefs were reinforced by our selective attention to "evidence" that supports our beliefs.

## Examples of Confirmation Bias

A clear example of confirmation bias is when someone who believes in extrasensory perception thinks about his friend and almost immediately gets an email from that friend. It reinforces his belief that what he thinks about is what happens in his reality. However, he ignores the very many times he has thought about that friend and many other friends without any of them calling, texting, or emailing him.

Another example of confirmation bias is when people support their favorite candidate and actively seek out examples of their "good" deeds to portray him or her in a good light. They are also quick to point out the "evil" deeds of the opposing candidate to paint him or her in a bad light. Perhaps, this behavior is best described in the following words, "Democrats will endorse an extremely restrictive welfare proposal, usually associated with Republicans if they think it has been proposed by the Democratic Party. Republicans will support a generous welfare policy if they think it comes from the Republican Party. Label the same proposal as coming from the other side, and you might as well ask people if they will favor a policy proposed by Osama bin Laden" (Travis and Aronson, 2007).

Apart from personal beliefs, confirmation bias can also affect decision making in the work we do. As Groopman (2007) pointed out, confirmation bias can lead to misdiagnosis of patients. A doctor can form an opinion or a hypothesis about what a patient's diseases and then seek evidence that confirms that hypothesis while consciously or unconsciously ignoring evidence to the contrary.

In 2015, the National Lipid Association's former president pushed for the use of the drug statin among the elderly to help in the reduction of cardiovascular occurrence (Thot, 2015). He cited one randomized control trial (the PROSPER study) to buttress his point but he overlooked another published randomized control trial (CORONA) which reported that statin made no significant impact on the reduction of cardiovascular events (DuBrof, 2017).

I'll like to cite one more example of confirmation bias as it affects our work and this is a very dicey topic for a lot of people. In the US, some (not all) law enforcement agents use their "discretionary" powers to treat people of color "differently" in places like airports, especially persons of Middle Eastern descent and Muslims. There is a phenomenon that has come to be known as "driving while black" in the US. These are clear examples of confirmation bias in law enforcement, especially in the US. This stereotypical way of thinking about black drivers among police officers in the US is as a result of confirmation bias. The police use legitimate reasons like broken tail lights to stop these black drivers and then seek evidence to confirm their preconceived notions about blacks. However, it is important to note that not all police officers engage in this behavior or share this faulty belief.

## Avoiding Confirmation Bias

It is a bit tricky to completely avoid falling into the trap of confirmation bias (or any bias for that matter) because we all have confirmation bias to some degree. However, it can be significantly reduced to lessen its impact on our day-to-day decisions. You will find the following suggestions helpful in avoiding confirmation bias.

1. **Don't be Afraid to Expand Your Mind:** Expanding your mind does not mean you will automatically be brainwashed by ideas you don't subscribe to. Permit yourself to temporarily suspend your bias against an idea and then become an impartial observer of the idea to see its merits and demerits. Don't just throw away an opinion because it doesn't fit into your current set of beliefs. Your ability to give other people the benefit of a doubt both in social and professional interactions will allow you to reach more rational conclusions and decisions.
2. **Be Open to Opposing Views:** As obvious as this may be, it really is difficult to accept. Have you wondered why people often argue vigorously and fight over opposing views? It is because of

the difficulty in being open to embracing ideas that conflict with theirs. And that is partly because they really don't know much about their tightly held ideologies. Someone who cannot explain his ideology is likely to be a die-hard fanatic of that ideology and can easily resort to blind arguments and fights instead of tactful explanation and presentation of their ideas. Part of being open to opposing views requires being humble enough to ask questions about your ideologies and how you came to accept them as true.

3. **Test Ideologies:** As much as it is advisable to welcome opposing ideas, you need to be wary of buying in wholesale on the ideologies that are sold to you. Don't just accept an ideology because you read it in a book or because someone famous proposed it. Exercise your mind – put opposing ideas to test; question them before accepting or rejecting them.

4. **You Know Some Things... But You Don't Know It All:** Your ego sells you the idea that you know it better. It's okay to think that way but you need to realize that you don't know everything and your way of reasoning (no matter how rational it appears to you) can still be fraught with a lot of biases and errors. Acknowledging this fact requires a lot of humility – a virtue that is not very common in today's world.

5. **Embrace Surprises:** When things happen that you least expected, don't dismiss them because they don't tally with your belief. Instead, begin to take a closer look into them with a view to refining some of your beliefs that were unsettled by the surprise. This is how new the frontiers of knowledge are expanded.

Keep in mind that your ideology is the filter through which you sift your world. The narrower your ideologies are, the more close-minded you become, and the less you are able to think for yourself or expand your thinking beyond its current capacity. The impacts of your ideology are not just on the work you do – your profession – but also on your relationship with your close friends and family, and on the day-to-day decisions you make. One of Charlie Munger's popular quotes reads thus, "Another thing I think should be avoided is extremely intense ideology because it cabbages up one's mind… When you're young, it's easy to drift into loyalties and when you announce that you're a loyal member and you start shouting the orthodox ideology out, what you're doing is pounding it in, pounding it in, and you're gradually ruining your mind" (Munger, 2007).

## Framing

What do you see when you look at a glass of water with the water level at the midpoint? Is the glass half-full or half-empty? The answer to that depends on how the information is presented to you. Usually, you think about what the pros or what you stand to gain versus the cons or what you stand to lose when faced with a decision. But how the gain versus loss is portrayed has a lot to do with what your final decision would be. Naturally, if you think you'll lose more by making a certain decision, you will settle for an option that cuts your losses. This is what framing does; it influences you to see how making a choice will reduce your chances of loses.

## *What is Framing?*

Framing is one of the cognitive biases that influence decision making based on how information or facts are presented. It is an alternative way of presenting previous information that significantly modifies a person's perceptions, assumptions, and decisions regarding the information.

Consider the following statements:

- If you are consistent with your medication, you're less likely to have a cardiac arrest.
- If you are not consistent with your medication, you're increasing your chances of having a cardiac arrest.

Even though both statements are mathematically equivalent, the way the statements were framed makes the second one appear more effective than the first. This happens almost daily in our lives. The essence of framing can be simply summarized as what you say is not as important as how you say it (or what you perceive is not as important as how you perceive it).

## Examples of Framing in Real Life

Framing is used in different facets of our lives to nudge us towards certain choices. In advertising, framing can be used to influence our buying choices. Here's an example that many people fall for. You see an item offered for a limited time as "2 for $2" and you quickly bought it like many other people. However, the unit price of the item is $1 and it is written (usually) in small print. There was no special offer, but it was framed to give that perception.

Dental care products are advertised in such a way that shows healthy gums, sparkling white teeth, fresh breath, and how that can make consumers more attractive to potential partners. Framed in such light, the next time the consumers think of buying dental care products, their minds race back to the advert and they become more open to buying that particular product. Also, advertisers usually avoid words like "overpriced" and "expensive" when showcasing high-end products. Instead, they emphasize words like "luxurious" and "plus." Even when they advertise low-priced products, they don't use words like "sturdy and cheap," instead they conveniently say things like, "dependable and affordable."

In economics, an investor is likely to put his money into a company that is said to have a 75% probability of making a profit than in a company is said to have a 25% probability of having losses. Technically, both statements are the same, but the way the information is framed influenced the obvious choice.

Politicians use framing all the time to make the opposition appear incompetent while emphasizing only their positive developments to frame the minds of the citizens towards giving them more votes.

One last example I'll like to share is a folklore that is popular among psychologists. It is a fictitious letter from a girl to her parents, narrating a series of unfortunate events that happened to her in school (Bronner, 2012, p. 69). She told them of how she suffered a concussion when she jumped out her a window in her dormitory during a fire outbreak. She informed her parents she was being cared for by a young man who witnessed the event and called the fire department and ambulance. She also informed them that the young man was not well educated, a different race and religion, and has a sexually transmitted disease that she caught from him. She's already pregnant and in love with him, and they intend to get married before the pregnancy begins to show. Finally, she informs them that she just made up everything she wrote, but that her grades are really bad.

This example may appear a little too extreme, but it perfectly highlights the use of framing to help her parents receive the same information from the right perspective. Certainly, having poor grades is a lot better than that entire catastrophic episode.

## How to Use Framing to Your Advantage

Deliberately framing a problem or a challenging situation can give you the perspective you need to make the right decisions. Your ability to decide whether or not a problem is worth solving depends on how you frame the problem. Equally, your success in making the right decisions depends, to a large extent, on how well you are able to deliberately frame situations to spur you into action. Leaving your brain to perceive your situations using your default perception process may lead to faulty choices because of the tendency of our brains to rely heavily on the first few pieces of data it has access to when we are faced with a decision.

Consider a situation where your spouse complains about how you give her too little attention because you are too consumed by your job and it is beginning to take its toll on your family life. You can think of the situation in the following ways:

- I have to choose between her and my job!

- I have to learn how to manage my time more.

Looking at the situation from the first frame of mind is likely to put you on the defensive. Instead of nudging you towards finding an amicable and mutually benefiting solution, it will lead you down the path of thinking she is selfish, too demanding, and ungrateful for your effort to cater to the family's needs. This is bound to lead you to make decisions and take actions that will cause more conflicts in your relationship.

But framing the situation from the second perspective is likely to make you open to finding a balance between your job and family life. This line of thinking can make you live a healthier, happier, and more meaningful life devoid of unnecessary conflicts in your relationship.

## *Retraining Your Thinking*

Considering how powerful the influence of framing can have on our decision-making and subsequent behavior, wouldn't it be nice to learn how to be deliberate in framing your perspectives? Break your mind's default framing using the following methods.

- When presented with a problem or message don't swallow it line, hook, and sinker! First, reframe the problem or message more than once if possible. Consider different reference points from where to frame and reframe the problem or message. Similar to using the inverted model, frame the situation, statement, or idea from a negative perspective if it is in the positive or frame it in a positive perspective if it is in the negative.

- Start thinking in terms of the quality of the questions you ask. I began this chapter by saying *"you can only see what you want to see."* What you see, the solutions you get, the ideas that occur to you, or the answers you get all depends on the quality of the question you ask. So, when you are faced with options, ask yourself multiple questions before deciding. Picking the first option that occurs to you is acting based on autopilot or your default mode of thinking.
- Be mindful of the context of your framing. Your thoughts can be misled if a statement or problem is worded wrongly. In the words of William Poundstone, "The stumbling block isn't the certainty effect per se. It's the way that smart people are influenced by mere words, by the way, the choices are framed" (Poundstone, 2010).
- One way to break free from default thinking (framing bias) is to understand that almost everyone you interact with has a different perspective about an issue even if you are both looking at the same issue. When you seek to understand other people's perspectives, it would help you to reframe a situation differently and approach it with a better understanding.
- Challenge your perspective! You can do this by encouraging contrary opinions and perspectives from the people around you. Let your colleagues, friends, and even spouse know that you are open to their honest views even if they are sharply in disagreement with yours. Renowned CEOs and captains of industries are known to surround themselves with people who think differently than them and this is one huge factor for their fewer mistakes and higher success rates.

Here are some practical steps you can take right now to begin to frame or reframe the situations in your life to help you tackle them with more zest and vigor.

- Start to think of the work you do as a "calling" instead of a "job." Framing your work in this light can lead to more commitment, engagement, and a higher level of satisfaction.
- We are more inclined to think more about what we are going to lose if a situation goes bad. Begin to see this as an advantage instead of a curse. That is to say, use your power of imagination to conjure up the worst-case scenario in your mind and begin to see all the negative impacts losing or failing can cause. Ask yourself if you can live with such negative impacts. I am not suggesting that you engage in overgeneralization (making a situation worse than it actually is). I am simply urging you to apply an earlier mental model I touched on while sharing the story of Charlie Munger in the previous chapter. By looking at what you are likely to lose you are more likely to take steps to correct it to prevent it from happening.
- Ask yourself if the status quo of your life (or any particular area of your life) is acceptable to you. Take a particular aspect of your life and flip it over; do you like what you see? For example, if you currently earn $500 per month, begin to ask yourself if that is the highest you can earn. Is this amount all that I am worth? Does this amount reflect my true capabilities and potentials? Can I not go beyond this amount? In other words, you are beginning to shift your frame from looking at the glass as half full to half empty. Before long, you will start thinking of ways to improve yourself to earn more money or diversifying your

resources (time, money, and energy) to generate more income.

## *Why Deliberate Framing Works*

Isn't the glass-half-empty analogy a negative viewpoint? Well, it depends on how you frame it! Negative and positive are our interpretations of neutral events. Remember that how information is presented can determine whether or not we think it is less negative. Besides, we tend to be more motivated by potential loss than by what we can potentially gain. This explains why many people tend to be contented with their life's status quo and will do all they can to keep it that way but will find it difficult to put in the required effort to go beyond their status quo. Usually, there is less motivation for striving to achieve a goal than there is for losing what you already have. Have you not heard the saying, "a bird in hand is worth two in the bush?" That is a perfect reflection of low self-motivation. And the reason is that they have accepted the perception that their glass is half full. That type of thinking or framing can keep you longer than necessary in your status quo – your comfort zone, even when the zone is no longer comfortable!

Deliberately framing your situation can mean the difference between chasing your goals and settling for your current lifestyle. Almost every man has dreams and aspirations, but the drive to pursue that dream and the ingenuity to think outside the box (of their peculiar mental model) is usually truncated by their perception of their current situation.

Framing your current level of success as "I have done well for myself" is likely to lead to contentment, relaxation, and letting down your guard (just for a tiny bit!), and eventually hitting a plateau. On the flip side, framing your current level of success as "There is still room for improvement" is more likely to keep your creative juices flowing. Have you wondered why great athletes break their own records? Have you wondered why successful businessmen and women keep outdoing themselves year after year? They refused to accept the perception that says there's no more world to conquer! They are continually in the process of framing their situations to make them want to achieve more than they have already achieved.

Framing does not work only for negative situations. You do not need to wait until a situation gets bad before you deliberately change how you perceive the situation. For example, you have put a lot of effort into your relationship and it is working out fine. You could frame that positive situation as "If I can do this much, I definitely can achieve far better results in other areas of my life!"

# Chapter 3: Let's Do It Like This... Or Wait... Maybe...

24-year-old Kelvin read the end-user agreement written in small print. His mind raced with several questions. Should he click the Agree button and take the huge risk of investing his hard-earned money or should he just click the Cancel button? How many times has he come to this crossroads? He has lost count. His salary from his job seems to be constantly shrinking compared to his responsibilities. And now that his wife is expecting a second child, he desperately needs another source of income. He had taken the advice of investment gurus to save up and invest in real estate crowdfunding to give him extra income. Moreover, since that is a passive investment, it would not affect his demanding job. How long ago was that? It's been three long years, and he's gone from one investment to the other and doesn't have any significant profit to show for it. Initially, he'll have some early profits, but before long, all he'll be left with are irredeemable losses.

He had read several motivational and self-help books. He set goals and put in his best efforts towards achieving his goals. But somehow, there doesn't seem to be any light at the end of Kelvin's tunnel. He had considered giving up but with mounting responsibilities and his wife recently quitting her job to be a stay-at-home mom, Kelvin is back at giving real estate investments another shot. Would he succeed this time? What does he need to do to succeed? What would help him make better decisions?

Like Kelvin in the fictional story, a lot of us are faced with situations that force us into making decisions whether or not we are well-prepared to make them. Some of these decisions are good, while for many, the decisions are mostly bad. But that isn't the only problem. Usually, in retrospect, we would think we've learned our lessons and then try again only to be greeted with another round of failure resulting from more bad decisions than good ones. So, how do you, like Kelvin, make the right decisions? Of all the hundreds of questions buffeting your mind almost daily on different subjects of your life, how would you know the right answers to give and the right choices to make? What do you need to know to free yourself from the trap of second-guessing yourself and going, "let's do it like this… or wait… maybe…?" Is there some special secret formula for making the right decisions? What do famous and successful businessmen know and use that the average struggling man doesn't know?

All these are the focus of this chapter. We shall take a look at the lives of a few men who are renowned for their successes. But our focus is not going to be on their wealth; rather, we shall pay more attention to how they were able to rise from the ashes of their several failures. Because, whether we want to admit it or not, the majority of successful people recorded a lot of heart-wrenching failures before they became successful at their various ventures. At the end of this chapter, you will understand that while there is no beeline to success, there are, however, ways of thinking that can give you an "unfair" edge over others who simply burrow through life armed with only hope. First, let us begin by studying the common mistakes people like Kelvin (and perhaps you too) make in decision-making.

# Common Mistakes in Decision-Making

## *Driven by Emotions (Rushing into Decisions)*

When you are angry and depressed or elated and excited, your decisions at those moments may not be rational. You may be under what is known as emotional hijack (or amygdala hijack) – where your rational mind is overtaken by your emotional mind and makes you respond according to what you are feeling in the spur of the moment regardless of the long-term effect of your response. For example, you are in a good mood and you offer to make a substantial donation for a project that you don't really care about before you have time to think through your decision. Or saying hurtful words in haste without pausing to think about it because you are angry, and then those words change your relationship forever.

Whether it is in your professional or personal situations, rushing into making important decisions can be a huge mistake. Jumping at the first alternative may not usually result in the best decision. Equally, making decisions without understanding the ramifications can be disastrous.

To avoid this, always hold off making decisions until you are in a reasonably stable state where you can think more clearly. You can deliberately take yourself out of such emotionally charged situations (take a walk or do something unrelated to the situation) to allow you to think more rationally.

## *Procrastination*

Making a decision can be a difficult process sometimes. To avoid this difficulty, many people simply postpone making the decision and get along with the seemingly simple things that don't require too much thinking (their default way of living). However, what many people don't realize is that deciding to postpone a decision is a decision in itself. The longer you postpone an important decision, the more difficult it gets to rationally make up your mind especially when making the decision becomes critical.

Part of the reason for postponing a decision is the fear of making mistakes. Own your decisions once you've made it. You may not get it right the first time, but mistakes show that you are attempting something instead of idling away in procrastination. Don't wait until you have to make a decision. Decide when you can boldly say, "I choose to."

## *Narrow-Mindedness*

This is where selective perception and confirmation bias discussed in the previous chapter comes into play. Not giving your mind enough room to think beyond your current level of perception can lead to huge mistakes in decision-making. For example, you are excited about a new change you want to make in your business. Four out of your 15 employees seem happy about the change, so you go ahead with implementing the change regardless of the opposing ideas raised by the remaining 15. Your mind was already made up and you were merely seeking confirmation for your bias instead of seeking honest input.

To overcome narrow-mindedness and biases, make sure that you are not making important decisions based on a single component without duly considering the bigger picture. Acknowledging your personal bias and your inexperience about the issue at hand will ensure that you keep things in perspective. Keep channels for new information open – avoid shooting from the hip! Gather relevant information and consider them first even if they seem opposed to your current perception. You may not accept the opposing views, but they can give you fresh insights on how to think inversely as successful people do.

## *The Halo Effect*

Like Kelvin, many of us listen to gurus the way younger children learn from parents, adults, and society – with our minds wide open to receive and act without scrutiny. Making important decisions based on what someone you hold in high regard tells you may not work well at all times. It is similar to confirmation bias except that this is more about people. Once someone has given you a few good pieces of advice in the past or is known to make sound judgments, we tend to take in everything they say hook, line, and sinker.

Be open to advise from credible sources, but also think for yourself. Keep in mind that the person whose opinion you respect may not share your identical problem or situation for which you are trying to make the right decisions.

## *Overanalyzing*

Analysis paralysis can occur from too much data to chew on. This stems from the desire to make perfect decisions. Overanalyzing will keep you focused on the trees while neglecting the forest! The big picture will be lost on you because your attention is engrossed in the details. Simply keep your eyes on relevant information that will give you useful clues of the future and not a bunch of historical data that only points to where you (and others) have been. Basing your decisions on out-dated information can be fatal. Select a handful of factors that are critical and forget all other factors – they are mere distractions. If your decision proves to be wrong or does not go as expected, re-examine your factors and make adjustments.

Always remember that there will be room for improvement. You don't have to see the whole staircase before you take the first step. Your decisions don't have to be perfect from the outset. You can always adjust, improve, and improvise as you go along.

## *Do-or-Die Mentality*

Approaching decision making with a do-or-die attitude often puts you under undue pressure. Kelvin, in our story, will find it difficult to make any rational decision in his current state of mind because he places his entire future on the click of one button! If you find yourself faced with a make-or-break decision, it is more than likely that you have made a series of bad decisions leading to that single decision. Usually, decisions made from this mentality are done to justify previous actions or to cover up past mistakes. In many cases, you will neglect your values (ignoring the right thing) while making this type of decision.

## *Rationalizing Away Reality*

Self-deceit is the worst form of deceit. Decisions made out of hope that current reality will bend to favor your decision is simply burying your head in the sand. No matter how unpleasant the realities on the ground are, you must take them into consideration while making your decisions. Kelvin would have to consider his financial standing, his growing responsibilities, and his current level of experience in real estate investing if he must make a sound decision. Ignoring his inexperience with regards to real estate investing in the hope that one single click will turn his fortunes around may be another financial disaster waiting to happen to him.

You need to be honest with yourself before making decisions, especially if they are important ones. I do not mean to offend your religious inclination or your belief in the supernatural, but I strongly suggest that you don't rely on hope or blind faith when making life-altering decisions. You have an inborn ability to reason – use it!

Okay, it's now time to examine the success stories of a few famous men. Remember to keep your attention on the mental models they used to achieve their successes.

# Elon Musk: An Embodiment of First-Principle Thinking

Elon Musk is a highly successful and audacious entrepreneur who needs little or no introduction. His net worth of $19.3 billion as of 2019 is a clear testament to that fact. Musk has some lofty goals and visions among which are to significantly reduce global warming and establish a human colony on Mars to reduce the risk of human extinction (Anderson, 2014).

His successes cut across various fields from PayPal in the financial sector to Solar City (energy sector), SpaceX (aerospace), and Tesla Motors (automotive). These are all revolutionary companies that will change human history forever.

Apart from a series of failures, in both his personal and professional life, as well as being fired from his own company while on honeymoon, Mr. Musk was faced with challenges that would have made any other person succumb to the popular way of thinking. But not Elon; his success wasn't just as a result of his incredible work ethic. It is a result of his ability to think like a genius about his challenges.

But how does all this make any meaning to you? Here's how. Elon Musk was able to strip non-essentials from big ideas, challenges, and problems and then gradually work his way up in building a solution. This brings us to the first-principles thinking.

## *First-Principles Thinking*

It isn't really about what Mr. Musk thinks that is the highlight of his success story. Instead, it is how he thinks about it. He simply doesn't accept that something should be done in a particular way because that's how it's always been done. He's really great at using the first-principles thinking to approach problems. So, what exactly is first-principle thinking? How did Elon Musk use it to solve problems? And most importantly, how can you use it in your life?

A first principle is a fundamental assumption or concept on which a method, formula, system, or theory is based. No further assumption can be reached beyond the first principle of a thing.

Let me put that in layman's terms. It is keenly questioning the assumptions you have about situations or problems and then building solutions about the problems and situations from scratch. This is how formulas and original solutions are derived – by stripping assumptions down to their fundamentals, to what is known as true, and then working back up.

One of Mr. Musk's multibillion-dollar companies, SpaceX, came into existence through the conscious application of first-principles thinking. Elon wanted to send a rocket to Mars in 2002; however, there was a huge challenge that appeared insurmountable. The cost of buying a rocket was extremely high – in the range of $65 million. Instead of giving up the idea because of insufficient funds (like most will do), or postponing the idea of sending rockets to Mars until he can save up for the project at a later date, he began to question the generally held assumptions about rockets. He began taking the problem apart by asking what the basic components of a rocket are and the cost of those components or materials in the commodity market.

He found that rockets are made of materials like aerospace-grade aluminum alloys, carbon fiber, copper, and titanium. His quest also revealed that these materials are a lot cheaper in the commodity market, about 2% of the cost of a finished rocket! Instead of purchasing finished rockets, he bought the materials and built his own rockets. So, what appeared to be an insurmountable challenge turned out to be the birth of a new multimillion-dollar aerospace company!

This is the result of being guided by mental models that generate the right thinking. Using first-principles thinking, Musk was able to drastically cut down the cost of launching rockets while still making profits. He refused to settle for the assumption that rockets are astronomically expensive to launch and created a more effective solution.

## How Does This Matter to You?

You may not be interested in developing innovative ideas, so how does using first-principle thinking apply to you? Well, for starters, it saves you from the trap of living by analogy instead of by thinking for yourself. Many people live by what can be best described as copy and paste. They see others doing things a certain way, and boom, they do the same without questioning the ideas, beliefs, and concepts. Sticking to old conventions and inherited ideas can limit your ability to think for yourself.

When you begin to take the time to consider how you approach your day-to-day problems, you may begin to find that you are merely regurgitating the so-called solutions you inherited from others. We learned this from when we were kids. Parents and grownups will irritably respond with "Because I said so!" to our too many questions. As adults, we got the same answer, "Because that's how it's always been done!"

Equally, our analogical thinking makes us envisage future development using a current form instead of function. For example, critiques of technology may scoff at the idea of flying cars failing to see that flying cars are already in existence in the form of airplanes. The form may be different, but the function it serves (air transportation) is the same. In other words, for you to be more effective in decision-making, ask yourself what the functional outcome of what you are trying to accomplish is, and then make the best of the function without so much worry about the form.

## *Applying First-Principles Thinking in Your Life*

Working with how others think means that we can only make incremental improvements. First-principles thinking means branching out from the norm and not living by analogies or conventions. Analogies are great – they help a cook, for example, to follow a recipe without bothering so much how the recipe came about. In that case, the analogy (recipe) saves the cook some time. However, the cook runs into problems when the situation requires a different dish. This is where a chef differs from a cook. The chef can think for himself and produce another recipe for the new dish. A cook is stuck without a recipe.

Thinking for yourself requires that you strip down assumptions to their basics. Here's how to do that.

1. Find out the genesis of your assumptions. What are your thoughts about a problem, challenge, or situation? Why do you think that way?
2. Challenge your assumptions. How do you know that what you think about a situation is true? Suppose you think the opposite?
3. Begin to look for evidence. Can you back up your thinking? What is the source of your evidence?
4. Seek other viewpoints. What do others think? How do you know that you are correct?
5. Consider the implications. What happens if I go wrong? What is at stake?
6. Cross-examine your earlier questions. Why did you think that way? Is that type of thinking correct? What have you reached from all your reasoning?

So, the next time someone says to you, "It's never been done before," take that as your cue to start striping down that assumption.

## *Ray Dalio: Decision Making with Second-Order Thinking*

Ray Dalio, founder of Bridgewater Associates, the biggest hedge fund firm in the world is no doubt a successful investor and philanthropist. With a personal net worth of $19.4 billion in 2019, there's definitely a few principles of right-thinking we can learn from him with regards to life and work (Forbes, 2019).

As with many successful people, Ray Dalio had to learn through several mistakes and seeming failures. To him, there's a lot more to learn from failures than from success. He learned one of his most painful lessons when Mexico defaulted on his loans in 1982. Being a world-renowned successful hedge fund manager doesn't come without its own price! But how did Ray go from being almost completely broke to donating $768.9 million to different philanthropic causes? He changed his thinking, that's how. Instead of thinking, "I want this to be true!"; he started thinking, "How do I know this to be true?"

However, one of the major changes he applied to his thinking that resulted in a major shift in his life and fortune was the second-order thinking. When his market prediction came true, he went all in and made a huge financial decision based purely on first-order thinking without considering second-order thinking. His company tanked, and Ray had to borrow $4,000 from his dad at one time. He learned his lessons and made a comeback. Today, his company, which almost went under, now manages $160 billion.

## *What is Second-Order Thinking?*

In simple terms, second-order thinking is a deliberate consideration of the consequences of your intended choices and decisions. It is thinking about possible future outcomes on more than one level before deciding on a course of action. It is a complex form of thinking. In contrast, first-order thinking is easy, considers only surface outcomes, and is commonly used.

Consider the following examples of first and second-order thinking:

1. Kelvin is trying to decide whether to invest in real estate, bonds, cash, stocks, or a mix? Currently, the market is on a downturn. Kelvin's first-order thinking would be something along the lines of, "Stay away from the markets! Investing is risky. The market is crashing, just save your money." If he's smart enough to think further, his second-order thinking would go, "The markets are currently down and that's making people panic. This means the stocks are a great bargain because they are grossly undervalued. I am still young and can take the risk. I'll invest."
2. A fat gangster, more than twice the size of Kelvin, is chasing him down a hallway. He gets to a staircase and has to decide whether to go up the stairs or down. "Go down. You'll move a lot faster when going down," screams first-order thinking. "Go up. You'll move slower but it'll be much more difficult for this thug to carry his weight up the stairs," says second-order thinking.
3. Kelvin is trying to lose weight and eat healthily. First-order thinking will make him cringe at the thought of going to the gym, lifting weights, and passing on his favorite chocolate cakes. Second-order thinking will focus on the benefits of living healthier, stronger, and leaner.

More often than not, deciding and acting from first-order thinking cost us the very thing we want or block us from getting them. They are like temptations that distract from proper thinking. Athletes who use drugs to enhance their performance didn't give second-order thinking a chance. They only focused on the immediate results their decisions will bring (fame and fortune) without giving thought to the consequences of their actions if they are found out (a ban from sports participation, health hazards, and a ruined reputation).

Lying to the people in your world can seem harmless and even make you achieve your agenda, but it is capable of destroying your relationships forever.

## *Avoiding Mediocrity*

How can you outperform others and even your previous performance if you keep thinking the same way? To reach uncommon decisions, you need to think beyond the first easy level where almost everyone thinks. Mediocrity results from a common way of thinking and acting.

Your thinking processes have to take an unconventional form for you to stand out from the herd. Using second-order thinking can help you access ideas that are different and can also help you to process your ideas differently than the average person would.

## *Being Deliberate About Your Decisions*

I'll like to suggest the following way through that you can apply second-order thinking in your day-to-day decisions.

1. Make a habit of asking yourself, "What happens next?" This opens your mind to think beyond the first-order thinking.
2. Try to think into the future and picture what the consequences of your decision would be in the short, medium, and long term.
3. Ask yourself how your decision will impact others and how they will respond. If it is a personal decision, how would your spouse or friend respond? If it is a business or career decision, how would your competition, employees, colleagues, or bosses respond?

Be wary of thoughts that immediately confirm your preconceived ideas or biases when you are faced with challenging situations. In Dalio's words,

"Failing to consider second- and third-order consequences are the cause of a lot of painfully bad decisions, and it is especially deadly when the first inferior option confirms your own biases. Never seize on the first available option, no matter how good it seems, before you've asked questions and explored." (Dalio, 2017)

## Jeff Bezos: Thinking on Your Feet

Have you ever bought anything on Amazon, maybe this book? If you have, you have transacted business with Jeff Bezos! Even if you haven't bought anything on Amazon before, Jeff Bezos hardly needs any introduction. I mean, almost everyone knows the man who, in early 2019, was named the world's richest man with a net worth of $113 billion (Forbes, 2019).

Mr. Bezos couldn't have successfully built an incredible company like Amazon that generates more than $24 billion annual revenue, hire the right kind of people to run his businesses, and amassed an incredible fortune for himself without knowing and applying a few mental hacks that the ordinary man usually overlooks or is completely ignorant of.

## *Deciding Before You Decide*

So, how do Jess Bezos and other successful people do it? In a world of constantly moving pieces, how do they know which piece will fit for what part of their personal and professional lives? Of all the several decisions they have to make, how do they know which is right and which is not? Well, first of all, successful people know that they don't have to make the right decisions at all times. This is one thing that keeps most people stuck; we want every decision we make to be the right one, and that explains why we don't easily change our minds. Because we have invested a lot of time, energy, and emotion into the decision, we want it to be right at all costs.

Here's what Bezos and other successful people do. They classify decisions into two broad categories.

**Category 1:** These are decisions that are almost irreversible. For example, quitting your job or selling your business. You will have to permanently live with the outcome of these types of decisions.

**Category 2:** These are decisions that can be easily reversed. A lot of the decisions you make daily fall into this category.

Erroneously assuming that all decisions are extremely important can keep you stuck longer than necessary. To improve your productivity and increase your worth before your boss, colleague, friends, or spouse, you need to be able to think on your feet. Taking too much time to make up your mind shows that you consider every decision as a Category 1 decision. It also shows that you desperately want to be right straight out of the bat! Doing that is essentially depriving yourself of the opportunity to learn from your experiences.

Successful people are not afraid of making a lot of decisions daily. It doesn't mean they've become so good that they don't make mistakes. It simply means they are willing to learn from their mistakes. For the highly successful leaders, business owners, athletes, entertainers, and so on, success comes with making a lot of mistakes. To the rest who are very careful to avoid mistakes, well, let's just say, being too careful is a sure path to a mediocre life.

So, the next time you need to make a decision, first decide if it is a Category 1 or 2 decision. You are not going to get all your decisions right and that is perfectly okay. The more you quickly make and execute Category 2 decisions, the faster you gather experience and understand how to make better decisions. Over time, the quality of your decisions will improve significantly.

## *Changing Your Mind... Quickly*

Mr. Bezos was able to quickly change his mind when necessary because he believes that consistency of thought isn't necessarily a positive trait. If something is not working, change your mind! You are not stuck with one pattern of thinking. If you are confused as to whether you are stuck in the same pattern of thinking, carefully examine your results. It was Einstein who defined insanity as doing the same thing over and over again yet expecting a different result. You definitely cannot solve a problem with the same mind-set that created the problem in the place.

Successful people don't cling onto a decision even when circumstances have changed. They are very flexible and quick to change their minds when they have ample evidence that suggests they are wrong. Perhaps that was one of Steve Jobs' great qualities. He understood that it was pointless holding unto an assumption in the face of changing circumstances. Tim Cook, Apple CEO had this to say about Steve Jobs,

"Steve would flip on something so fast that you would forget that he was the one taking the 180-degree polar opposite position the day before. I saw it daily. This is a gift because things do change, and it takes courage to change. It takes courage to say, 'I was wrong.' I think he had that." (Cook, 2012)

## *The Mirage of Definite Thinking*

You must develop the habit of continually revising your understanding especially if a problem you thought you had solved keeps resurfacing. Nothing can get you more stuck than trying to be always definite in your decisions. It keeps you fixated on all the seemingly important details you need to sort through while neglecting the big picture of the situation at hand. You must give up the need to be right all the time.

So, don't be afraid to make decisions because you don't want to go wrong. Going wrong or failing on Category 1 decision only makes you wiser. This is what Jeff Bezos has to say on failing,

"Failure and invention are inseparable twins. To invent you have to experiment, and if you know in advance that it's going to work, it's not an experiment. Most large organizations embrace the idea of invention, but are not willing to suffer the string of failed experiments necessary to get there."

Did I mention how many times Elon Musk attempted a rocket launch and failed? Did I mention the millions of dollars he lost on each of those failed attempts? I would rather leave those details to your imagination. But failure didn't stop Mr. Musk from refining and making better decisions either.

# More Mental Models for Making Better Decisions

## *The Bayesian Thinking*

The work of Thomas Bayes, an 18th century English minster led to what is known as Bayesian thinking. In simple terms, this is the core of Bayesian thinking. When you encounter new information or learn something new, you should take into account your prior relevant knowledge and how it validates or negates the new information. Given that a lot of your prior information and knowledge are useful, you shouldn't simply discard them because you learn something new. Equally, given that we in a constantly changing world, you shouldn't discard new information because it contradicts your prior information. This means you should take into consideration all prior relevant information (what statisticians call a base rate) when making decisions. There are a lot of statistical analysis and calculations that can be used to arrive at probabilities of things being true or not, but I will not bore you with such computations. My goal is to help you apply this and the other mental models in the decisions you encounter in your daily life and not to take you through the hypothetical processes of these models.

Bayesian thinking is particularly useful when you are faced with making decisions involving uncertain situations or predicting a likely outcome. It is almost always a gross mistake to make decisions in uncertain situations without pausing to ask yourself what you may already know that can help you better understand the reality of the uncertain situation. For example, you invite a handyman to fix a broken faucet in your kitchen and he begins to snoop around the house. Later in the day, the local news reports a case where a repairman returned to a house where he had previously worked to rob. You are perplexed and begin to worry that this handyman may come back and rob you. You can go ahead with that assumption and begin to frantically take precautionary measures that can cost you time, money, and effort, or take a pause to apply the Bayesian thinking before taking any action in the uncertain situation.

To apply the Bayesian thinking to the above situation, start by asking how many times repairmen have been reported to rob a house and how likely is that to happen in this instance. Are you basing your fear on a single piece of evidence (the news report) or it is a frequent occurrence? How many repairmen are robbers and how many are honest? By relying on previous information and comparing it to the new information, you can determine the likelihood of the outcome, in this case, the repairman coming back to rob you or not. You can lock your doors or install alarm systems, but getting worked up over that piece of new information isn't the best use of your time and can push you into making poor decisions like calling the police to investigate an honest repairman.

You can apply Bayesian thinking in the workplace too. For example, a colleague named Sam, whom you suspect is envious one of your direct reports named Kelvin, begins to complain to you about Kelvin's poor attitude towards finishing a project. You can immediately confirm your earlier assumption that Sam is indeed envious of Kelvin, or take a pause and think about the situation. Is Sam in the habit of complaining about Kelvin or any other colleague for that matter? Is Kelvin actually being sluggish about the project? Is it out of place for a colleague to complain about another's poor work attitude? This line of questioning can help you better understand the reality of the situation without jumping to rash conclusions or leaning toward confirmation bias.

To help you remember how to use the Bayesian thinking, keep the following in mind when you are about to make a decision in an uncertain situation:

1. Remember the things you know prior to the new information.
2. Imagine that your conclusions are wrong. How would that affect your personal life, work, and others who are directly affected by that conclusion?
3. Review and update your knowledge incrementally. Discarding everything you know about a situation prior to obtaining new information could prove fatal.

## *Loss Aversion*

Would you expect a farmer to sit all day watching and waiting for a seed he planted to sprout? Definitely not! But many people do just that. When you take a quick peek at your investment for the umpteenth time in one day, for example, or when you continuously check on your new romantic partner to be sure that their feelings for you haven't changed, you are like the farmer urging his seeds to grow! The reason we do that is that the pain we feel by losing something is far more than the pleasure we feel by getting it.

In Chapter 2, I mentioned that many people would prefer to maintain their current status than putting in the required effort to attain a higher status. This is because of what psychologists call loss aversion. We hate losing. But how does that affect our ability to make more right decisions? The more you see losses, the greater the psychological pain you experience, and the higher your chances of making a bad decision especially during the worst and challenging times.

I could go into all the theories and details of scientific research on how our brains are affected and react to the several stimuli we get about perceived losses and gains but that may not be very beneficial to you. What I am primarily concerned with is how this can help you improve the quality of decisions you make.

Whenever you are in a situation that requires you to present information to others (clients, customers, colleagues, family, friends, and so on), always remember that people are interested in less risk and more gains; people want to be assured of gains even when they are taking risks. Therefore, tailor your information to gains rather than losses, for example, offer discounts instead of surcharges or extra charges. Offer guarantees for products and services instead of caveats. Offer love and assurance instead of warnings and insinuated threats. However, if there is significant uncertainty in a situation, present the information, but don't focus too much on the possibility of failure or unpleasant outcomes. Be more focused on potential successes.

## *Reverse Thinking*

We brought Chapter 1 to a close with a short story of Charlie Munger and how he used the reverse or invert thinking. Briefly, let us look at how you too can apply this mental model in your daily life.

Armed with the understanding that reverses thinking is simply looking at a problem from an inverted angle, here's a practical example on how to use it in a work situation:

1. Firstly, define the problem you are trying to solve. For example, your sales are significantly falling and you are trying to increase it.
2. The next step is to invert the problem. Think from the reverse angle instead of how to solve it. What exactly do you need to do to ensure that the situation gets worse? How can you take a great product or service and make sure that it doesn't sell? You may begin to consider things like, making the buying process very complex, using a cheap and unreliable computer program, web service, or app for the sales, not making enough cold calls or downplaying the role of advertising campaigns, offering only

one type of payment method, not providing adequate customer support, and so on.
3. The final step is to see how to avoid the pitfalls you have identified in Step 2.

Here's another example that shows how you could apply this in your personal life. Suppose you are trying to improve your relationship with your teenager. Think of what would guarantee that the relationship grows worse?

- Infrequent communication.
- Talking to your teenager only when he or she has done something wrong.
- Spending little to no time with them.
- Not being there for them and not taking an interest in their activities.
- Breaking your promises to them.
- Putting them down in front of their peers.

Working to avoid these things is an easier way to guarantee a healthier relationship with your teenager than spending time worrying over how to improve the relationship.

When you begin to feel stuck about how to move forward, perhaps it is time to start thinking about how to go backward or how to not go forward – invert, always invert!

# Bottom Line

There is something about success that is undeniably connected to failure. Unfortunately, when we think of famous people, our attention is usually on their results without much consideration for the series of failures they went through and the mental toughness that saw them through the tough times. Of course, they are financially successful people who didn't have to go through massive failures to become wealthy, and if you are born with the proverbial silver spoon, then money struggles may sound alien to you. However, success is not only about money and fame. Failure can also be in relationships, bad habits, health and fitness, and so on.

When you encounter setbacks in any aspect of your life, think more about how a shift in perspective can help you and less about how much of a failure you are. Easier said than done, I know, but that's how successful people think. They get knocked down more times than they care to admit but still get back up. Your name may not make the list of top 100 successful men of your time (and that may not even be your goal), but you definitely are successful if you can understand and apply the wisdom shared by these highly successful men.

# Chapter 4: This Can Be Done Faster...

How can you shorten the time it takes for you to do the things you do without compromising quality? Better still, how can you significantly improve productivity and at the same time drastically cut down the time you put into your work? How do you optimize your productivity to achieve over-the-top success?

For many people, the answer would be to develop an incredible work ethic, but that would mean putting in more hours in your work and can lead to burnouts. While I am totally for having a healthy work ethic, I do not subscribe to the thinking that suggests that you need to work long hours to be efficient and more productive.

A small business owner can pour all his efforts and waking hours into his business project, but working round the clock as an entrepreneur cannot yield greater and better results than a competitor who can assemble a team to handle a similar project in far less time because the team can collectively put in more man-hours. That is one way to work smarter instead of harder. The entrepreneur may be busy throughout his waking hours, but being busy doesn't necessarily translate into being productive. As Adam Grant, author of *Give and Take*, puts it, "If you want something done, ask a busy person. The old saying rings true, but it also spells doom for that busy person" (Grant, 2014).

However, improving productivity isn't just about managing your time alone. It also involves effectively managing your energy –

spending less and less of your energy while still generating the maximum benefits possible. What other ways can you work smarter instead of harder and longer? The answer to that and the previous questions are what this chapter is designed to answer using mental models that can help you improve efficiency. But first, let's take a brief look at what most people do that prevents high productivity.

# Thing You Do That Prevents Productivity

### *Working Overtime*

As earlier mentioned in the preceding paragraphs, working for longer hours does not automatically equal higher productivity. If anything, working for longer hours tends to reduce your productivity because you are susceptible to burnouts. When are you likely to have brilliant ideas and clear insights? Is it when you are buried in your work with your mind and body all worked up or when your mind and body are relaxed, calm, and off from desperately trying to figure out how to solve a problem?

### *Not Having Adequate Sleep*

Do you bring work back home? Do you take your gadgets (phones, tablets, laptops, and so on) to bed? Do you deprive yourself of adequate sleep in a bid to get a head start on the next day's tasks? If you do any of these, you shouldn't be surprised if your productivity isn't getting any better. Sleep recharges your body and mind – both of which you need to be efficient at work. Great leaders and successful people all maintained a habit of having adequate sleep because they understand the immense benefit it gives your body and all its various systems. Some great minds and leaders even included napping during the day as part of their daily routine. Leonardo da Vinci, Thomas Edison, Winston Churchill, President John F. Kennedy, President Ronald Reagan, John D. Rockefeller, and many other successful people are known for sleeping for short periods during the day (Hyatt, 2016).

## *Allowing Distraction*

What does your computer screen look like – cluttered with icons, completely iconless, or having a couple of icons? How many tabs do you have opened at the same time on your computer? How about your phone, how many apps do you have installed and how many do you actually use? Modern life comes with its blessings and curses, heavy distraction being one of them. You cannot expect your productivity to improve if you are constantly distracted by your gadgets. To help get you less distracted, unclutter your computer and phone; only keep programs and apps that are really useful to you. Turn off your phone or turn off all notifications until you are through with your tasks.

## *Saying Yes to Irrelevant Tasks Too Often*

Usually, no one wants to be seen as the bad guy so we are inclined to agreeing to tasks that are irrelevant to the results we seek. When you give people the impression that you are responsive to every request, you open yourself up to a flood of never-ending requests and saying no becomes difficult. Before saying yes to a task, take the time to evaluate whether it can lead to greater productivity or it would just be a waste of your time and energy. In the next section when we explain the mental models that can improve our productivity, we shall take a look at the Pareto principle to determine what to say yes to and what to say no to. But for now, suffice it to quote Warren Buffett on saying "no" as stated on the BBC Worklife website: "The difference between successful people and very successful people is that very successful people say 'no' to almost everything" (BBC, 2014).

## *Doing Everything Yourself*

One of the number one causes of burnout is trying to do everything yourself. When you fail to ask for help or build a system that makes your work more efficient you are slowing down yourself, using up more of your time and energy, and ignoring the leverage that can significantly increase your productivity. If there are tasks you repeat often, it is in your best interest to seek ways to automate that task to save yourself time, energy, and money. Automation and building a system is more efficient than multitasking because multitasking does not allow you to give your very best to any individual task. Instead, your attention is scattered all over the place trying to do everything at the same time. You do not know everything, nor should you try to. There principle known as the Circle of Competence (more on this later). Become good at what you do, even if it is just one thing, but allow others who are also good at what they do to assist you to attain your goals more efficiently than only you could ever do.

## *Trying to Get It Right the Very First Time*

It is okay to put your best effort into your work, but you should not become obsessed with perfection that you waste valuable time on trying to get things done perfectly from the very onset. The more attention to pay to perfectionism the lesser your productivity because you are focused on the nitty-gritty and paying less attention to the big picture, you spend too much time than required on problems and tasks, and you are always waiting for the perfect moment. There is no perfect moment to execute an idea than now. If you ever find a so-called perfect moment, you can be sure you are already too late!

## *Relying on Guesswork*

Making decisions without having reliable data is taking unnecessary risks. You cannot optimize productivity and maximize efficiency through guesswork. Taking time to do your research will save you a lot of pains, regrets, and wasted efforts. If you cannot find reliable data, you can examine your own results and determine what the best cause of action would be.

The next two sections of this chapter are focused on mental models that can help you optimize your productivity and improve your systems. Note that these mental models are not limited to only these two functions. I have only categorized them this way for the purpose of convenience, logic, and the flow of this book. They are very much applicable to other areas of life. Let me quickly add here that using mental models the way a kid in school recites his multiplication table is not the proper use of mental models. Your ability to know which mental model to use for any given situation shows your true knowledge and understanding of its function. As Charlie Munger puts it in his 1994 speech entitled, *A Lesson on Elementary Worldly Wisdom*:

"Well, the first rule is that you can't really know anything if you just remember isolated facts and try and bang 'em back. If the facts don't hang together on a latticework of theory, you don't have them in a usable form. You've got to have models in your head. And you've got to array your experience both vicarious and direct on this latticework of models. You may have noticed students who just try to remember and pound back what is remembered. Well, they fail in school and in life. You've got to hang experience on a latticework of models in your head." (Munger, 1994)

# Mental Models for Optimizing Productivity

### *Circle of Competence*

"I'm no genius. I'm smart in spots, but I stay around those spots" (Tom Watson Sr., Chairman, and CEO of IBM, 1914 – 1956).

The things you think you know are quite different from the things you know. If you build your life around the things you think you know, you may find that you are like the proverbial jack-of-all-trades who is incompetent in any of the trades. The circle of competence simply means that we all have areas where our knowledge and skills have been fully developed through experience and through some study. We are good at some things but not everything. Building your work and life around those areas where you are very competent will guarantee high productivity.

Perhaps the story of Thomas Watson Sr., the former CEO of IBM between the years 1914 to 1956, explains the idea of the Circle of Competence more clearly. After working for only one day as a teacher, he gave up the job and went for a one year course in accounting and business (Wikipedia, n.d.). He took up a job as a bookkeeper in 1891 earning just about $6 a week. His first job as a salesman was selling pianos and organs and making about $10 weekly. Dissatisfied, he quit and began selling sewing machines for a while, then peddling loans, and then finally started a butcher shop which failed afterward. That left him broke, without a job or any investment.

Watson had gathered experience in sales and knew that if given the right opportunity, he would do well in sales. He saw that opportunity when he met John J. Range, the Buffalo branch manager of National Cash Register – one of the leading selling organizations of the mid-1800s. Watson persisted until he was hired by Range in 1896. Range mentored Watson into a fine salesman who became the most successful salesman in the East. His earnings went from $10 to $100 a week. In 1914, Watson was hired as the general manager of Computing-Tabulating-Recording (CRT) Company and was made the president of the company after just 11 months. He doubled the company's revenue to $9 million, and in 1924, he renamed CRT to International Business Machines (IBM).

What are the takeaways from this story?

- Stick to what you are good at; you'll make more impact in your area of competence.

- If you keep jumping from one method of doing things to the other, you'll waste a lot of time and energy. Get good at applying a few important methods and your productivity will shoot through the roof.
- You may have the basic ideas of doing a thing and want to improve on it. That's okay. Devote time and energy to the learning of skills that will make you more productive.
- Don't be afraid to say you don't know a thing if you don't know it. However, if knowing it will greatly improve your odds of success in life, you should go ahead and learn it.
- Define a clear perimeter of your competencies and keep yourself within that perimeter. Gradually increase that perimeter over time to include areas that are absolutely necessary for your success.
- Never fool yourself into assuming that you can do a thing if it doesn't fall into your clearly defined perimeter.

**Bottom line**: Identify the area or a few areas where you are great and apply your most effort there. You will accomplish more and achieve greater things by limiting your focus to your circle of competence while allowing others who are skillful to compliment you in the areas you know little to nothing about.

## *Pareto Principle (The 80/20 Rule)*

Do you find yourself busy all day long but accomplish far less than the efforts you put into your activities? If that is the case, your unsatisfactory accomplishments are not an indication that you are lazy or not putting in the required effort. It, however, indicates that you are giving your effort to tasks that have low value or impact on your overall output. In most cases, you are assigning the same amount of importance to all your tasks and activities instead of focusing on only the very few that are guaranteed to double your output.

If you live your life by inverting the principle of garbage in, garbage out such that you put in your best efforts into every single activity that comes your way, perhaps it is time you considered modifying attitude a little bit with the Pareto principle which is also known as the 80/20 rule.

The Pareto principle states that about 20% of all causes results in about 80% of all effects. In simple terms, this means that of all your activities, only about 20% of these will account for about 80% of your results.

To break this down a bit further, if you itemize 10 things on your daily to-do list, only about two items on that list will have the greatest positive impact on your day in comparison to the other eight items put together. Given this to be true, wouldn't it be wise to prune your activities to the most vital and then give more attention and energy to those since they yield the greatest results?

The important thing in the 80/20 rule is not the exact percentage but that you should understand that in very many cases, a cause is not directly proportional to effect. This is especially true for productivity; a relatively small proportion of the causes (effort, time, attention, manpower, and tasks) usually yield the most effects.

The Pareto principle is applicable in almost every area of life. For example, only a small portion of your customers will account for a greater percentage of the total revenue your business generates. Recognizing these customers and paying more attention to satisfying their needs can significantly improve your revenue. The key to using this principle is for you to find out the primary cause of a particular result and then optimizing the result using the primary cause.

World-renowned motivational speaker and self-development author, Brian Tracy, shared an interesting story on his blog that captures the essence of the 80/20 rule. It was about one of his friends who wanted to double his income within three to five years using the Pareto principle (Tracy, 2018). The friend found that he spends equal amounts of time on both his high- and low-profit clients. He gave all his clients the same level of energy and devotion. On discovering the 80/20 rule, he carefully examined his client base and separated the high-profit clients from the low-profit clients. As expected, only a small percentage of his client base fell into the high-profit group, leaving the larger percentage in the low-profit group.

What the friend did next was both decisive and life-changing. He called in other professionals in his field and politely, strategically, and carefully handed off the low-profit clients (who represented only 20% of his business) to them. Next, he concentrated his energy and best efforts on the remaining smaller percentage that represented 80% of his business profits. He also began searching exclusively for new clients who matched the profile of his high-profit clients. His goal was to find those whom he could offer high-quality service in return for high profits.

The result of this move was incredible. Instead of achieving his goal of doubling his income in three to five years, his income doubled in only one year of using the Pareto principle to manage his time and energy.

We can also see something similar to the 80/20 principle in the story of Mike Flint, the personal pilot of Warren Buffett. Flint wanted to clearly define his career priorities, so he could maximize his focus and master his priorities. Mr. Buffett offered a two-step process for him to achieve his goal.

1. He asked Mike to write down 25 of his top career goals, which Flint did.
2. He asked Mike to carefully review the list and then circle out five of the most important goals from that list and have them as his second list. Mr. Flint complied as directed.

Mike Flint was determined to immediately start working on his second list – the top five most important of his career goals. Then, Mr. Buffett asked what he intends to do with his first list of top 20 items. Mr. Flint said his top five list is his primary target, but he'll give his attention to the list of top 20 items from time to time as he sees fit. At this point, Mr. Buffett gave him the most important lesson of the two-step process. He told Mr. Flint never to pay any attention to the list of 20 items and to avoid that list at all costs until he accomplishes his top 5 most important goals.

The lesson? Eliminating unnecessary activities will help you maximize your focus and energy. The activities that yield little to no results appear important to us unless we take time to thoroughly evaluate and handpick the ones that actually lead to greater results.

Here are some key points to keep in mind:

- A large number of your unproductive activities take up most of your time and energy. Invert this, and you'll figure out what tasks you need to focus on.
- Usually, tasks that produce the greatest positive impact appear the hardest. Tackle them first because the payoff for accomplishing them outweighs the results of accomplishing a multitude of other valueless tasks. Stop postponing your valuable tasks for the day.
- Doing many small irrelevant tasks is more appealing than tackling one or two major tasks. Don't give in to the temptation of clearing the irrelevant task first. As Brian Tracy puts it, look for the biggest frog and eat it first.
- Also, not all mental models will generate the greatest impact on your life. Find those that are really relevant to your goals and lifestyle and then apply them constantly.

**Bottom line:** Not everything in your life and work deserves equal attention and effort. To significantly reduce busying around and eventually improve your overall productivity, use the Pareto principle to discover the tasks and activities that have the greatest impact on both your personal and professional life and then concentrate your time, money, and energy on those activities.

## *Minimum Viable Product (MVP)*

Have you seen the number of useless mobile apps on app stores lately? They are all representative of someone's idea that was not tested before launching into the market. Those apps were developed on the assumption that there was a need for their use in the marketplace. Time and effort were put into their development, but it didn't meet the user's needs and, therefore, didn't sell as expected. Instead of an increase in productivity, the developers experienced the exact opposite. But no developer has failed unless he or she gives up on their idea and refuses to go back to the drawing board to trace where the error lies. The higher your ability to quickly detect your errors, the faster you will be at correcting and making necessary adjustments. This is an important fact to keep in mind when trying to improve productivity, go into any creative venture, or start up a new business.

Contrary to what the name suggests, a minimum viable product is not necessarily a product at all. Instead, it is a process for testing your ideas and assumptions to ensure that there is an actual need for your idea (and product).

The MVP test process can be broken into two tests.

1. The first test is to determine what your riskiest assumption is.
2. The second is to figure out the smallest and simplest experiment that can put the assumption to test.

If you don't use the MVP process especially when coming up with some new idea, you may discover to your utter dismay that you've wasted energy, money, and a whole lot of time on an idea that is of no benefit to anyone. For example, before devoting several months into designing and developing a mobile app, a business idea, or even a lifestyle change for yourself and your spouse, test whether or not others are interested in that idea. Go round your potential app users or whatever idea it is you are developing and figure out if there is a need for what you want to create. If there is none, it may be a bit heart-breaking, but you have saved yourself time, energy, and money. If there is a need for your idea, the MVP process continues in small increments until your product or idea is matured and has a steady growth.

No matter the current level of your productivity, there is no harm in going back to the drawing board and using the MVP process to optimize your productivity. Remember that testing your ideas is a continuous process, regardless of whether it is in your personal or work life.

For many successful people, their success usually began with failure. But they understood something very important, and it was that failure is feedback. One of such people is Bill Gates, founder of Microsoft, multiple times world's richest man, and currently the second richest man on earth with a net worth of $103.7 billion (Forbes, 2019). Gates's first company known as Traf-O-Data failed. As a matter of fact, during the first demo of that business, the machine didn't work! Gates, alongside his business partner, Paul Allen, went back to the drawing board and continued testing their ideas and assumptions until Microsoft was born.

But for some other people, success begins with a failing streak! Such was the case of Sir James Dyson, the British inventor with a net worth of $5.4 billion (Forbes 2019). His first, second, and up to 5,127 prototypes for a bag-less vacuum all failed. Talk about sticking to your vision! Dyson is a modern-day Thomas Edison who didn't consider his many failed attempts as failures but 10,000 ways his ideas won't work. Dyson went back to the drawing board each time he failed until he got it right. In his words, "There are countless times an inventor can give up on an idea. By the time I made my 15th prototype, my third child was born. By 2,627, my wife and I were really counting our pennies. By 3,727, my wife was giving art lessons for some extra cash. These were tough times, but each failure brought me closer to solving the problem" (Dyson, 2003).

**Bottom Line:** While it may be great to stick to your ideas and work relentlessly to come up with something that is of benefit to you and others, you can avoid the colossal waste of time and resources by testing your idea with incremental development steps.

## *Division of Labor*

That no one can do everything on their own is no new knowledge; in spite of this, we still fall into the trap of trying to accomplish everything on our own. Imagine a large household where only the mother goes about doing everything from cleaning to laundry and cooking, mowing the grass, taking out the trash, and just about all the house chores. Other members of the household would become redundant and the mother would be worn out. Over time, her overall output will start to decline due to continuous burnout.

Unfortunately, this scenario can play out at work especially if you have a small business or you are a start-up. It is expected that over time, start-up's expand to hire more manpower to allow for division of labor and division of work. The two are similar but not the same.

Division of labor means separating work into different tasks, roles, and steps which ultimately results in the specialization. Division of work refers to breaking down work into different tasks with the goal of scaling yourself and your business. Nevertheless, both are often used interchangeably. For the purpose of this book, I use both meanings when I refer to the division of labor.

I do not intend to lecture you on this fundamental principle of economics, so we shall not go into the nitty-gritty of it. All the same, if you can put this one principle to work in your professional endeavour, you will begin to see significant improvement in your productivity because you are not just dividing work, but you are equally building an efficient and interdependent system. By allowing people to handle different aspects of your work, they will specialize in those areas and form a formidable team of experts.

On the flip side, having just one person that is the go-to guy for every aspect of your business is not healthy for your business even if the go-to guy is yourself. Self-sufficiency is not a positive trait when it comes to running a business that involves hiring other employees. Instead of leading to greater output, it causes burnout, overdependence on one person, and redundancy among the others.

Applying the principle of division of labor can also be in the form of asking for help. This is particularly true if you are an employee. Don't bury yourself under a mountain of tasks working yourself to stupor just to complete them alone. Even if you are an expert in your field, learn to delegate some tasks (if you have the power to do so) or ask for help from others. Arrogance is a negative trait that can prevent you from asking for help. Arrogant people will prefer to suffer silently than simply ask for help. If you are in business, arrogance can cost you a lot of money!

Asking for help lightens your workload, gives you time off from work to do other equally important things, decreases your stress level, and gives you the time you need to get out of your own way.

Perhaps one of the leaders who masterfully demonstrated the use of division of labor was Henry Ford, who, at the time of his death, was worth $100 million (Forbes, 2017). Before Ford's advancement in automobile production, cars were previously produced by craftsmen. Typically, the craftsmen are highly skilled individuals who are very knowledgeable about every aspect of cars including the physics of cars, design, mechanics, metallurgy, engineering, and so on. Many of the craftsmen could build a car from scratch to finish by themselves – they were that good.

Then came Ford with his assembly line, which is basically the division of labor. He put together a small team that designed cars as well as map out the assembly process. Then another team – a larger one built the cars. Usually, the larger team is made up of both skilled and unskilled workers. The process was so simple that just about anyone can be included in the larger team to help build a car even if they are so uninformed that they have never seen a car before!

The entire process was faster, more efficient, cost less, and increased the production of cars. Also, there was no clash or overlap of knowledge and skills. Each person knows only what he needs to do his job well and that was sufficient to accomplish the task. There was no need for any single assembly worker to know every detail about building cars. In fact, an assembly worker could focus only on building wheels without knowing what a complete car looks like – as long as he can screw parts together, he'll be okay. This leads to specialization as each worker gets used to his part of the work and that in turn led to a higher quality of job output.

**Bottom Line:** Your work and personal life get easier if you apply the principle of division of labor. Allow others to do what they do best and focus on specializing in what you do best. That is a more efficient way to live.

## *Incentives*

Incentives are rewards that are used to motivate people. The concept is built on the idea that we are likely to do what is in our own best interest. Providing the right incentive can alter how people behave. The key phrase here is the right incentive. Finding the right incentive requires that you know exactly what will motivate people and then aligning what you intend to achieve with what will motivate them. For example, a parent promises to buy his child their favorite toy if they got good grades. The child is interested in getting the new toy so they'll concentrate more on their schoolwork and perform better because they want the reward.

As adults, our motivations differ, but there's one common motivator among many adults, and that is money. Promise an employee a promotion or a raise, and he'll be willing to put in extra effort into his job. This was clearly demonstrated by FedEx employees who were supposed to handle overnight shipping services. Initially, it was difficult for FedEx to keep up with delivery schedules because employees moving packages from one plane to the next wasn't fast enough, and the planes were delayed.

To solve this problem, FedEx introduced an incentive. It was no longer going to be "payment per hour" but "payment per shift." That means that no matter the number of hours the employees moving packages put in, their pay would remain the same. In other words, they could finish their work sooner and go home, yet be paid the same amount. The night shift employees saw no reason why they shouldn't work faster and FedEx got what it desired – an efficient overnight shipping service. It was a win-win situation for all.

Non-monetary incentives can also be used to boost productivity in your business. A very good example of aligning incentives with your goals can be seen in the Lambda School cofounded by Austen Allred. What is spectacular about Lambda School is that it aligns its business ideas with the motivation of its students. Students who are accepted into the school's program don't pay a dime to the school until they graduate, and the school gets them a job that pays at least $50,000 annually. After this, the school can begin to deduct a small amount from their monthly income for up to two years (Indie Hacker, 2018).

But Austen Allred didn't just start Lambda School on a platter of gold. He had the misfortune of watching his business implode, and he ran into debts. He then began learning some life-transforming lessons that helped him put his entrepreneurial experience to good use and recovered his lost fortune at the same time help others change their lives with the Lambda School. And by the way, he learned those lessons from Charlie Munger and Jeff Bezos!

Okay, so should you start promising your employees mouth-watering rewards to get them triple your revenue? Well, incentives have to be right. If you overdo it to make people meet unrealistic goals, they may end up cutting corners and eventually jeopardize your business. This was the case with Wells Fargo when in 2016, the company was fined several millions of dollars for creating unauthorized accounts for clients without their consent (Shapiro, 2018). Wells Fargo employees wanted to meet unrealistic quotas, so they cut corners and landed the company in a financial scandal.

So, what are the takeaways from these stories?

- As a leader, you can modify the behavior of your group to achieve your goals if you carefully align your goals with the incentives you offer to your group.
- Be sure to be clear on what you want if you are using incentives to motivate employee performance. Let them know that you are interested in increased revenue generation, but not to the detriment of the company.
- Money is a great way to motivate people, but it certainly is not the only way to offer incentives.
- You can combine incentives with loss aversion power to increase the chances of compliance. For example, instead of positively motivating an employee, you could imply that certain privileges will be withdrawn if they fail to meet a

goal.

**Bottom Line:** Others are likely to put in more effort if they have the right level of motivation. Use that right level of motivation to steer them towards your goal.

# Mental Models for System Thinking

## *KISS Principle*

What better model to start with than one which teaches the simplicity of a system? KISS is an acronym for Keep It Simple Stupid. It originated back in 1960 when Kelly Johnson, an American aeronautical and systems engineer, handed a few tools to his team of engineers and challenged them to keep the design of the jet aircraft they were building simple such that an average mechanic under combat conditions can repair the aircraft with only those tools (Wikipedia, n.d.). This KISS principle does not imply stupidity; rather, it means keeping system designs simple, while being able to perform functions optimally, is the best form of sophistication.

You don't have to be an engineer or a mechanic to use the KISS principle. Here's how you can apply it to your life and work to optimize productivity.

1. **Time Management:** It is easy to feel overwhelmed when you want to do everything at the same time because your mind is focused on the complexity of handling and accomplishing multiple tasks within the shortest possible time. KISS the overwhelmed feeling by making a list of the

things you need to do in their order of importance and begin to prioritize them. As you complete tasks, cross them off the list to give you a sense of accomplishment.

2. **Relationships:** Keep your relationships with others very simple by taking what they say at face value. Stop wasting your time and energy on trying to figure out if they have some hidden agenda. Simply accept their truth and move on with your life. Also, say the things you mean, and mean the things you say. Stop complicating your communication; it's a sheer waste of time.

3. **Problem Solving:** If you identify a problem, don't wait for someone else to resolve it. Even if you can't fix it or it is not your job to fix it, you can take steps to resolve it by simply pointing it out. If you let mind games to encroach into your work, it will complicate issues that can be resolved long before it became critical.

4. **Sending Messages:** Whether it is hand-written, text, verbal, or by email, be concise. Leave out unnecessary details. It saves valuable time for everyone. Also, it prevents miscommunication.

5. **Work and Life Balance:** To enjoy personal or family life and your work life, there must be a clear boundary between the two. Focus on your work when it is time for work. Keep work out of your family or personal time. Don't complicate things by mixing the two – it doesn't result in more productivity. Instead, creating and respecting the boundary between the two can lead to productivity at work and a happier version of you and your family life.

6. **Health:** Instead of fussing over what diet to choose, simply

asking yourself what types of food are healthier will point you in the right direction. Exercising doesn't necessarily have to be in a fancy gym. What physical activities do you enjoy doing? These are things that can easily be your form of exercise.

**Bottom line:** It doesn't make your personal life or work life easier to complicate things. Whether it is a process, system, or technique for doing a thing, always remember this: keep simple tasks as simple as possible. The ultimate form of sophistication is simplicity.

## *Checklist*

Imagine setting up your projector and screen for an important business presentation and then realizing that you forgot to bring along the projector cord! Failing to close a deal because you forgot something as small as a cord may not be that much of a big deal – you could close a better deal the very next day, but forgetting a surgical tool inside a patient you operated or operating the wrong body part (yes, it happens) can lead to serious complications, irreparable damages, and even death.

Question: Why do we forget the most common things? Why do we for routine tasks that we repeat even almost daily?

Short answer: We have limited memory and attention.

Long answer: Complex tasks, repetitive tasks, and tasks that involve too many steps tend to be difficult for our brain to remember from start to finish. It is not that we do not know what should be done, but it is our brain's inability to retain every single detail of what needs to be done.

This is why a checklist is a powerful tool in that it stimulates thought. It outlines the number of things (steps, items, processes, and so on) that needs to be completed during the performance of a task. This limits errors and accidents as well as increases consistency and accuracy.

The checklist is not a sophisticated piece of equipment that costs staggering amounts of dollars. It is probably the cheapest tool you could ever get. It is almost free! Just a piece of paper, yet it can and is saving lives, businesses, and careers. Imagine the number of doctors and pilots that would be out of a job, serving jail terms (for negligence), or paying heavy fines if not for the power of this simple but effective tool.

One glaring example of the negative impact of not using a checklist especially during handling complex tasks is that of a two-year-old boy who was accidentally castrated by surgeons (The Guardian, 2019).

The boy who had an undescended testicle was scheduled for a routine operation that shouldn't take more than 30 minutes. However, after a grueling two-and-a-half-hour wait, his parents were informed that a camera had been mistakenly inserted into the wrong testicle and had damaged the healthy testicle. This meant that their son had been castrated. Of course, the hospital offered their sincerest apologies and also launched an investigation. This could have been avoided if the surgeons religiously followed the checklist.

While a doctor can offer his sincerest apologies for depending solely on his memory instead of a checklist, a pilot does not have that option. His life, crew members, and everyone aboard his airplane will be at a huge risk if he fails to use a checklist.

But is a checklist meant for only doctors and pilots? Certainly not! Nor is it limited to closing business deals or helping you to deliver a powerful presentation. Your checklist could be something as simple as your daily to-do list, grocery or shopping checklist, wedding checklist, packing checklist, moving checking, and so on. Depending on your memory to remember these details can slow you down, lead to mistakes – grievous ones – and appearing incompetent.

A checklist gives you a sense of accomplishment. As you cross things off your list, you get the inner satisfaction that you are making progress, and you'll naturally want to cross everything off. This increases your productivity level. It is also easier to delegate or enlist the help of another person when you have a checklist. The other person will know exactly what it is you want them to do since they are all written down. Additionally, a checklist helps you to be more organized knowing exactly what steps to take when performing a task.

**Bottom Line**: To make your tasks a lot less complicated, go over the things you do repeatedly at home or at work. Once you've identified them, create a checklist of all the steps required to perform that task. Now go ahead and begin to use that checklist. It will help you to minimize errors and increase the speed with which you complete your routine tasks.

# *Redundancy*

How often have you heard the saying, "Don't put all your eggs in one basket?" Take the advice because it is good advice. Risking everything in a bid to secure a single venture doesn't really show thorough thinking and negates the second-order thinking. This is where the principle of redundancy comes in handy.

In Engineering, redundancy is the idea of including additional components into a system to checkmate system failure. It involves duplicating a system's critical components to increase the reliability of that system. In layman's terms, it is simply providing backups or backup systems that ensure the continuous functioning of a system even after a failure occurs.

For example, having more than one source of income in a family, including a spare tire in your car, backing up data in external hard drives, and so on. The main purpose of redundancy is to significantly reduce (or completely eliminate) any negative impact that can occur when a system fails.

How can you use redundancy in your daily life? And in what way does it improve productivity in your professional endeavor?

- Consider backing up critical information relating to your business not just on any hardware but using cloud programs. Also, create redundancy for critical parts of your business like getting a backup generator for your business (and home too).
- You can begin to think of ways to generate extra income or create an emergency fund just in case some unforeseen event

happens and you lose your only source of income.

- If you are making an online presentation, for example, you could include both audio and text-only options for your users. The same goes for producing user manuals; you can include a paper manual alongside the audio version in case the audio doesn't work.
- If you are a business owner, you would understand that overdependence on an individual employee can result from specialization. To checkmate this, you can complement the principle of division of labor with the principle of redundancy. Here's how to do that. Identify the critical areas of your business – those areas that a single failure can result in the complete shutdown of your business. During your hiring process, enlist at least two people who can competently handle each of those critical areas. Of course, only one of them should man those areas while the other will handle other tasks. In the case where the employee handling the critical area is indisposed, you can fall back on your backup employee to temporarily handle the critical area.

**Bottom Line:** Take some time to think about the critical systems that exist in your life. Try to figure out what you would do if any of these systems fail and begin to put these backup plans in place. The earlier you begin to do that the lesser your chances of running aground would be in case of a system failure in your business or in your personal life.

## *Bottleneck (the Theory of Constraint)*

The weakest link of a chain is the strongest point on that chain. If anything goes wrong with that weakest link, then it doesn't matter how strong the other links are; that chain is coming apart. This is the fundamental idea behind the theory of constraint or the bottleneck principle.

Every system – your physical body, your car, your company – has some constraints, but there is one constraint that is tighter than every other one. That constraint is called the bottleneck. The bottleneck is the point of greatest congestion that is capable of slowing down the entire system. It is similar to the weakest link on a chain – fix the bottleneck and the entire system will work better. Fix other constraints without first of all tackling the problem of the bottleneck, and it would just amount to a waste of effort as far as the entire system is concerned. For any improvement to affect the entire system, there is a need to first identify and remove the bottleneck.

Here is a simple example that shows how a bottleneck can slow down an otherwise efficient system. Let us assume it takes you under 15 minutes to drive to your place of work, but it takes another 45 minutes or more to find parking, it means that finding parking is a huge bottleneck in getting to work. Buying a better car will be an effort in futility because it doesn't address the bottleneck.

Whether you are focused on personal development or concerned about improving your work, you must first understand that these things have different interconnected parts that make them all function as a whole. Your life may seem to you as if it is in shambles, and you are worried about fixing your life using different self-improvement programs. But not everything in your life needs fixing. If you do not identify your personal bottleneck, you will waste too much time and effort shouting into the wind. It may be that your bottleneck is your thinking process. Once that is fixed, every other part of your system will fall into place. In other words, more effort is not exactly what you need. What you need is to effectively apply the effort.

For example, if a task involving five steps takes about three hours to complete but more than two hours of that time is spent only on one of the steps, then shortening the time it takes to complete that one step will significantly improve the time it takes to complete the entire task.

Some of the common causes of bottlenecks in a work setting are:

- Waiting for information – especially if that information is critical to completing a task and the person to provide the information isn't forthcoming.
- Working in a team – this is especially true if one or more members are dragging feet on their part of the work.
- Perfectionism – as much as it is important to do a great job, constantly tweaking it to make it perfect can result in a huge waste of time.
- Handling unpleasant tasks – this is one of the causes of procrastination. You are likely to waste too much time getting started on a task that you don't enjoy doing.
- Difficult tasks – a task may not necessarily take much time to accomplish, but getting to understand how to handle it may take up too much time and effort. For example, putting

in five hours of research time for a task that can be completed in 30 minutes like writing a dissertation on a topic you don't really understand.

To identify and eliminate bottlenecks, consider the following recommendations:

1. Try to figure out where you procrastinate. Most of the time, procrastination results from activities that are not mentally stimulating for you and can eventually lead to a bottleneck. You can remove this bottleneck by automating that task using software or apps. You can also consider outsourcing such tasks.

2. Identify your creative blocks. Sometimes, we spend too much time on a task trying to figure out the best way to solve them. This can slow us down. You can eliminate this by splitting your creative tasks into two phases: idea-generation phase and idea-refining phase. Trying to accomplish both phases at the same time can lead to a creative block. First, gather as many raw ideas that are relevant to your task without bothering about tweaking them. After that, take the time to piece them together and refine them into a coherent whole.

3. When working in a group, what areas do you depend on others to complete your task? You may not have complete control over this, but you can speed up the process by taking precautionary measures to ensure that others are on the same page as you. Communicate early with team members. When you get a request to complete a task as a group, make sure to add extra hours (or days) to the deadline to take care

of possible delays in the project completion.

Removing one bottleneck alone may not automatically fix every constraint in a system. However, it is the first step in allowing us to see other constraints in a proper light. As you work on eliminating only one bottleneck at a time, your entire system gets better over time.

**Bottom Line:** Concentrate your effort on fixing your bottleneck first. Ignore every other so-called solution for other constraints. They don't impact the entire system. Remember that you can get your entire system working faster by fixing just one bottleneck.

# Chapter 5: Getting Want You Want... Like This

In this final chapter, we are going to focus our attention on how to use mental models to improve our communication, particularly in the art of persuasion. You don't have to be a salesperson, a businessman, or a professional negotiator before you can effectively persuade others. There are quite a number of mental models that you can use to enhance your ability to think better during negotiations and persuading others, but we are going to consider only a few of them in this chapter. Before then, let us consider the common communication mistakes that people make in an attempt to persuade others to see their point of view.

## Common Persuasion Mistakes

It is important to first distinguish between the different types of persuaders. Briefly, we all fall into one of these three categories:

1. **Detectives:** These are people who have a deep understanding of the art of persuasion. They employ the principles of persuasion and are honest in their attempts at creating a win-win situation for themselves and those whom they persuade. They don't rely on only one communication approach for every person or people they encounter. Instead, they take their time to do the groundwork to get a good understanding of the mindset of their audience and then approach them accordingly. They do not come across as pushy and coercive in their persuasion even

though they are assertive and know when to shift ground to allow mutual compromise. They don't set out to get the other person to agree to their position. Their mindset is always set on finding a middle ground that is beneficial to all involved.

2. **Smugglers:** These are people who understand what the correct principles persuasion are but prefer to cut corners by manipulating the other person or their audience. To the smugglers, following principles slows down the process of getting what they want, so they can lie, withhold critical information, exaggerate information, or distort the truth to get their way regardless of what their manipulation will cost others. Smugglers are those who are quick to twist the idea that the end justifies the means to suit their selfish agenda. They are not limited to corrupt politicians alone. Abusive spouses, manipulative bosses, dishonest salespersons, and many others fall into this category.

3. **Bunglers:** These are people who do not understand the principles of persuasion are, so they miss great opportunities to effectively communicate their point of view. At every opportunity, they simply bungle their way through and fail to get the results they seek. Some of them may intuitively know one or two things about the techniques of persuasion, but they lack the skills to put them to effective use. They do not necessarily manipulate others like persuasive smugglers do, however, they just don't know how to persuade people.

Now let us consider some mistakes that bunglers and smugglers make during persuasion.

## Confusing Great Arguments for Persuasion

Presenting your point with sound reasoning and a lot of logic doesn't necessarily mean you will win the other person over. You need to make the other person see your position by connecting emotionally with them. As you know, emotions defy logic most of the time, so great arguments alone don't always work. Lacing your words with expressive and figurative language is necessary to tilt the odds in your favor.

## Starting Out Too Strongly

Beginning with a strong stance is simply giving the other person a reason to object. Many people start out their persuasive process with a strong case and then try to push the other person over with a lot of enthusiasm and persistence. This is almost always guaranteed to fail. Begin your persuasion without giving the other person something to fight against. Find a mutual ground and gradually nudge the other person towards your point of view or request.

## Refusing to Compromise

Many people think that a compromise means surrendering their position. If you understand the principle of reciprocity, particularly the rejection-then-retreat technique you would know how to use compromise to your advantage. I'll explain how to use that technique in the next section of this chapter. When you refuse to shift ground, you are telling the other person that it is either your way or no other way. A compromise tells the other person that you are flexible and willing to listen to their concerns and viewpoints.

## *Thinking Persuasion Is a One-Off Event*

Unless you are a persuasive smuggler who uses persuasion as a hit-and-run tool, persuasion cannot be used as a one-off event if you want it to yield a continuous effect. This is particularly true when you are trying to persuade a group such as your team, employees, entire family members, or an entire organization. Persuasion is a process that involves building credibility, stating positions, testing the positions, making compromises, and a continuous repeat of these processes until a mutually beneficial position is reached.

## *Assuming Your Message Is Understood*

When you present your position without giving room for questions or input, you are assuming that your position has been accepted. If you have given a presentation, for example, give those who listened to your presentation the chance to ask questions no matter how powerfully logical your arguments are.

# The Psychology of Persuasion

To increase our understanding of how to persuade others, let us take a quick look at Dr. Robert B. Cialdini's work on how social psychology intersects with marketing. His book, *Influence: The Psychology of Persuasion*, is widely considered one of the best works in the field of persuasion. The book focuses on six key principles that can be used to positively influence customers' behavior. However, we can apply these principles in our daily lives to help us improve our communication as it relates to persuading others. So, even if you are not trying to sell anyone any product or service, learning these principles can put you in an advantageous position. By the way, you can sell your idea and perspective to a loved one, friend, and colleague.

## *Persuasion Principle #1: Reciprocity*

Imagine that your car won't start when you are already running late for work. Your neighbor gives you a ride to your office even their route is totally different from yours. You are grateful for their help, but you'll be on the lookout for a way to return the favor. Why? Reciprocity! It is an unwritten social rule that when you receive something good, it is expected that you reciprocate with a good gesture too. This is why we seem to behave nicer to those who are nice to us. Quantity or size doesn't matter in reciprocity; you may offer a total stranger an ordinary pen to write with when they need one, and in turn, they link you up with someone very influential.

Almost every business uses this principle to get potential customers to make purchases. It is no surprise to see free newsletters, ebooks, trial versions of products, webinars, reports, and so on target at offering prospects a taste of what they can get if and when they eventually make a purchase. Doing something nice for someone first puts them in the uncomfortable position of wanting to return the favor because if they don't, they'll feel shame on some level (whether real or perceived) and they'll be deemed ungrateful.

How does this apply to your daily life? To get others to be more receptive to you and increase your chances of persuading them, always be nice to them. The least they can do to return the favor is to listen to your proposition. It is easier to get someone to shift ground if they are morally indebted to you in some way. The key is to be the first to act positively towards them so that they "owe you one," and then you can call in the favor. This is applicable to people you know both on a professional and social level.

Persuasion is easier if the other person or people trust you. Sharing something important with someone is also another way to make them reciprocate by trusting you more. Be careful though not to give out information that others can use against you in the future.

Another way you can use the principle of reciprocity to persuade others is by asking for a favor that you know cannot be easily fulfilled. Then, when the favor cannot be met (an outcome you already envisioned), you make a second minor request which is what you originally wanted in the first place. Since your second request is significantly lesser than the first, it is easier and more likely to be fulfilled. This is known as the rejection-then-retreat technique. The idea behind this technique is that you are seen as willing to shift ground and come to a compromise even when it means sacrificing your first option. The other person will feel more inclined to reciprocate your compromise and sacrifice by fulfilling your request.

Keep in mind that the principle of reciprocity is intended to build trust that results in mutual benefits between people. This can only be true if you use this principle genuinely devoid of any agenda.

It is quite easy for those who do not understand the art of persuasion (bunglers) to confuse contracts with reciprocity. Feeling obligated to return a favor is very different than doing something based on some condition. A contract is generally in the form of I will do X on the condition that you do Y. Don't assume that someone who enters a contract with you is obligated to do you any favor or is open to considering your viewpoint. He or she is only bounded by the terms of the contract and not any social norm.

## *Persuasion Principle #2: Consistency and Commitment*

Usually, we all want to appear to behave consistently with our commitments. Once we make a choice, especially an open one, we'll go to great lengths to maintain that image of ourselves. This means that if someone can get us to make a commitment, they can easily persuade us to do what appears consistent with that commitment even if that thing isn't really what we originally signed up for. The internal pressure we feel is usually linked to our desire to be seen in good light which is similar to seeking external approval.

The key to using this principle is to first get the other person to see themselves in a new (usually higher) light. Once you get their self-image in that new position, they are more likely to comply with a lot of your requests that help to maintain that self-image. For example, getting a customer to make their first purchase of something dubbed "exclusive" is a way to get the feeling that they belong to a higher income class. It would be easier to get them to make other expensive purchases since they would not want to be seen as inconsistent with their status.

You can use this principle to get others to agree to your requests especially if you can get them to make an open commitment or a written one. This can also work very well with getting colleagues in the workplace to behave in ways that are in keeping with their commitment. Asking a colleague what their goals and priorities are and then channeling your requests to conform with those goals and priorities will make it difficult for them to turn down your requests.

Another way to use this principle is to ask someone to do something instead of telling them. When you ask and get a yes, it increases the likelihood of the person doing what you want. Consider the following statements:

1. "Please, inform me on time if you can't keep the appointment."
2. "Will you please inform me on time if you can't keep the appointment?"

The first statement simply tells a person what you want them to do and is less likely to make the other person keep the appointment. The second statement is a question, and it is framed in a way that engages consistency because the question appeals to their sense of commitment.

Do not try to use the principle of commitment and consistency to trick people into an agreement. Instead, see it as a tool to improve your chances of persuading others to agree to your genuine cause. In order to use this principle effectively, you must develop the ability to align your proposals and request with what others see as valuable. In other words, if your agenda is self-serving, it will be difficult to get others to see that your proposal will be beneficial to them. And even if you trick them into an agreement, as a persuasive smuggler would do, it will be difficult to keep up act unless you have the misguided understanding that persuasion is a one-time event.

It is important to also know how to break yourself free from this way of thinking if someone is using this principle to make you agree to almost everything they want. First, you need to be sure of what your true values are and don't be carried away by approval-seeking behavior. If you feel internal pressure to behave consistently with some prior commitment which is no longer in keeping with your core values, do not hesitate to turn down a request. Don't be trapped by external social pressure and internal psychological pressure to do or agree to what you don't want to.

## *Persuasion Principle #3: Social Proof*

Social proof, which can also be called herd mentality, is overdependence on what others around us are doing. Many times we look to how others behave to know if a thing is right or wrong especially in situations of uncertainty. If others are doing something, it is reasonable to consider it socially acceptable. After all, none of us want to be out of touch with the acceptable norm.

The need to fit in is our way of avoiding judgment. Marketing companies understand this, which is why they dub their products as the number one selling product! It makes sense for you to go for that product since the people buying can't all be wrong, right? Testimonials are also included in advertising where people who are just like you enjoy the benefits of product or service. All these are geared toward persuading you to do business with them.

How can you use social proof to persuade others in your life if you are not a sales representative or selling anything? First, understand that if you can show that a good number of people agree or accept your idea, it becomes easy to use that as social proof to persuade others. For example, instead of just telling someone to behave in a particular way, show them that all the other people in their group are already behaving that way. In other words, you are shifting their attention from the unwanted behavior (without necessarily judging it) to the wanted behavior by pointing out the positives of the wanted behavior. It works both at home and in the workplace because no one likes to be the odd one out, especially if what you are proposing doesn't contradict their core beliefs in a strong way.

A little caveat here – do not compel people to do want they truly don't want to do, especially if they are not violating any rule by being unique. Persuasion is not about getting every single person to agree with what you propose or to fulfill your request 100% of the time. Respect people's views and learn how to make compromises if that will make them shift ground. Persuasion reduces conflicts in your personal and professional relationships with others. If you are trying to persuade people and the conflict level in your relationships is on the rise, it shows you are not using the persuasion principles correctly.

## *Persuasion Principle #4: Liking*

In ancient times, a messenger who brought bad news was killed! Why? It is for the same reason you like people who bring you pleasant news and tend to dislike people who are known to bring bad news even when they are not the cause of the bad news.

The principle of liking simply means that we like those who like us and are more inclined to listen to their suggestions or fulfill their requests. A salesperson who spend too much time describing how great his product or service is and all the benefits that customer can get from using his product or service may miss out on his opportunity to persuade the customer if they don't like him. Quite often, the difference between making a sale or not is whether the other person likes you. This is why a customer can bypass several stores selling an item he or she wants to buy just to get to a particular store because he or she likes the owner of that store.

Ignoring the principle of liking is throwing away a huge chance of connecting with your audience and making them pre-approve you. When people like you, they are predisposed to hear you out and receive your message.

Highlighting similarities increases your chances of being liked than emphasizing differences. This is where empathy and rapport building works magic. Giving compliments, especially genuine ones, can also help other people like you better. A compliment is akin to pleasant news, which makes the receiver likes the bringer of the pleasant news more. Many con artists have used compliments to distract their marks and get their way because we tend to be suckers for flattery, even if it is not genuine.

Taking the time to learn a few things about the person you want to persuade is a good way of connecting with them. You can't offer a genuine compliment about a person's positive traits if you don't know anything about them. Attempting that would give you away as a phony and ruin your chances of influencing them to do what you want.

Here's one other technique you can use to tilt people toward liking you more: improve your halo effect. The halo effect is a cognitive bias that makes us take one characteristic (or a few) and forms an opinion about a person, an organization, or a brand. Have you wondered why we tend to be shocked when a good-looking person behaves badly or a shabby-looking person turns out to be a successful millionaire? It is because we use one characteristic (in this case, their appearance) to judge their entire personality.

Marketing companies use the halo effect when they use a charismatic and attractive person in their marketing campaigns. Usually, they will get celebrities to use or wear their products. Since a lot of people like the celebrity, it stands to reason that they will also want to buy the product the celebrities endorse.

So, how can you improve your halo effect? Start by coming off as confident even if you don't have an attractive look in your own estimation. Don't neglect to work on your appearance (good nutrition, moderate exercise, and adequate sleep). Also, always put your best foot forward. It doesn't matter if you are meeting people face-to-face or through a medium like your website or blog, always think about the impression you want others to have about you and then channel your efforts towards making your personal brand reflect that image.

## *Persuasion Principle #5: Authority*

This principle relates to our collective tendency to be easily persuaded by people in authority. You'll have certain reservations and may even out-rightly object if a person with the wrong credentials asks you to do a thing. However, if someone with the right credentials asks you to do the same thing, you are most likely to comply. For example, if a stranger tells you to take a certain drug for your ailment, you'll probably not listen to them. But if that same stranger is in a doctor's uniform with a stethoscope around his neck, you'll probably consider his advice. You may not heed his advice but the sign of his credentials (uniform and stethoscope) made you give him the benefit of the doubt.

This was how we were raised as children. Parents, teachers, and other adults rewarded us for obeying them and punish, scold, or show displeasure when we disobey them. So, we are conditioned to obey constituted authority. And by the way, that's a good thing – better than its polar opposite, anarchy.

When you try to persuade others, especially if the other person or your audience knows little to nothing about you, it is helpful if you say a few things about your credentials. Let them know why they should take you seriously. Be careful not to overdo it though as that can make you appear desperate.

## *Persuasion Principle #6: Scarcity*

When the availability of an opportunity appears limited we tend to place more value on it. This is the basic idea behind the scarcity principle. The principle is somewhat similar to the loss-aversion mental model. The reason this principle works so well is that we tend to believe that things that are scarce are better than things we can easily acquire. We want something other people don't have or can't have because we want to be the ones who stand out.

"Limited copies available," "This offer is time-sensitive," "This is the limited edition." Do you see how this works? Deadlines and limited availability are used to make something appear more valuable and makes it easier to persuade people to seize the opportunity. Advertisers use these types of lines to persuade people into taking action immediately because not acting immediately may mean they would have to wait and possibly miss out entirely. And no one wants to miss out.

The more your information or idea appears scarce, the more likely it is that you can persuade others to want to listen to you. Become less eager to get other people to see your point of view. Being readily available makes you appear desperate and too eager. Learn to keep your enthusiasm in check. Have you ever wondered why women play hard to get? Scarcity! The harder it is to get her attention (within reason), the higher the value a man places on her. Be assertive and confident about your position.

# The Power of "Because": The Mental Model of Reason Respecting

One powerful way to get people to do what you want is to give them a reason to do it. When you tag your reason with the word "because," it can significantly increase the odds of getting others to comply with your request **because** it explains why they should. People usually resist change even without consciously realizing it. But when you give others a reason to do something different and highlight the reason with the word "because," it becomes easier to persuade them to do what you want. Consider the following statements used to encourage action from your website visitors:

1. "Call us now."
2. "Call us now because this offer is limited."

The first statement tells your website visitors what to do without a reason. The second statement tells them what to do and why they need to do it. You are giving them a reason (valid or not) to take action.

Take your mind back to when you were a little kid when your parents will tell you to do something like cleaning your room and you asked why. Even as a child, you resisted change. But when your parents would say, "because it's good to have a neat room", "because you're a good boy," or simply, "because I said so," you complied whether or not you understood the reason for their request.

We seem to need a justification to take action regardless of whether the justification is valid. The Copy Machine Study in the late '70s is a relevant example. Psychologist Ellen Langer headed a study in 1978 gathering data from a busy college campus photocopy center. Back in those days, Xerox machines were used for making copies and a lot of people waited in line to make copies in that photocopy center.

The study participants were given three different questions that were carefully worded to test people's response. They asked those waiting in line if they could skip the line and make copies. The following are the three questions and the responses as recorded in the study (Langer, 1978).

1. "Excuse me, I have 5 pages. May I use the Xerox machine?" Only 60% of the sample population said yes.

2. "Excuse me, I have 5 pages. May I use the Xerox machine because I have to make copies?" 93% said yes.
3. "Excuse me, I have 5 pages. May I use the Xerox machine because I'm in a rush?" 94% of the sample population said yes.

The first request had a low positive response because there was no reason given. The second and third request had very high positive responses because a reason was given. However, note that there was only a 1% difference between the second and third groups of responses even though the third reason is more valid than the second. There was a 93% positive response without minding if the reason was bogus or not. "Because I have to make copies" is not a valid reason! Of course, you want to make copies! Why else would you be waiting in line in a photocopy center? This shows that we are somehow programmed to respond more favorably to reason than a bland request.

So, whether you are trying to get clients to agree to your proposal, get people to work with or for you, asking for favors from family and friends, or when you need just about anyone to do something for you, consider using the word "because" in your persuasion **because** you now know how powerful a tool it can be.

# Warren Buffett: A Few Practical Lessons in Persuasion

The third richest man in the world (Forbes, 2019) and one of the most successful investors of all time, Warren Buffett is an incredibly persuasive individual. Psychologist Robert Cialdini explains why people easily pay attention to Mr. Buffet (and it isn't just because of his $79.4 billion net worth!)

In his book *Pre-Suasion: A Revolutionary Way to Influence and Persuade,* Robert Cialdini shows that great communicators (like Buffet and Munger) first prepare the minds of people to accept their message even without knowing what the message is. This is done through what Mr. Cialdini describes as pre-suasion: "The process of arranging for recipients to be receptive to a message before they encounter it" (Cialdini, 2016).

So, how does Warren use pre-suasion to persuade people? And most importantly, how can you use pre-suasion in your work and personal life? Here's how: first of all, establish credibility, disarm your audience, and then create a sense of unity. Here's how he demonstrates these steps.

## *Establish Credibility*

There are several ways to establish credibility. One effective way Mr. Buffett uses is to show how believable and human he is. At every Berkshire Hathaway's annual shareholders meeting, Warren Buffett, alongside his partner, Charlie Munger, shares a short video that portrays them as honest and straightforward people. Usually, they make fun of the duo and humanize them. The goal of the video is to demystify their personalities and remove any notion that makes them look like know-it-alls and arrogant.

Also, during the questions and answers session, questions are allowed from not just the audience but also from financial journalists who have not been telegraphed beforehand. This is an open display of honesty and reinforces that in the minds of the audience.

The key lesson here is to come across as a relatable human who is ready to let his foibles show without feeling embarrassed or belittled by his humanity. In other words, making others feel that you can be accessible is a vital persuasion tactic. Equally, even if you have established prior believability, you need to make others see you as honest by being open about your processes. Keep in mind that persuasion is not the same as a deception; therefore, your credibility must be seen as genuine.

## *Admit Mistakes*

Many people would think that admitting your mistakes is counterproductive when you are trying to be effective at persuasion. But it isn't. Warren always admits his mistakes even in the presence of the shareholders of his company. In many instances, he begins his messages to audiences by admitting the mistakes his company had made in the previous year. For example, in his letter to shareholders in 2012, he began by saying, "for the ninth time in 48 years, Berkshire's percentage increase in book value was less than the S&P's percentage gain" (Stillman, 2017).

Admitting mistakes puts you in a good place to drive home your message because it first makes the other person or your audience to see the human side of you and also establishes you as a trustworthy source. You can prepare the minds of your audience to receive what you are about to persuade them about with this technique. Robert Cialdini explains that each time Mr. Buffett admits his mistakes, it opened him (Cialdini) up to be more receptive and to deeply process what Buffett had to say next.

## *Create a Sense of Unity*

The idea you are trying to share with others or persuade them to accept is not as important as trust. If others don't trust you, they are not likely to accept your message and see things from your point of view. Buffett understands this and demonstrates it by making his audience feel they are part of his trusted group. Mr. Cialdini (2016) mentioned that he found Warren Buffett's 2015 message to shareholders of his company disarming. Mr. Buffett began his message by saying, "I will tell you what I would say to my family today if they asked me about Berkshire's future." This is a great way to gain the shareholders' trust. He gave the shareholders a sense of unity by using such personal connotations.

You can use this technique – making others feel they are part of your inner circle – to make people trust you more. The more other people feel they are part of your group or carried along on important issues, the more trust they have in you. A quick word of caution here: do not use this technique to trick people into trusting you. A truthful disclosure should be used as a smart means to earn trust instead of a shrewd way of getting people to believe what is untrue.

# Conclusion

Your life does not get better than the quality of your thoughts, beliefs, and general perception. For any area of your life to improve, there is a need to adjust the thinking processes applied to that area.

We have seen how successful people do not rely only on hard work but also on smart thinking. Unconventional thinking or thinking out of the box is almost impossible if you do not open your mind to learning and accepting mental models. No matter how long and hard you work on coming up with a different decision or behavior using consensus thinking, you will simply be reinventing the wheel and at best, be making very insignificant incremental changes. Unconventional thinking may not be popular and may even be difficult and risky, but that's your best bet to making high-quality decisions that are capable of transforming your life, career, business, and relationships.

Knowing as many mental models as possible is a good thing; your ability to apply them to the various situations in your life is a different ball game entirely. I am not implying that you shun the quest for learning about different mental models. Instead, my emphasis is on knowing how to use them to solve your peculiar issues. Of what use is reading and accumulating knowledge if you cannot properly apply them in real life?

But the application equally requires a thorough understanding of the models. This means you need to be able to take a model and evaluate its usefulness in your situation before applying it. Applying a mental model to your situation because it worked for someone else, does not guarantee that you will record any form of success.

You must first understand the nature of your situation and the combination of mental models you need to tackle the situation.

It doesn't matter the number of self-help books you read or the number of seminars you attend; you must develop the habit of thinking for yourself. Depending only on robotically applying the things you learn from books, seminars, and other sources, you cannot handle the peculiar intricacies of your situation. That type of application has its limits of improvement. When you can take the lessons from the stories in this book, combine them with the principles explained, and then see how you can tailor them to meet your specific need – improvising where necessary, only then can you be said to have mastered how to use mental models to improve your life.

Your previously held assumptions can help ease the process of making routine decisions in both your personal life and professional endeavors. However, they can also constitute stumbling blocks upon which you constantly trip on your journey to a broader, better and more beneficial way of thinking. It can be a bit tricky to decide which of your previously held assumptions are beneficial or otherwise. Whatever you do, do not dismiss all your assumptions, concepts, and beliefs because you have found something new and better. Keep in mind that new truths tend to build on existing truths. Do a thorough mental house cleaning if you have to, but do not throw the baby out with the bathwater. I strongly recommend that you should take the time to carefully analyze how you came about your beliefs and determine if they are actually serving you or disempowering you and limiting your ability to think beyond their boundaries. A beneficial assumption or belief is not dogmatic;

instead, it empowers you to think beyond your current state. It does not forbid you to reason beyond a certain point neither does it fetter you to consensus reasoning.

As you apply these and many more mental models you will eventually come across, keep an open mind about your definition of failure. If things don't work out the first time, it doesn't automatically mean you should throw the baby out with the bathwater! Perhaps Elon Musk has one of the most powerful quotes on failure. In his words, "There's a silly notion that failure's not an option at NASA. A failure is an option here. If things are not failing, you are not innovating enough" (Musk, n.d.).

Always have it at the back of your mind that the men you idolize in terms of success had (and still have) rough patches too. History is dotted with people who were considered failures during their trying moments but whom we now refer to as successful people. In 1985, Steve Jobs was considered a huge "public failure" when he was kicked out of Apple, a company he founded. Walt Disney was considered "not creative enough" and therefore fired from a newspaper. He later founded a film studio that soon went bankrupt. Steven Spielberg was considered unfit and was rejected twice from the film school at the University of Southern California.

These people didn't define failure as fatal. They understood that what they needed to do was to take a closer look at the thinking process that led to such failure and make the necessary adjustment. Thankfully, this book covers several methods you can use to correct flaws in your thinking process.

Here is one final caveat before I bring this book to a close: it is easy to drown in the sea of information. Do not spend too much of your time trying to figure out the exact mental model you need for every single situation in your life. Remember the advice of Jeff Bezos on prioritizing decisions. Not all decisions deserve the same amount of time and energy. If a decision can't be easily reversed, you will need to consider it very carefully. But spending all day considering every single decision you have to make very carefully means you won't ever get to decide on anything!

Sometimes you need to think on your feet. You cannot afford to tell your boss, for example, that you need more time to come up with a yes or no answer to a minor decision (because you want to figure out which mental model to apply!) That will not put you in a good light and reduces your chances of getting any advancement in your career.

Don't allow the fear of deciding wrongly stop you from making any decisions at all. You are going to make mistakes! That is a given. Make peace with that fact and come to terms with learning from your mistakes. I did not write this book with the intention of making you completely avoid mistakes in your life. However, one thing is clear, the more you can put these time-tested principles to work in your life, the fewer wrong decisions you will make. The fewer mistakes you make during decision-making, the better your quality of life both on a personal and professional level.

It is my sincere wish that you would find the time to really study these mental models until they become second nature. That is only when you will reap the tremendous benefits of these mental models. And that also is when you can begin to think on your feet using this smart way of thinking.

# Part 2: Memory Improvement, Accelerated Learning and Brain Training

*Learn How to Optimize and Improve Your Memory and Learning Capabilities for Top Results in University and at Work*

# Introduction – Know Your Brain

Have you ever felt the fascination of reading printed words?

Not so fascinating? It is if you think about the million other things that happen at the same time in your body.

While you comprehend the written words, your heart keeps on beating, and you can feel the air on your skin. Your eyes know when to blink, and your lungs keep on breathing for you.

There is one headquarter where all of it is controlled at once.

That headquarter is your brain.

Your brain gives the needed rhythm to your heart, controls the temperature, and does a billion other things. In addition, you can read and remember what you have read too.

Every activity, which you can or cannot control, is managed by your brain. That is why your brain does not sleep. Even when you are in your bed giving yourself a good night's sleep, your mind keeps on working. Your brain helps you get a sound sleep. Shutting down unnecessary activities, repairing cells and keeping the crucial events in check. These are a few of many jobs your brain does when you go to sleep.

## *How Does Your Brain Work?*

Your brain has three major areas:

- Cerebrum
- Cerebellum
- Brain Stem

The most significant part of your brain, with two left and right divisions, is called cerebrum. This part of your mind controls your thinking ability, language comprehension, eating, memories, senses, drinking, body temperature, sleeping, and hormones.

Inside the cerebrum, you have your cerebellum, which is not more than a pear in size. But the job of this section is vital. Your muscle movements are managed here. In addition, your ability to coordinate your body functions also comes from here.

Your brain has its extension to your body through the spinal cord, which makes the complete nervous system of your body. Neurons in your brain are 100 billion, creating a vast network in your whole body.

## *How Do We Learn Things?*

Learning is how any living organism survives. We, as humans, have enhanced learning abilities in the living kingdom, so improved that we have not even understood it all yet. Our genetics and surroundings decide what we learn and how fast we can learn those things.

For example, if you read a chapter of your book every day, eventually your brain will adapt to this activity. Your reading ability will improve, and you will start remembering most sentences of that chapter.

Similarly, a worker, who has to attach the right information label to the right product, gets efficient with his or her work with practice. It all happens due to our brain's ability to learn and adapt to new things.

There is no doubt that learning is the most critical skill your brain offers. You can improve your verbal intelligence, enhance your working memory, learn new languages and do more; all because your mind lets you do so.

Every time you stretch your abilities, your brain network changes substantially to help you adapt. That is why something that seems impossible becomes more straightforward day-by-day. Moreover, eventually, you get comfortably efficient in doing that activity.

At the beginning of learning something new, your brain has to put an effort to concentrate and control. Practice trains your mind to adjust networks on a large scale. Therefore, with time, the effortful activity of the brain reduces, and the new system manages the operation on its own. That is how things get simple to remember, and actions get more comfortable for you. That is the process of how your brain reaches the automated level of skill. The brain activity enhances every time you practice something, which tends to improve the effortlessness.

Let us dive into the technicality of learning things.

Practicing an activity increases a synapse's strength in your brain. Two neurons keep being activated repeatedly. That creates a permanent link between those two neurons. This process is known as long-term potentiation. Because of this process, every time, the first of the two neurons is activated, it automatically activates the second one.

Researches on rats have shown that learning new things also increases the size of the brain. New protrusions, known as dendritic spines, get larger to help a rat find food through a tunnel during experiments.

Briefly, our brain develops more neuron connections, we learn more, and that learning becomes permanent information stored in our brain network. We have to think less when remembering or doing something.

## Can We Enhance Our Learning Abilities?

"Believe in yourself" - you must have heard that a thousand times from your peers, your parents, and teachers. How about you modify this and make it-

"Believe in your brain."

Your brain can learn anything and become a master of that skill. From understanding complex data every day, to memorizing a long list of formulas for exams, you can do it all. Just put your faith in the brain and neuron network it has up there in your head.

The science of how the brain learns is all about facts, so you can believe in that and give yourself a chance to learn anything you like. Nevertheless, it is not only related to understanding the scientific concepts, but it is also linked to applying that science to lets your brain learn efficiently.

There is an external process as well as an internal process of learning. The external means such as training, guides, tutorials, and others help you begin the learning process. These are great during the initial phase, but you have to go beyond and allow your brain to practice internally. If you are getting information without practicing to solve tasks or problems, it will not help. Your mind requires actual tasks to practice and build strong neuron networks. Therefore, you need to ACTUALLY do it and fail a thousand times to become a master.

## *Using failure for productivity*

You must have heard this a thousand times - experiencing failure and overcoming it makes you stronger. If that is true, you can utilize failure to improve your productivity.

For example, a university student can work on math problems, without understanding the concepts in the first place. The student can look at the question first, then, analyze the ideas to find out a way to reach the right answer. However, getting the correct answer is not the ultimate goal here. This approach helps in finding out new ideas about the problem. It is also possible to find a new way of solving that question. The work approach for such types of questions will become more comfortable for the student. Hence, it will enhance productivity. That is how you utilize failure for productivity.

Similarly, suppose you have a new machine you need to work on, which comes with a user manual. Instead of using the instructions, you can figure out the functions on your own. You will try to fail, but a personal quest for the right solution stays in your mind for a long time. You sustainably learn things.

Another important thing about learning ability is the period you choose. Most people tend to involve too much in their learning process, once they get a grip of their concentration. However, an obsessive approach to learning only gives you a temporary solution.

To learn and retain knowledge, you should focus on choosing a longer period of learning. Spreading the learning process allows your brain to form long-term networks of neurons. Students of every age utilize this approach without even knowing it. The habits of revising chapters, quizzing and other methods are popular to learn and retain knowledge. Just distribute this approach within a long period, and you can enhance your learning ability.

The science behind distributed learning is pure. You give sensations to similar neuron networks from time to time by practicing something. Your brain receives stimulations in small and short sessions, which is why the process of skill development and learning becomes more comfortable. Therefore, instead of giving 4 hours to a project in one day, you can give 15 to 20 minutes every day and master it in a week.

## *Your senses and learning*

Experiences become memories, and every thought in your body gives you a unique ability to experience things. Your eyes give the experience of sight, your ears let you experience hearing, the skin gives a background of touch, and you smell with your nose and taste with your tongue.

Think about it, if you once sip a very hot coffee, your brain stores that experience as a memory. So, when the next time you are about to have a sip, your brain tells you to be cautious. That is how your senses assist in creating a memory, which becomes learning. The more feelings are involved in an experience, the better the mind it creates. That is why students, who look at the text and say it aloud, revise more effectively.

If an action is happening in your head only, it stays virtual. Only your artistic skills are enhanced with virtual experiences. The brain creates neuron networks when you provide real-world experiences. Therefore, using your skills in real life is very important. Use a foreign language and work on your data evaluation method daily. That is how you can learn and retain that knowledge as well.

When bringing your rehearsal approach to the real world, context matters too. Your brain gives importance to learning things, which becomes a matter of your survival. For example, your accounting skills will get stronger and faster if you use it to manage your taxes, savings, and investments. Your brain knows that finances matter to you. Hence, you will learn faster.

How can one define memory? How do they work inside our minds?

Through this book, you will have a better grasp of its fundamentals and workability. By the end of this book, you will find yourself more familiar with this world of memories and the functioning of brain activity.

## *Brief Introduction about Your Memory*

Everything that you are is a collection of memories stored in your mind. Every second, you are creating new memories and using them. You store them in your mind and can recall whenever required.

From brushing your teeth in the morning to remembering complex information related to your projects, you do it all.

The human memory is a center of fascination for scientists, psychologists, and philosophers. But, understanding your ability to create memories can help you too.

You already know how experiences help in memory creation and memories let you learn effectively. So, if you see the process of memory creation, memory storage, and organization, you can increase your brain capacity.

So, let us talk about memory in detail!

# Chapter 1: Memory: An Evidence Of Your Existence

Your memory is your way of understanding the surroundings. Every time you experience something, your brain tries to make sense of it by looking at the stored memory. If no memory is available, it creates a new consciousness and stores. The process happens every second, which builds your personality, knowledge, and skills.

So, it would not be wrong to say that your memory is the evidence of your existence.

## What is Memory?

In an overview, a memory is a process through which your brain acquires, stores and recalls information. There are different types of memories, making this process extremely complex to study.

Three memory processes include:

1. Encoding- obtaining information
2. Storage- storing that information
3. Retrieval- recalling that information

Unfortunately, human memory is full of flaws. We tend to forget things or remember things differently. In many situations, we encode the memory incorrectly, which disturbs the other two processes. Most issues with losing memory are minor, such as leaving your car keys, forgetting to switch off the lights and others. However, complex flaws in the ability to create memories can result in mental diseases and have a huge impact on someone's life.

## *Formation of Memory*

Your experiences encompass millions of minor and significant details. It is all information for your brain. For working without breaking down, your mind decides to filter information and prioritize memory creation. That is why info has to be useful to become a memory in the first place. If your brain thinks that information is not helpful for you, it tends to forget it.

That is the reason why some students do not seem to remember the concepts taught during classes. It is all about how interested you are at retaining information.

Once you make information usable, it gets encoded as a memory in your brain. Then the storage process occurs, which allows your mind to store that memory. However, you do not stay aware of the stored memory, unless you recall it. That is exactly like working on a project and saving it in a digital folder. You do not keep remembering the data in your head 24/7, but it comes back as soon as you have a purpose for it. That is what retrieval of memory is.

The storage and retrieval of memories are the reasons why you have conscious and unconscious awareness. The storage process keeps the minds in your unconscious perception, and the retrieval process brings it back the conscious awareness, whenever you require it.

But, as said before, it all depends on the quality of information encoding.

## *The Period of Existence of a Memory*

Your brain has a wide diversity when it comes to creating and keeping memories. Some memories last for a fraction of a second, while others stay with you for years. That is logical, as you would not want to remember the name of a restaurant forever, where you only went once to have a meal. Every time you walk on a busy road, your brain sees every tiny sign, numbers, people's faces, their dress color, and a billion other things. All these pieces of information can be important right at that moment. However, you will not need them longer than a fraction of a second. That is why the diversified period of existing memory matters.

Memories can be as brief as a fraction of a second. Your senses provide information about the surroundings, and your brain uses them to help you handle a situation.

There are short-term memories as well, which last for about 20 to 30 seconds. You think about something or focus on certain information, which turns into short memories. That can also be the encoding process. The importance of a short-term memory decides whether it can become a long-term memory. If not, they fade away in the vast mental database in your brain.

When you obtain important information, it can stay as a stored memory for days, months and even years. These memories remain in your unconscious and come to conscious awareness when you recall. The period of existence depends on how many times you keep recalling a memory.

For example, if you are revising a chapter for an upcoming test, the encoded memories can last for weeks and months, depending on the revision. However, you start losing the grip after the test. That is why regular revision becomes necessary. On the other hand, a memory of a date with your partner can stay for months and years.

## *Memory Retrieval – How It Works*

Memory retrieval is precisely what a student does during an exam to answer questions given. The same process is tried on a daily basis in the life of knowledge workers, data analysts, and managers.

The success of memory retrieval depends on the cues available in the surroundings. Useful signals trigger the retrieval process, which successfully brings the memory back to conscious awareness.

Depending on the cue or clue, memory retrieval has four types:

- Recalling

Recalling is the process when you retrieve memory in the absence of any evidence or signal. The surroundings do not help in triggering the retrieval, so, you have to rely on your ability to bring back a memory. This type of retrieval takes place when you are taking a test or giving a presentation in front of your seniors.

- Recollection

You recollect a memory when the surroundings offer you some clues in the form of logical structures. Partial information stays available, which triggers the process of memory recollection. For example, if a test contains essay or passage questions, it allows a student to utilize the given information to remember the rest of it. Hence, he or she can answer these questions. Recollecting memory is usually easier than memory recall.

- Recognition

In some cases, you have all the information hidden in the surroundings. The brain allows you to recognize the right information by triggering its memory. For instance, a test with multiple-choice questions gives the correct answer along with other options. A student needs to recognize the right answer. Similarly, if you reach a street, which you visited years ago, your recognition of that street will help you make the right turns.

- Relearning

Relearning something enables you to retrieve the stored memories. Every time you relearn, it strengthens your ability to recover that memory. That is the reason why you do not have to learn the whole chapter when revising it. An overview allows your brain to retrieve all the memory encoded in the first place.

## *The Three Stages of Memory*

First introduced by Shiffrin and Atkinson in 1968, there is a stage model that divides memories into three stages.

- Sensory memory

This memory stage usually involves visual and auditory information. Generally, visual information lasts for 1/2-second only. On the other hand, you can keep auditory details for 3 to 4 seconds. The brain gives prioritized importance to sensory memories. Just a few of these memories move to the next stage of memories.

- Short-term or conscious memory

This stage is also called active consciousness or your conscious mind, things that you are presently thinking about or aware of. They are part of your dynamic memory. Sensory memories are created automatically. But, when you start focusing on particular sensory memory, it becomes a short-term or active memory. These memories last for about 20-30 seconds. Then, most of these memories fade away. However, if you are attentive enough, some active mind reaches the next stage.

- Long-term or unconscious memory

Long-term memory includes memories that you are not working with but may want in the future. The stored memory is also known as unconscious memory. That is because they stay outside the present awareness of your mind. But whenever required, the memory comes back to your consciousness.

## Why Do We Forget?

Forgetting is a common flaw in the process of human memory generation and retrieval. We tend to forget things.

An ideal memory would never let you forget anything that you experience. Imagine that! You will not have to read one chapter twice to memorize it or struggle with the same information every day as a data manager. This flaw is the reason why we all have to work on our ability to remember essential things more efficiently.

But, do not take forgetting as an error. It is a flaw, but a beneficial one. Your brain needs space to perform without breaking down.

That is why it tries to forget and remember for various reasons. Time is one of the biggest reasons that triggers forgetting. Information fades away if you do not bring it to your consciousness with rehearsal.

There are four fundamental reasons why we tend to forget things:

1. Failing to retrieve
2. Interference among memories
3. Failing to store
4. Deliberate forgetting

- Failing to retrieve

How many times have you felt that your brain has wholly forgotten something? Or you have the information somewhere in there, but it is not coming to the conscious mind. That is known as retrieval failure.

If you are unable to retrieve a memory, it can mean two things:

- You have not been practicing that memory lately.
- You do not give importance to that memory.

Mostly, time vanishes memories or reduces its print in our brain. This happens if you do not practice or retrieve a memory from time to time.

On the other hand, some memories stay intact even if you do not rehearse them. This occurs when a long-term memory is too important to forget for your brain.

- Interference among memories

Another reason why you forget is the interference among your memories. This takes place when you store new memories that overlap or contradict existing memories.

There are two situations when your memories can interfere with each other:

- The old memory is so strong that you feel unable to remember a new one similar to that. This is called proactive interference. For example, if a knowledge worker processes the same type of data for years, it becomes a strong memory. Hence, such a worker has to work hard to memorize a new process of working on a different data set.
- A new memory contradicts or competes with an old memory making the retrieval difficult. This phenomenon is called retroactive interference. For example, a student can learn the wrong approach to solving a problem. But, when the right path becomes visible, it interferes with the process learned previously.
- Failing to store

In many conditions, you cannot remember something because you have not encoded its memory correctly. If memory did not reach the long-term stage, it is impossible to remember it.

This also happens due to the prioritization of details conducted by your brain. For example, to remember a way to your classroom, you do not have to remember the color of the wall in the hallway. Only important details are stored by our brain to make long-term memory useful and reliable.

But, the same thing can divert your attention and lead to incorrect or no information stored about an experience. Hence, you cannot seem to retrieve that information in the future.

- Deliberate forgetting

Sometimes, we forget things because we want to. This usually happens to the memories associated with disturbing events or traumatic experiences. Our brain knows the anxiety we feel when a bad memory comes back to conscious awareness. To minimize the trauma, your mind takes charge and eliminates those pieces of information. The process involves suppression of memory to unconscious storage and forgetting it altogether.

There are arguments regarding the concept of suppressed memories. However, that is mostly because of the difficulty of studying memories, which are not detectable in the first place.

Forgetting things is not entirely avoidable. But, now that you have the reasons attached to it, you would know why you have forgotten something. Also, you can look at informational pieces critically and decide how likely you would forget or remember them. If a memory seems difficult to recognize, you can work on rehearsing and practicing it regularly and keeping it a part of your retrieval memory.

# Chapter 2: Memory Types and Their Need

You have already gained a glimpse of memory types in the previous chapter. However, there are more types, and every class has its importance in your everyday life.

## Types of Memories

Human memory has three main stages according to the Atkinson-Shiffrin model:

- Sensory memory
- Short-term memory
- Long-term memory

Modern studies have given sub-divisions of long-term memories. But first, let's understand how sensory memory works.

### *Sensory Memory*

Lasting for about 1/2-second, you get sensory memory from your ability to see, hear, smell, touch, and taste. These memories form to offer an instant understanding of the environment. Hence, their purpose is lost within a fraction of a second. You deliberately ignore these memories, or your brain forgets them automatically.

## Short-term memory

When you actively pay attention to something, it becomes a part of your short-term memory. You focus on sensory memories to increase their existence period to 20-30 seconds. That is how short-term memories come into existence.

In an overview:

- Short-term memories do not require active maintenance as they last for 20-30 seconds only.
- You can just think about seven or so things at once, which limits the short-term memory.

## Period of a short-term memory

The period of short-term memory is increasable to 1 minute or so. This is possible through an active working or rehearsing the memory. For example, people keep repeating a new phone number until they find a piece of paper to write it down. Without constant repetition, you are more likely to forget a new phone number within seconds.

Even the repetition or rehearsal can take your short-term memory to a certain extent only. After 1 minute or so, your existing memories start interfering with the short-term information.

Using the phone number example again, if you do not find a piece of paper early enough, your brain will start recalling other phone numbers stored in your long-term memory. The old memories will interfere and displace the new memory, and you will forget the phone number.

With enough time given to the rehearsal of short-term memory, you can move it to the long-term stage.

## *The capacity of your short-term memories*

You can have about 5-9 items in your short-term memory. Beyond that, your brain starts getting confused and losing track of thoughts.

Your short-term memory is a bit different from the working memory you have. While short-term memories provide temporary information storage, working memories allow you to collect, organize and rearrange information temporarily.

So, working memory is a temporary form of a long-term memory process. In addition, short-term memory is a part of your working memory.

## *Long-term memory*

Your long-term memory stores information in your unconscious awareness and allows you to use them whenever required. This storage requires maintenance with practice and rehearsal to keep the stored memories detailed. However, some memories stay fresh even after months and decades without practicing them at all.

So, there are two types of long-term memories your brain works with:

## *1. Explicit memory*

You generate an explicit memory by consciously practicing something. For example, if you memorize a phone number or your credit card pin, it would become a part of your explicit memory.

Now, there is a type of explicit memory, which is known as declarative memory. This memory type includes all the factual information pieces. For example, when you recall faces, event dates, or instructions about a game, they come from the declarative memory storage.

Declarative memory has three types too:

- **Episodic memory** - This includes recalling all the facts associated with your experiences in a sequence. Such memories are usually related to times, emotions, places or things that have contextual importance.
- **Semantic memory** - Semantic memory is more structured as compared to episodic memories. This type includes facts, knowledge, concepts and other structural information your brain stores. Regardless of the presence of personal context, you remember things as facts through this memory type.
- **Autobiographical memory** - While episodic memory can include event memories in a sequence, autobiographical memory stores events that are more personal. This type of memory is usually similar to episodic memories. However, it involves more individual events, instead of a sequence of events.

## 2. Implicit memory

Implicit is a more unconscious form of memory that impacts your behavior or thoughts. You do not remember a memory, but it changes the way you behave or think. For instance, your childhood memory of certain places does not come back. But if you see that place again, you know where to go. That is what an implicit memory does to you.

There are two types of implicit memories:

- **Procedural memory** - This memory allows you to remember actions and tasks. Your skill in doing something is called procedural memory. So, you know how to brush your teeth, drive or wear clothes.
- **Emotional memory** - Certain implicit memories can trigger emotional responses. The emotions can come along with procedural and declarative processes.

Interesting Facts about Long-term Memories

1. **Long-term memories mostly stay outside your conscious awareness.** Most often, you recall your long-term memories in the working memory zone to utilize them for a purpose. In some situations, you have control over recalling, while other times the process occurs on its own due to environmental cues.
2. **Frequently accessed and used memories are more likely to stand strong in front of time.** The memories you recall become powerful. But all the memories that are not retrieved become weaker with time. Usually, our brain tends to replace old, unwanted memories with new ones.

## *How a Short-term Memory Becomes A Long-term Memory*

Due to the minor duration of short-term memory, important memories are transferred to the long-term collection of memories.

One common approach is memorizing information in chunks. This method is a memory training approach, which you utilize to learn things in small segments. For example, a manager can divide informational pieces into groups. Each group can contain a similar set of information. This way, memorizing becomes easier.

If you have a list of 10 formulas, learning them in sets of two would seem easier than memorizing them separately.

Rehearsal is also a valid option to turn short-term memories into long-term memories. You revise, review and analyze information repeatedly. This gives your brain a chance to remember things for a long time. This approach, however, requires consistent rehearsal from time to time. Students, managers and knowledge workers can utilize this approach to make everyday memory sharper and retain critical information.

According to the Atkinson-Shiffrin model, all-important short-term memories become long-term, automatically. The duration of long-term memories also differs regarding their importance and practice. Working on your neural networks certainly helps in improving your ability to store long-term memories and accurately retrieving them.

## *How A Long-term Memory Changes*

To understand memory in your brain, you can think about the memory of a computer. Information is stored in a computer's hard disk and retrieved whenever required. The same thing happens in our brains. Different environmental cues trigger just the retrieval.

Every time you retrieve your memory, it changes. This is a common concept of information processing. You recall information and work on it, which tends to change the form of that long-term memory. This happens due to the upgrades provided to the same neural networks every time you recall a memory. Your long-term memory becomes a part of working memory, which begins the encoding process again.

This shows that you can change your long-term memories, for better or worse. Details can change, and you can improve or weaken your memories. It all depends on what you do with memory after recalling it.

There is another reason why long-term memories change- interference. Your brain does not keep memories in a static form. So, it can't give you back an exact piece of memory every time you recall. So, to resolve this flaw, the brain searches for similar memories to fill the gaps in the required memory. This can fill memory with misinformation and interfere with the stored long-term memory. So, you tend to believe that you are right when you are not.

How many times have you thought you answered a question correctly, but it was not the case? It is common among students. You mix information in your head and create new information, which seems right.

## *Visualization and Memory Techniques*

With the clarity that long-term memories do change, you need to work on memory training to save yourself from memory interference. Visualization is the best approach to remembering things correctly.

When you see images, it helps your brain collect every tiny detail associated with it. So, retrieving visual memories becomes easier and accurate. This is probably the reason why most memory tools and techniques utilize the visualization power of the brain. Most techniques give weird imagery to help people memorize situations and sequences faster.

A great visualization capacity of a person is called a photographic memory.

A person with photographic memory holds the ability to retain and recall detailed visual information accurately.

It is popular that a person with photographic memory stores memories in the form of still imagery. Therefore, whenever recalling, this person can look at the details of that image memory in his or her mind and recollect information. However, that is not the actual way photographic memory works.

To experiment, you can ask a person with a photographic memory to remember text on a page and rewrite it backward, using his or her photographic memory. No one can do this.

As you already know, our memories are not a static collection. They are like pieces of puzzles stored in a box. So, when a person recalls a memory, he or she utilizes different puzzle pieces to create the whole picture. Small bits of memories are easy to store and easy to retrieve which is what our brain does to collect information in long-term memory efficiently. This ability to collect and retrieve memory pieces can differ from person to person. We all have different attentive personalities, which tends to divert the ability to look at the details when collecting information. But, at the same time, it is also possible to improve your photographic memory by working on visual techniques and tools.

Overall, visualization is a great way of remembering information. The memory does not work like still photographs, but it can collect small bits of imagery like separate informational pieces. So, you can utilize images to enhance your ability to remember things.

# Chapter 3: Memory Preferences and Brain Waves: Accelerating Your Learning Channels

## Different Memory Preferences a Person Can Have

Our surroundings offer us different kinds of information. We obtain information via sight, sound, and feeling. These different types of memories are known as:

- Visual memory - what you see, such as facial expressions, printed materials, body language, and more.
- Auditory memory - what you hear or say, such as sounds, spoken words, and more.
- Kinesthetic memory - what you feel, such as actions, emotions, smell, taste, movement, and others.

However, we are not equally sensitive to all three types of memory channels. One person's memory preference can differ from another.

In humans, about 40% of people get more memories through visuals. About 30-40% remember feelings, which is a form of kinesthetic memory. Lastly, about 20-30% of people memorize through the auditory channel.

So, we all have our preferences when it comes to memorizing. Or, you can say that your mind has a choice when it comes to learning things. Finding your most sensitive memory channel can help in memory improvement and accelerated learning. This is true for everyone: from a knowledge worker, a manager to a university student. After all, we all have to memorize and deal with memories.

## Visual Memory – Are You More Sensitive To What You See?

From college to career, your visuals constantly help you memorize things. Visual memory assists in learning activities, skills and allows you to form short-term as well as long-term memories.

Visual memory is your ability to recall memories in the form of imagery. If you are sensitive to visuals, your memories often include images. For example, a student with visual memory preference can visualize the text written on the pages of his or her book when remembering.

For a visually sensitive person, short-term memory stays full of imagery. It is like your brain clicks pictures all the time and allows you to store them in your neuron networks for a few seconds. People who lack visual memory tend to forget visuals very quickly. For example, such a student might struggle when copying notes due to not being able to collect and store short-term visual memories.

Your long-term memories also contain small puzzle pieces in the form of imagery. People with a strong visual memory tend to recollect imagery even after months or years. Generally, we all utilize visual memory to remember directions to our office or college.

The concept of a photographic memory has come from visual

memory only. If you look at an image, it allows your brain to look at the details regarding objects, sizes, depth, color, shadows, and other components. That is how a visually sensitive person looks at the world. He or she keeps on storing small pieces of images as groups of memories. Hence, when recalled, all the right pieces are aligned together in the brain, and a visual appears in a person's mind.

As the imagery is stored in pieces, the chances of clearly remembering the whole memory are not 100%. It depends on how sensitive you are to visuals. The degree of remembering visuals differs from person to person.

## Why should you work to accelerate visual memory?

If you are a student, a knowledge worker or a manager, you constantly have to work on visual materials. Charts and diagrams are the realities of modern-age study and work environment. Visualized data is used to make the analysis process quicker and effective. You might spend time comparing diagrams, creating concept maps, and doing other tasks that require visual memory.

If you are a student of biology, you need to have a clear and strong visual memory to identify body parts. You have to learn and remember different muscles, bones, organs and other parts of the body. You need a strong visual memory brain training to become a successful doctor.

When you study statistics and look at concepts, your visual memory allows you to interpret the correct meaning. If visual memory is not exercised enough, your ability to make sense of a visualized data will reduce with time.

You have to have visual memory to clearly understand a lecture. Why? A professor, when giving a lecture, makes different postures and changes his or her facial expressions. You need to understand these visual clues to learn the concept taught during a lecture.

Similarly, you need visual sensitivity at every step of your life. Even if it is not your memory preference, you should indulge in brain training to increase your visual memory.

## *Auditory Memory – How Much Do You Remember From What You Hear?*

Auditory memory is another sensory memory type. Your sense of hearing receives various sounds and turns them into electrical charges. That charge reaches your brain via neuron networks, where sound images are created. Sound images are a type of mental concept created with sound.

Depending on your sensitivity, your brain can replay sound memories for a small period. Common examples of auditory memory include:

- Your ability to remember someone's name in one attempt.
- Listening to music and remembering the notes and words.
- Replaying other people's voices in your mind.

## *We listen and interpret other people's voices*

Every time you listen to someone, you interpret that person's voice. Just like the facial expressions and body language, the tone of voice says a lot about a conversation. Our mind allows us to understand people by figuring out their voice tones. Some people have more sensitivity towards this mental ability and tend to remember voices for a long time.

Suppose your friend is telling all about his happy mood, but you still know that he is not happy. How? The words are all right, but your brain is catching on the facial expressions as well as the anxiousness in his voice tone. Similarly, you figure out when a person is angry, sad, happy, nervous or concerned. This ability is a superpower no matter what you do in your life. From personal, educational to professional life, you can grab every opportunity and behave appropriately by knowing how a person is feeling.

If you have a strong auditory memory, you can remember people's voices from just one conversation. When people call, you instantly figure out who that person is just by hearing their voice. Surely, this is common when you spend a lot of time with someone. However, auditory sensitivity enhances this ability, and you remember most voices you hear.

## *We all have a musical memory*

Both musicians and non-musicians can have musical memory. Some people remember music better than others. This is also a sign of auditory memory preference. Musicians tend to remember the tone of instruments, different pitches, and tunes. Non-musicians, who enjoy listening to music, remember their favorite songs, tune, and words altogether.

## *We recognize non-musical sounds*

An experienced mechanic can hear the sound of your car's engine and recognize the problem. Not every mechanic can do that, but some develop higher sensitivity toward auditory memory. Their brain allows them to collect a new sound image and match it with an old image of the same kind. Hence, they figure out if your car has trouble or not.

## *Can you learn with your auditory memory?*

Short answer - **YES**.

However, it depends on how attentive you are to sounds. For example, most students read and memorize, but tend to forget their lectures immediately. They either remember a few things or do not remember anything at all. However, some students tend to remember everything explained during a lecture. Students with high auditory memory tend to listen more and do not give too much importance to making notes. They simply want to focus on hearing every word uttered by the lecturer.

It is exactly like remembering the dialogues of your favorite TV series. But, just like a TV program, visuals help the audio too. For example, it is difficult to figure out the difference between "Won" and "One" if you do not have any context or visuals to help you.

There are auditory brain training tools for accelerated learning using an audio approach. So, yes, you can learn effectively with the help of auditory memory. You would require improving this memory. The key is increasing the storage and retention capacity of sounds in your mind.

## Kinesthetic Memory – Do You Remember What You Feel?

With Kinesthetic memory, you tend to remember a feeling of something. It is a comprehensive awareness of your physical and mental presence. The movements of your body, even tiny muscular movements become a part of your memory. The more sensitive you are towards movements and feelings, the higher your ability to make and retain kinesthetic memory.

With heightened kinesthetic memory, you tend to store experiences regarding emotions or movements. This memory helps in learning activities such as typing faster or feeling the excitement of data evaluation. If you like to walk every time you read, it is associated with your kinesthetic memory. You have associated learning chapters with your movement of walking. Hence, it helps you memorize things faster.

People with strong kinesthetic memory tend to move a lot. Moving legs, tapping the pen on the table and other movements keep their brain and memory active which is why physical tasks become easier for such learners. If one of your hobbies includes physical activity such as sports, running, dancing, swimming or anything else, it means you have a heightened sense of kinesthetic.

Kinesthetic memory creates coordination between your body and the space around it. That increases body and mind coordination and offers you faster reactions.

# Brain Waves – the Different States of Your Mind and Learning Capacity

Everything you feel comes from the mental state created by certain waves in your brain. The feeling of happiness, sadness, and other emotions depend on brain waves. Understanding and controlling brain waves are necessary to learn anything. Certain mental states are better to learn faster, while some do not allow you to focus.

Most people spend their lives thinking that it is the external world changing their personalities. So, if you are not able to memorize a chapter, it is because of the upsetting thing your girlfriend said earlier that day. Sure, external elements send information to your brain, but you can control how to deal with that information. Your mindset, beliefs, and thoughts are just common results of brain waves.

In your brain, neural waves create different conscious states. Therefore, if you know those states, you can work on them and control your mindset more effectively.

Your mental state depends on 5 kinds of brain waves:

## 1. *Alpha waves - for deep relaxation at 7.5 to 14 Hz*

When you close your eyes, your mind reaches a level of relaxation. This state occurs when you daydream or meditate. You can look at it as a light meditative state when your mind generates alpha waves. These waves increase the visualization of your mind. Your memory creating skills heighten, you learn faster and imagine vividly.

Alpha waves put you right at the gate of your subconscious. So, you can stay conscious and concentrate better to maximize your ability to learn. Your intuitions become stronger and stronger as you get closer to the maximum state of alpha waves at 7.5 Hz.

## 2. Beta waves - for reasoning and awaken consciousness at 14 to 40 Hz

Brainwaves on the beta scale allow you to stay alert and awake. Your consciousness stays logical and obtains the ability to critically reason and evaluate the surroundings.

Beta waves help you go through all the tasks during any day. However, these are the waves that let you feel anxious, restless and stressed-out.

When you have beta waves running in your brain, it becomes your inner critic. The loudness of this critical voice depends on the strength of beta waves in your brain. The stronger the waves, the higher stressed you feel during a day. Most students and professionals function with beta waves and stay stressed out.

## 3. Theta waves - for sleeping and light meditation at 4 to 7.5 Hz

Beyond alpha state, you reach a light sleeping stage of theta waves. These brain waves also create a state of dream. Achieving theta waves in your brain can help you develop a strong spiritual connection with yourself and the universe.

Though it is a sleeping state, your mind obtains profound creativity and vivid visualizations. You attain inspiration. This is the reason why your dreams seem so real as if you are experiencing them.

The boundary of Alpha-theta is attained at 7 to 8 Hz. This is a perfect state to program your mind, utilize maximum creative power and making conscious visualized changes in your mind. But none of this action puts any stress on your mind like the Beta waves. Your body stays relaxed.

## 4. Delta waves - for deep sleep at 0.5 to 4 Hz

Delta waves are the slowest brain waves that allow you to stay in deep sleep. No dreams occur during this stage of sleep. You reach the maximum depths of meditative states and lose all sense of awareness.

Delta waves take your brain to its unconscious level. Your brain obtains access to the unconsciously present information, but you do not feel aware of it.

This state of mind is essential to heal and regenerate. Your mind and body go through a healing process during this state of sleep.

## 5. Gamma waves - insight wave beyond 40 Hz

The most recent discovery in the field of brain waves is the gamma waves. The research works are at their initial stages, but gamma waves are believed to be associated with exceptional processing of information and incredible insight.

So, it seems clear that you need to achieve Alpha waves to increase your capacity to learn. However, if you want to memorize things, Theta waves can help along with the Gamma waves, as they offer IQ increase and exceptional cognitive functionality.

When you ask- When can I learn it at my full potential?

It depends on the type of learning you want. Is it memorizing formulas, facts, and information? Or, is it about learning a skill or a process?

Learning a skill or a process is best possible if you reach the Alpha state of mind.

Therefore, the next logical question is - how can you get to the Alpha state of brain waves?

Alpha is the only state in which you feel extremely relaxed and stay awake at the same time. The alpha waves are the reasons your brain feels relaxed. Nevertheless, triggering that state requires some effort.

It is important to attain this state if you want to learn something. Without a relaxed mental state, your mind feels worried and stressed about things that actually do not matter.

Here is how you can reach trigger alpha waves in your brain:

## *1. Let your body and mind relax*

It sounds simple, but it takes a lot of effort to relax your body and mind.

First and foremost, you need to choose a suitable time — no need to rush things or worry about everything around you. So, pick a time when you can focus on relaxing your body and mind. If you feel worried about something, write it down and put it in a box. This technique will help your mind focus on relaxation.

Getting comfortable is another factor you should care about. A comfortable place where you can lie down would be perfect. You can sit as well, but lying down helps in achieving the alpha state faster. However, the comfort level is important. In addition, make sure you do not fall asleep.

After getting a comfortable space, you can get rid of the environmental distractions. So, switch off your mobile phone, close the doors, windows and your eyes. Even remove the clock to avoid hearing its repetitive sound. However, you can listen to slow, soothing music if you feel like.

Now, you can start removing all the clutters from your mind. The thoughts will keep running, so do not fight them. Follow a gradual approach and look at those thoughts from an observational point of view. At the same time, increase your concentration on the surrounding silence or on the tune of the music you are listening to. Eventually, your thoughts will start fading away.

## 2. *Manage your deep breathing*

Slow and deep breathing is an important approach to reaching the alpha state. Ideally, you can inhale a deep breath via your nose and exhale slowly via your mouth. You can also choose only one pathway to inhale and exhale air. But make sure you keep the pace slow.

To take deep breaths, you can focus on breathing via the diaphragm. The diaphragm is located a little below the chest area; you need to focus there when breathing. You can start the process by putting one hand in the middle of your chest and one hand on the diaphragm area. Then, breathe by moving mostly the hand you have put on the diaphragm area.

Increasing deep breathing is not necessarily possible at once. So, you can try mixing deep breaths with normal breaths initially. Try taking a normal breath after every deep breath. Eventually, keep increasing the numbers of deep breaths and reduce normal breathing.

Many people find it easier to attain deep breathing by counting. The process involves counting 1-7, as you inhale air. Then, you can count 1-8, as you exhale. This way, you can monitor your breathing, make it slow, and even.

Small deep breathing sessions with tiny breaks can also help. You can set a timer and manage your breathing for 9 to 10 minutes. Then, stop for 5 minutes and begin the process again. In two to four attempts, you can reach the desired deep breathing level.

### *3. Visualize yourself in a peaceful place*

After relaxing and attaining deep breathing, you can take yourself to a peaceful place. This is like daydreaming. The imaginary place in your head should be peaceful.

For example, you can imagine yourself in a small cottage amidst green hills. Keep your eyes closed and start walking towards the mountain from the cottage. You are still not there in the right state of mind. This is just the construction process. You can include your senses by looking at the details of the sight you are imagining. Try touching leaves, listening to the sound of falling water and smelling the moisture. Eventually, you will reach the alpha state.

Now, that you know how to attain the right mental state to learn efficiently, it is time to learn some mnemonics.

**Mnemonics** are methods utilized for accelerated learning and memory improvement. The term 'mnemonic' has come from Greek culture. Anciently, there was a goddess named Mnemosyne in Greek culture. She was known as the goddess who grants memory. The modern mnemonic techniques have been derived from there. Hence, mnemonics are techniques used for brain training to enhance memory.

When it comes to memorizing difficult stuff, mnemonics become a great strategy. This includes using rhymes, acronyms, association approach and plenty of techniques to utilize your visual, verbal and other kinds of memory sensitivities.

With the right mnemonics, you can easily memorize the following stuff:

- A long presentation
- Vocabulary
- Facts
- Speeches
- Phone numbers
- Ideas
- Faces and names
- Numbers

And more!

Whenever you want to learn something new, your limited memory becomes a hurdle. That is when mnemonics come into play, allowing you to accelerated learning with certain patterns. These strategies do require some practice initially, but once you master them, they take your memory to a whole new level of excellence. You obtain an organized and well-coordinated network of information in your brain. This way, remembering becomes an easy job for you.

# Chapter 4: Visual Mnemonics: Tools & Techniques

The most effective mnemonic strategies include visual imagery. From making lists to developing links and memory palaces – you can use your visual memory and learn faster in plenty of ways.

Here are some great visual techniques you can leverage:

## The Journey Method

Given in the popular book **How to Develop a Perfect Memory** by Dominic O'Brien, the Journey Method is quite effective in memorizing through journeys and places.

In the Journey Method, you use familiar places as anchors for things you want to remember. Then, these anchors are arranged in a serial order to create a journey of memories. For example, you can utilize your classroom, office, or room to develop a mental visualized journey of memories.

This method works effectively because of the familiarity of the places you use as anchors. So, no need to say that you need to pick highly familiar journeys. For example, you can choose your route to the office or college as a journey for memory.

Here is how it works-

Suppose you want to memorize the whole periodic table for a college presentation. So, you will need some anchors for the elements in each group.

1. Start by making a list of all the interesting things available in your room. This can include your desk, laptop, bookshelf, bin, drawer, and others. Make sure you choose distinguishable objects.
2. Now, divide that list in the clockwise order. So, scan from the left and reach the right side to memorize the sequence of every object you have selected.
3. In your mind, put elements of the first group in the first object from the left. So, H, Li, Na, K, Rb, Cs, and Fr can go on the desk.
4. Put the elements of the next group in the next object available in the sequence present in your room. Hence, Be, Mg, Ca, Sr, Ba, and Ra can go on your laptop.
5. Do the same thing in a sequence from left to right.
6. Eventually, you will create a memorable anchor for elements in every group.
7. Visualize this until you become confident about the memory.

Effective use of this technique requires deciding your anchors and journey in advance. The sequence of the landmarks should be clear in your head. Then, you can easily link them with information and make memorable associations. Choose the most memorable landmarks when creating a mental journey.

This approach can help you memorize events, experiments, people, objects and other elements.

For example, if you want to memorize the sequence of a presentation at work, you can use this method.

1. Select your office building as your mental journey.
2. From entering the office building to reaching the conference room, decide the required number of anchors. So, you can pick the entry gate, reception, lift, main office, your office, and conference room.
3. Now, make a list of presentation sequence you want to follow and include in the mental journey.
4. At the entry gate - welcoming everyone present during the presentation.
5. At the reception - introducing the purpose of the presentation.
6. Lift - going through every step of concepts of that presentation.
7. Main office - describing the importance of the presented information for your company.
8. Your office - explaining your personal views on the idea presented.
9. Conference room - closing with an overview and thanking everyone.

That is it! You will remember the whole presentation without even using your fingertips. Your mental journey, from the office entrance to the conference room, will let you go through every aspect of your presentation step-by-step.

The method is flexible, so you can easily change the anchors and information, as per your requirements. However, it is important to follow a sequence when deciding these. That is the whole point of the Journey Method.

# Linking

Linking is another tool you can use to memorize lists of objects, places and other types of information in a fixed sequence.

This method involves a fun process of using your creativity in making mental imagery for items on a list and creating a memorable sequence.

Let's find out how it works-

Suppose you have to memorize a list of items in the same order. You can write those elements in the fixed order and assign every element to a mental image.

For example, let's consider that your list contains the following items:

- Firefighter
- Chef
- Apple pie
- Pirate
- Cowboy
- Soldier
- Pizza
- Trouser
- Spider

You can memorize it by using the following linking approach:

1. Pick one image for every item on the list. So, your firefighter can be sitting on a couch watching TV.

2. Link every image with the other somehow. For instance, the FIREFIGHTER, sitting on a couch watching master CHEF on TV.

3. Go through this mental sequence 2-3 times to memorize.

And there you have it! You can use this linking approach to remember any list, no matter how long it is. Dominic O'Brien also gives this great method in his book **How to Develop a Perfect Memory.**

This method is effective because of the visualized and emotional approach it utilizes. You already know that our brain is wired to respond quickly to visual cues and emotional cues. Hence, the creative freedom of picking your mental scenarios allows you to retain the created links in the correct sequence.

But there's a catch here! This method works only if you give yourself complete creative freedom when creating mental pictures. To do so:

- Do not change the first image that comes to your mind. The first image is the image that stays permanently.
- Stop judging yourself if an image is weird or strange. We are human with a complex mind, so embrace it.
- Try associating a strong emotion with your images such as surprise, excitement, shock or any other.
- Associate with a moving image such as fighting, swimming, dancing, running or any other.

Keeping the given tips in mind, you can make this linking method extremely effective for your memory improvement. With practice, you become better at this, and your mental images become brighter and clearer. Therefore, you can begin accelerated learning with this approach.

For exams' preparation:

Students find revision process hectic before exams especially if your exam syllabus is huge with many chapters.

In that case, you would want to utilize the linking method to memorize concepts in the right sequence.

Suppose you have to memorize a diagram, which contains the following elements in a sequence:

- Two men
- One girl
- Four tall buildings
- Three small houses
- A garden
- Five trees
- One main road
- Six interconnected streets

To memorize this diagram in the same sequence, you can follow the linking method:

1. Two men - fighting with each other.
2. One girl - shouting to call the police.
3. Four tall buildings - giving shadows to the fighting men.
4. Three small houses - where policemen are standing.
5. A garden - where two men are fighting.
6. Five trees - shredding leaves slowly.

7. One main road - many cars honking loudly.

8. Six interconnected streets - bulls chasing people.

If you observe, all the imaginary scenarios contain strong imagery and have connections with each other. You have to do the same to make every item a strong memory. Then, go through it once by visualizing. If you forget one or more items, try modifying their images in your mind. Follow the same process until you memorize the whole sequence.

Initially, it can seem complicated, but practice will give you necessary brain training for faster learning.

At work:

Linking is not limited to students preparing their exams, even managers and knowledge workers can utilize this approach at work.

What if you have to pitch a product to a client? Your boss has put his faith in you, so you cannot miss any detail or look nervous when presenting that product.

In that case, you have to make a clear sequence of every element associated with that product. Only then, you can confidently present the product and convince your client to buy.

Suppose your product involves the following specifications in a sequence:

- Beautiful design
- Affordable price
- Durable body
- Low maintenance

- Customer support
- Warranty

This is quite a small list, but you can utilize linking for long lists of items too. The process is the same as mentioned before. You have to associate each item with an image in your mind and visual it all in a sequence.

So:

1. **Beautiful design** - a BEAUTIFUL girl dancing slowly, wearing a golden dress.
2. **Affordable price** - the golden dress looks dull and CHEAP.
3. **Durable body** - the dancing girl suddenly starts doing PUSHUPS.
4. **Low maintenance** - the music stops, so a mechanic comes and picks up the equipment.
5. **Customer support** - the dancing girl, is talking to the mechanic.
6. **Warranty** - the mechanic is fixing the sound equipment right there on the dance floor.

With similar mental images, you can create a sequence of actions to memorize a difficult list of things when working.

Learning words in a foreign language:

Known as an expert on the practical use of mnemonics, Dr. Michael Gruneberg has derived this approach called Linkword. His techniques are similar to the linking approach, which helps in learning words from German, French, Italian and Spanish languages.

His Linkword books include clear mental pictures, which readers can use to learn foreign languages. Hundreds of words are divided into small groups of ten words in each group. Every group is some category, which allows you to make sense of each.

Then, you get clear imagery ideas of linking words with mental pictures. For example, to remember "Hummer," you are advised to picture a funny lobster because Hummer means lobster in German. Similarly, there are unique examples of imaginary visuals for hundreds of words to visualize and learn foreign languages faster.

## *The Memory Palace*

The memory palace is a modern version of the Journey Method given by Dominic O'Brien. However, it has been famous since the ancient Roman era with the name Method of Loci.

A new version is appreciated because it has more fun elements attached, which makes this version effective for many people.

To remember a list of information, you choose a familiar place instead of a journey. For example, you can choose your home, your office, your kid's room or any other place you are familiar with. Then, you create a crazy story involving that place and the elements of the list you want to memorize.

So, if your list has items:

- Oranges
- Apple juice

- Paper cups

You can imagine your kid's room and create a memory palace like this:

1. You enter the room, and your kid is juggling four oranges at once.
2. The floor is filled with apple juice.
3. Hundreds of paper cups are visible in the pool of apple juice.

Sure, this is a small exercise, but it can go to any length depending on the size of the list you have.

## 5 Steps to Successfully Create and Utilize the Memory Palace

### 1. Create your palace

The most important part of this technique is the place you pick in your mind. The palace should be visible in your mind. So, choose a place you are most familiar with. You should be able to visit every corner of that place in your mind. That is why picking your own house seems the best option. You know your home in detail, so the memorizing part becomes easier.

After picking a place, you need to think about the route you want to take when you are visualizing it. A route is better than looking at a static image. You can start walking from room to room and recall things that you remember in every room.

Here are more examples you can use to create a memory palace:

- Pick a street you are most familiar with and follow a sequence you generally follow. So, driving to your workplace, walking to the supermarket and other rides can become a memory palace.
- We all remember our former schools so that they can become a great choice of the memory palace. You can even pick your current institution and use classrooms, the library, and other elements to make a route in your mind.
- How about indoors at your office. You know every corner there, so make your office cubicle, conference room, and other places a part of your memory palace.
- For more soothing scenarios, you can imagine yourself jogging in a green surrounding where you frequently go.

## 2. *Figure out distinctive features*

Choosing a palace in your mind does the first job only. You have to enhance its clarity and detailing in your mind. For that purpose, it is important that you go through the palace mentally repeatedly to pick distinctive features.

Start by closing your eyes and noticing the first thing you see when looking at your memory palace. Is it the color of the surface, or the front door of your home? Keep going through the mental route and analyze everything you see mentally.

Make sure you choose a fixed process when analyzing your memory palace. For instance, if you look left and move to the right, do that every time you are in your memory palace. The same thing is required with the turns you take and the elements you seek in a sequence.

Keep creating a mental note of every element that you see. This will enhance the visibility of your memory palace through your mental eyes.

### 3. *Practice visualizing the palace repeatedly*

The Memory Palace technique can only work if the elements are imprinted perfectly. So, practicing is key here. If you are already sensitive to visual thinking, this process will not seem difficult. Otherwise, you can:

- Go to the place, follow the same route physically, and keep saying every feature you see.
- Make a list of every feature you see in the selected route, then, follow the same route in your mind to find all those features. Even now, you can say the names of the features you see.
- Follow your point of view every time you are mentally walking through the memory palace.
- When you think you are ready, do it once again to be sure about the features of the route.

### *Assign memories*

Now that you have a clear memory palace with distinctive features, you can assign those features with memories and memorize them. The assigning process is the same as the Journey Method. You can be as strange as possible; it all depends on how easily you can remember that mental picture.

## *4. Repeat and repeat!*

After the first four steps, you become ready to memorize things using your memory palace. However, the technique is still new to you, so it would be better if you constantly repeat and practice. Do not just go to the memory palace only when you want to memorize something. Keep using the mental route and see if the assigned memories come on their own as soon as you see the associated features.

Stay relaxed during the whole process, and you can successfully create and utilize the memory palace technique.

## *Association or Memory Pegging*

When you attach a memory to a mental visual, it is called a memory peg, and the process is known as memory pegging or association. This method, however, is more effective when you want to memorize abstract items such as concepts, numbers, names, and words. Everything that does not hold emotional value to us. This method has also been given in the book How to Develop a Perfect Memory by Dominic O'Brien.

You take abstract items and associate them with things that matter to you such as objects, locations or people.

Here is how it works:

1. You allow your mind to soak abstract information for a while.
2. Calm yourself down to reach a relaxed state.
3. You ask yourself - what do I remember when I say this

information?

4. You create a chain of mental images, which leads to a vivid memory of that abstract information.

The process requires truthfulness and the absence of resistance. You need to be genuine with the images that come to your mind. Do not hold back. You can be ridiculous, crazy, extraordinary, unusual, animated or anything else — no need to judge yourself or try to stop from controlling the trail of thoughts. Just go with the flow and see where it takes you. The first instincts will give you the best memories to retain knowledge. That is an essential key to memory improvement.

And remember, if it seems boring, you're doing it all wrong!

**Association method works because** you allow your brain to flow freely. Abstract ideas are difficult for our brain to store because they stay disconnected from our important memories. For example, a student does not feel any emotional attachment to a mathematical formula, but he does feel happy when playing a video game. So, associating the formula with that video game can help. The brain can create a permanent memory network and bring the memory back through the same route.

If a student wants to use association for brain training, he or she can do this for example:

You want to memorize the word "Strenuous," which means "difficult."

1. "Strenuous."
2. I am thinking "Strength."

3. Strength reminds me of the "Hulk."
4. Handling the Hulk is pretty difficult for others in the movie Avengers.
5. Hulk is STRENGTH; Hulk is DIFFICULT.

Students can use this technique to associate abstract information with things that hold importance in their brains. This way, exam preparation can become way easier than usual.

Even professionals can utilize this process to make their work easier. For instance:

You want to remember the name of every client who would be present in a meeting.

1. "Ryan."
2. I can think of a party where I saw a kid "Ryan." He was holding a big lollipop.
3. This gives a picture of the client "Ryan" holding a lollipop in his mouth.

As mentioned before, you can be as ridiculous as your mind allows you to be — no need to restrict your mental images.

Association is pretty much a combination of linking approach and the Journey Method. You can link an abstract idea with a more memorable one. Or, you can create an imaginary, but familiar scenario. Nevertheless, there's a catch. You can't choose associations given by other people as your own. Of course, sometimes it works, but mostly it does not help you create a long-term memory. The association has to be your creation so that it automatically creates a memory network in your brain. Your connection matters.

## *The Dominic System*

Another great visualization exercise for brain training from Dominic O'Brien. In his book **How to Develop a Perfect Memory**, he has explained his Dominic System to provide ready-made links of associated memories to memorize large numbers.

This system is great for students and professionals who have to memorize large numbers on a daily basis.

Here is how it works:

An abstract idea is associated with a person, an action or an object, which is known as the **PAO System**.

1. You take single digits from 0 to 9 and associate them with single alphabets A, B, C, D, E and so on.
2. 0 becomes A, 1, becomes B, and so on.
3. Now, digit pairs from 00 to 99 are replaced with letter pairs, using a significant association.

This will create a ready-to-use system for you to remember any number, no matter how large it is.

**The process works** better and better as you practice it. Regular use allows you to remember the associated letter with every digit. So, you can create real-time visuals in your brain and memorize large numbers faster.

**For students**, this method is exceptionally effective due to the presence of numbers in all major subjects such as mathematics, physics, chemistry, and others. Even topics such as history and geography require number memory. In history, you are supposed to memorize exact years of events. In geography, you have to memorize coordinates along with the name of places.

Here is how it can work for you:

You want to memorize the year 1954 of the Civil Rights Movement.

- 19 = BJ = **B**ig **J**am/ all over the city.
- 54 = FE = **F**lying **E**agle/ in the sky.

Similarly, you can memorize larger numbers using the same method. Just use the letters and create your associations using the same process.

**For people at work**, this method can make data analysis and its use more convenient. When you are good with numbers, people take you more seriously. So, using this method seems effective for knowledge workers and managers too.

Suppose, you want to memorize sales data which includes a large number. Then, you can use the same method and create useful associations to memorize that number. Similarly, you can memorize multiple passwords, security codes, and other valuable numbers.

For instance, you want to memorize your computer password, which is 2569.

25 = CF = **C**at **F**lying/ in a balloon.

69 = GJ = **G**o **J**oker/ find Batman.

When you have an odd number, pairing all of them is not possible. Do not worry! There is a solution for that as well:

1. You can divide digits 1-9 and turn each one of them into objects.
2. 1 becomes a candle, 2 becomes a swan and so on.
3. Make zero a football.

Done! You have all the numbers associated with objects that look like those numbers. The shape of the object is critical here. It should remind you of the number you are associating it with.

So, now, you have both versions of the Dominic System. Make sure you practice them frequently to become better with time.

## *Reviewing*

Dominic O'Brien has another book called **You Can Have An Amazing Memory.** In this, he explains the use of reviewing in creating long-term memories of important things.

The process is simple:

1. You come across any information.
2. Review that information once, and then leave it for a while.
3. Then, you review that information 5 times at intervals of 48 hours, 7 days, 30 days, and then, 3 months.

The purpose of distributed reviewing is to allow your brain to refresh that memory repeatedly until the neural network becomes permanent. Therefore, this approach is more about patiently following the process and letting your mind soak every detail of the information.

The keys to successfully using this method are:

1. Giving yourself the proper time to visit your mental route when reviewing.
2. Stopping at every route station and letting the details sink in.
3. Finding weak links and working on them every time you review them.

So, there you have it! All the visual mnemonics to help you in accelerated learning. Now, you can reach the level of photographic memory.

# Chapter 5: Verbal Mnemonics: Tools & Techniques

You can also leverage your auditory sensitivity to memorize stuff with the following tools and techniques.

## Coding mnemonics

To remember difficult numbers, you can utilize the sense of sound too. The numbers such as security numbers, contact numbers, important dates, and others can become impossible for some people to remember generally.

Imagine you talked for hours to a potential client and gotten his number. But the next moment, you cannot even remember a single digit. Such situations can occur and become painful in every professional's life. Similarly, students lose important marks in test papers just because of one silly mistake of adding a wrong date or a year.

But numbers are easier to remember if you focus on the sound they make when you say them out loud.

For example:

- 0 = z, s or c (0 sounds to start with z, s, or c)
- 1 = w or v
- 2 = t, u, o (u and o because it ends with a sound of u or o)
- 3 = th
- 4 = f, ph,

- 5 = fy, phi
- 6 = sh, ch
- 7 = ss, sey
- 8 = I, ay
- 9 = n

That is how you get the sound of each digit from 0 to 9. Then, you can choose relevant words using the same sounds and associate them with the numbers.

**For students**, this coding method can help in memorizing geographical facts, mathematical formulas, historical dates and more. Similarly, **knowledge workers** can use this method to learn passwords, security numbers, or important data while preparing for a meeting or presentation.

For example, if you want to learn:

1. Amazon is 3990 miles long.
2. The Nile is 4140 miles long.

You can utilize the coding mnemonics like this:

1. Amazon- 3990 = th-n-n-s = Thanos nose
2. Nile- 4140 = f-v-f-s = favorite fist

It does not have to be meaningful. If it makes sense to you, then, you can memorize the numbers. Focus on the sounds of the numbers. That is most important in this technique.

# Acronyms or Chunking

Chunking is a process you can use to group items, information, and ideas in an organized manner. The purpose is to make things easier to remember. The same process is utilized in creating acronyms.

The acronym process allows you to make your own words using the initial letter or initial two letters of every word you want to remember.

For example, the combination of colors present in sunlight is called VIBGYOR:

**V**iolet

**I**ndigo

**B**lue

**G**reen

**Y**ellow

**O**range

**R**ed

So, you can create your acronyms whenever you have a big list of words to memorize.

## *Acrostics*

When you want to remember words in a particular order, the acrostic approach works as well. You can create a sentence in which every word will start with a letter representing the word you want to remember.

For example, if you want to memorize the seven continents:

1. North America
2. South America
3. Antarctica
4. Europe
5. Asia
6. Africa
7. Australia

You can make a sentence using the first letter of each continent's name.

So, it can be:

**N**ever **s**ound **a**dult, **e**ven **as** **an** **a**dult.

Each first letter here is representing the beginning of each continent's name. You can do the same with other groups of words you want to memorize. If you want to memorize certain abstract words associated with your business presentation, this method can help. The process is fun and stays on your mind.

## *Rhyming*

Rhyming is about arranging words in such an order that words with similar sounds get equidistant places. The meaning of the sentence changes, but the sound and the words help you remember better. Then, you can rearrange the original order after memorizing it.

Here are a few examples:

If you want to memorize - Columbus started his sail in 1492.

This sentence has a popular rhyming form - **In 1492, Columbus sailed the ocean blue.**

You can create your rhymes to remember information if it suits you.

# Chapter 6: Food for Your Memory

Until now, you have understood how complex your brain functionality is. The process of developing neural networks is a consistent task, which your brain does.

If your brain keeps on performing, you can memorize anything and create long-term retrievable memories. However, that is possible only if you keep having the required nutrients.

Just like your body muscles, your brain also requires nutrition to stay healthy and work at maximum capacity.

There are specific nutrients that come from specific food and beverages. This chapter will give you a complete understanding of how certain food and beverages affect positively on your brain's function and memory.

## 1. Fatty fish

No other food can top the nutritional value offered by fatty fish to the brain.

Such fish types include sardines, trout, and salmon. They all contain omega-3 fatty acids, which is highly beneficial for brain and memory power.

Our brain contains about 60 percent of fat, and about 50 percent of brain fat is omega-3. This type of fat is utilized to create nerve cells and brain cells. At the same time, this fat assists in memory creation and learning.

You already know that learning new skills is about developing neural networks and strengthening them consistently. The process becomes easier when your brain receives an optimum amount of fatty acid.

There are plenty of other benefits your brain attains with fatty fish foods.

One of them is the slow decline of mental capacity as you age. This is also because of the nerve cells and memory construction generated with the help of an omega-3 type of fat.

You can include fatty fish in your diet in broiled or baked form to obtain the maximum quantity of omega-3 fat. This will promote gray matter in your brain, which includes nerve cells of the memory, emotions, and decision capacity.

## 2. Coffee

If you are a coffee drinker, you can feel glad because it is beneficial for your brain.

Coffee contains two kinds of components that help your brain - Antioxidants and caffeine.

A controlled quantity of caffeine in your body provides a temporary boost to your brainpower. This component is known to block adenosine in your brain, which causes sleepiness. Hence, you feel alert and awake.

At the same time, caffeine triggers serotonin and other neurotransmitters that make you feel happy. This way, you can improve your mood and feel positive. And a positive attitude is a must in accelerated learning. So, you can understand the importance!

According to studies conducted on caffeine, researchers have found that it enhances concentration. Concentration is a must-have trait for students, managers and knowledge workers.

## 3. Dark-colored berries such as blueberries

Among plenty of health benefits, dark-colored berries usually contain anthocyanins. This compound stays available in blueberries as well and offers antioxidant and anti-inflammatory effects.

Oxidative stress is one of the common reasons why our brain loses its capacity with time. This type of stress triggers the degeneration of neuron networks. With age, this problem causes low memory efficiency. In the worst-case scenario, an oxidative state can turn into neurodegenerative diseases as well.

Having enough blueberries and other dark-colored berries can help you have an ample amount of antioxidants. They work to control oxidative stress along with the restriction of inflammation.

The antioxidants of blueberries reach your brain and help in brain cell communication. This component is accumulated between the brain cells, which provides a comfortable path for brain cells to communicate with each other.

You can include blueberries in your cereal every day. Or, make smoothies with some blueberries to gain antioxidants.

## 4. Turmeric

Turmeric is a spice that looks yellow. Usually available in curry powder, this spice is a major source of curcumin.

Curcumin holds the capacity to reach your brain cells easily and provide anti-inflammatory and antioxidant benefits.

This compound allows your brain to have a strong memory. The signs of depression go away when this compound triggers dopamine and serotonin in your brain.

Regular use of turmeric in your food provides enough curcumin to enhance the neurotrophic factor of your brain. This factor is responsible for the growth of brain cells. This is an important brain health benefit because our brain cells start dying as we age.

You can include turmeric in the spices prepared for veggies and meat dishes. Some people also like to make turmeric tea to gain curcumin.

## 5. Broccoli

Broccoli contains vitamin K, antioxidants and plenty of other plant-based compounds. Vitamin K is fat-soluble, which has an important job in our brain. The brain utilizes this vitamin to create sphingolipids, which is another kind of fat required for healthy brain cells. This way, broccoli can enhance your brainpower and memory.

Along with vitamin K, you get antioxidants that further support your memory and brain performance. With just 1 cup of broccoli every day, you can obtain the require RDI or Recommended Daily Intake.

## 6. Pumpkin seeds

Some valuable elements become available to your brain with regular intake of pumpkin seeds. These elements include zinc, magnesium, copper, and iron. Every element has its purpose regarding brain health and memory power.

With Zinc, your brain strengthens its nerve signals. Hence, the connection between neurons stays strong. Plus, regular intake of pumpkin seeds allows you to enhance your learning process. The new neuron networks form faster, so you learn faster.

Magnesium is another beneficial element that enhances your memory and learning capacity. It keeps your brain protected from neurological diseases, migraines, epilepsy, and depression as well.

Pumpkin seeds are also a great source of copper that increases the capacity of sending nerve signals. The optimum amount of copper helps nerve networks to work efficiently and create memories that last for long periods.

Iron is also a necessary requirement to keep your brain function in top-notch condition.

All these micronutrients are available in pumpkin seeds. So, you can give yourself a lot of brainpower by adding this ingredient to your meals.

## 7. Dark chocolate

You can enjoy dark chocolate and drinks made with cocoa powder to obtain plenty of brain-boosting nutrients such as antioxidants, flavonoids, and caffeine.

Flavonoids are a combination of multiple antioxidant compounds that come from the plant. The flavonoids obtained from chocolate reach brain areas where memories and learnings are stored. The neural networks get stronger quickly with dark chocolate's flavonoids, which helps in accelerated learning.

Along with memory strength, dark chocolate also affects mood by driving positive feelings.

## 8. Nuts

Nuts and brain health are associated and backed by various studies. Nuts usually contain antioxidants, healthy fats as well as vitamin E. All three nutrients are directly related to our brain health. Vitamin E increases the strength of cell membranes in our brains. Hence, the brain becomes protected from free radicals that are known to decline memory power.

Among all kinds of nuts, walnuts come on top when it comes to brain health. Walnut contains omega-3 fatty acids. And you already know this fatty acid improves the brain's health and memory power.

## 9. Oranges

Do you like orange juice? If yes, then you are gaining an important nutrient for your brain.

Oranges and all other tangy fruits include vitamin C, which is an antioxidant. It fights against the brain free radicals that attack brain cells. Hence, your mental power stays strong for a long time.

Other sources of vitamin C include kiwi, guava, tomatoes, bell peppers and strawberries as well. You can make smoothies, salads or have a glass of juice to gain enough vitamin C for your brain.

## 10. Eggs

With eggs, you gain folate, choline, vitamin B6 and vitamin B12. And they are all associated with brain health.

Enough quantity of choline promotes the creation of acetylcholine, which works as a neurotransmitter. This neurotransmitter ensures your relaxed mood and allows your mind to remember things accurately. A high intake of choline is a necessity to increase your memory power. However, most people do not get enough.

Egg yolks contain high choline content to help you gain the benefits. With one egg yolk, you get about 112 mg of choline. Men need to have about 550 mg of choline every day. On the other hand, women require about 425 mg every day. With that, you can decide the number of eggs in your daily diet.

Eggs will also give you vitamin B6 and vitamin B12. These vitamins keep your brain away from depressing thoughts and increase memory holding capacity. B12 has a special power of controlling sugar content in your brain.

## 11. Green tea

Green tea is a healthier alternative to coffee to have ample caffeine in your brain. The benefits are similar such as brain performance, focus, alertness, and the ability to increase memory.

Along with caffeine, green tea also provides L-theanine, which is a type of amino acid. This amino acid works on improving the activity of GABA neurotransmitter, which allows the brain to feel relaxed. Hence, green tea is advised when you want to attain a light meditative state by promoting alpha brain waves. You can concentrate better and improve your creativity levels without going to sleep.

You can also use green tea for antioxidants and polyphenols that help the brain stay protected from neurodegeneration.

## 12. Avocados

Avocados are also a great source of brain fats, folate, and vitamin K. These components working together protect from blood clotting in your brain. Cognitive functionality stays top-notch, which assists in concentrating and building long-term memories.

Along with vitamin K, avocados also contain vitamin B and C. Their low sugar and high protein contents are one of the rare nutrient combinations you find in fruits.

You can make smoothies with avocados, include them in baked

dishes, and other forms to enjoy the taste and improve brain health.

## 13. Beets

A not so favorite of many, but beets score top marks when it comes to brain health and performance. The presence of natural nitrates in beets helps in keeping a steady flow of blood in the brain. Hence, your brain functionality enhances, which allows you to stay alert and feel focused.

## 14. Bone Broth

Bone broth has been known to improve brain health since ancient times. The broth included in your recipes allow your body to obtain various amino acids such as glycine and proline. These amino acids increase the immune system and memory building capacity.

## 15. Bananas

As you already know, potassium promotes the generation of brain fats. And bananas are a perfect source to obtain high potassium content on a daily basis. You can make delicious banana smoothies and give your brain enough potassium to work on nerves, brain cells, and the heart as well.

# 16. Spinach

Spinach contains high quantities of nutrients such as folate, beta-carotene, and lutein. All these components are known to work on brain function and prevent dementia. Regular inclusion of spinach helps in boosting concentration.

You can have 2 cups every day in the form of salad, juice or any other form. Many people use sweet fruits with spinach to make delicious salads.

## How Sugar Impacts Your Brain

Being the control room of your body, your brain requires a lot of energy. So, the availability of an optimum quantity of glucose is necessary for humans. Glucose works as a fuel to run all the activities in the brain. But just like a vehicle, there's always a limitation on the quantity of fuel you can have. High sugar content in your diet can lead to negative impacts.

Understand this - a small amount of sugar stimulates your brain to ask for more. So, when your brain asks you to have more sugar, you lose self-control and keep eating more and more sugary food. And that increased quantity reduces your cognitive skills. Sugar gives a sense of reward by stimulating the associated section in your brain. That is why your brain craves for more and more sugar to keep having that feeling.

According to dietary science experts, food types such as fatty, salty and sugary can make people addicted. This addiction can lead to overeating, loss of cognitive control and increased weight. Plus, thinking about eating all the time does not allow your brain to think about other valuable stuff such as learning or memory training.

It all started to keep early humans alive with a calorie-rich diet. The stimulus helped in selecting high-calorie food, which helped in the survival of early humans. However, the scenarios have changed now, and the same stimulus is making people diabetic, obese and reducing brain functionality.

Increased sugar in your body holds the capacity to damage blood vessels. That damage impacts your heart and brain as well. In the brain, vessels associated with your ability to see can get damaged. If you get diabetic, your brain cells lose their performance progressively. So, your ability to learn goes down, motor speed reduces, and memory building capacity decreases as well.

Eating high sugary food regularly can lead to diminishing mental capacity. It increases the HbA1c levels in your brain, which causes brain shrinkage. This is possible even if you do not get diabetes. Anyone who has a high consumption of sugar every day can say goodbye to optimum cognitive function. Other associated impacts involve hypertension, hyperglycemia, insulin resistance, and enhanced cholesterol levels. In addition, it all reduces your overall brain health.

So, the ultimate question is - how do you save your brain from sugar?

You cannot stop sugar intake completely. But, you can choose better versions of sugar. For instance, using refined sugar or food with added sugar are bad choices for your brain's health. You can satisfy your need for sugar with fresh fruits. You cannot even choose too much honey, agave or maple syrup, as they all contain concentrated sugar content.

# Chapter 7: Physical Fitness for Improved Memory and Brain Function

Your brain is connected to your body. So, if your body is in its peak condition, your brain does not have to put too much pressure on various functions. Your physical health directly impacts your brain function and increases your ability to concentrate and hold memories.

Sitting all day trying to solve a problem is not the best way to sharpen your learning skills. You need to combine it with good physical exercises to improve brain training and information processing.

Let us understand the science behind physical fitness and its connection to your brain's health.

You know that your heart rate increases when you indulge in a physical workout. That increased heart rate allows more oxygen to reach blood cells, which reaches every body part including your brain. More oxygen in your brain assists in triggering healthy hormones. As a result, all the existing brain cells perform at a higher rate and new neural networks are developed at the same time.

Experts call it brain plasticity, which is the growth of neural networks in your brain. Working out stimulates the process of brain plasticity. Various cortical areas obtain new connections between brain cells, which improve memory power, concentration, and overall brain function.

With exercise, you can experience these changes occurring in your brain. Refreshed happy mood instead of depressing thoughts, better focus and many other benefits help you live and learn effectively. Moreover, your brain can effectively fight insulin resistance, inflammation, and other degenerative factors. The chemical condition in your brain stays balanced, which helps in the long-term survival of neural networks and brain cells.

Here are all the brain health advantages you can expect from physical exercise:

## 1. Stress reduction

A hectic day at work, or the pressure of an upcoming exam. You can release your stress with a good workout session. Walk, jog, or head to the gym for some weightlifting. All kinds of exercises release feel-good hormones in your brain, allowing you to think positive thoughts and feel refreshed. A component called norepinephrine increases in your brain when you exercise. This component balances the stress, allowing you to get a better perspective of things. So, you can refresh yourself with a good workout and get ready for another round of working at the office or preparing for your exam.

## 2. Increased happiness

People, who exercise feel happier than the people who do not. And happiness is associated with a healthy mental state, which lets you focus and promotes accelerated learning. Exercise triggers the release of endorphins in your brain. Using this hormone, your brain gives you feelings such as euphoria and happiness.

Regular exposure to stress can lead to depression. However, exercise keeps on balancing it with endorphins. Hence, your mind feels elevated above anxiety and depression. You do not have to spend hours lifting a weight. Simply 20 to 30 minutes of regular exercise can give you protection from anxiety, depression, and stress.

## 3. Confident personality

Whether you are a student, a knowledge worker or a manager, a confident personality is a necessary trait to thrive in your career. Nevertheless, you can't feel confident if your brain does not allow you to. Confidence comes from self-esteem for your mental and physical capacities.

With regular workout, you get to see a better version of yourself both physically and mentally. In addition, that improved self-image leads to a confident personality. No matter what your body weight is, or how old you are, regular exercise lets you believe in your abilities.

A confident personality is important in life, especially if you want to learn things constantly. For students, memory improvement and learning provide better scores in exams. For professionals, learning is about reaching higher designations. You can do all that only if you have confidence in your capabilities, including appearance and mental capacity. And that is exactly what physical fitness does for you.

# 4. Protection from gradual cognitive decline

No one wants it, but our age decreases our ability to memorize and even think properly. In the worst-case scenario, cognitive decline reaches the level of Alzheimer's. Brain cells die, and brain functions gradually stop working.

While Alzheimer's is the extreme condition, cognitive decline is common in almost every person. People, with some knowledge of cognitive decline, think that it begins after crossing the age of 45. This is true, but you have to start worrying about it way before to protect your brain functions.

Exercising regularly prevents the degeneration of brain cells. Beginning at an early age, you can exercise to increase the healthy chemical content in your brain. Hence, your brain obtains the capacity to support the hippocampus that plays a big role in the functions of learning and memory.

# 5. Development of new brain cells

If you invest time in cardiovascular exercise, it is helping your brain by developing new cells. More cells mean higher brain performance. High-intensity workout enhances a type of protein in your brain, which is called BDNF. This protein is derived in your brain and improves your mental capacities. You can think faster and go to deeper levels of the thinking process. It also improves your decision-making capacity and enhances your ability to learn new things faster.

New brain cells promote the development of new memory networks in your brain. Hence, applying all the memory tools and getting results can become easier if you spend time gaining physical fitness.

The production of new brain cells majorly takes place in the hippocampus area of your brain. This happens due to the increased oxygen content that reaches your brain through the blood pumped by your heart. The new cells in your brain's hippocampus create better conditions for memory building and neural connections. Hence, learning gets easier. This increased brain cells can improve your ability to memorize vocabulary or learn new skills for the job.

## 6. Controlled addictive behavior

All kinds of addictions are related to your brain. An imbalance in the brain chemical leads to addiction. Regular consumption of sugary food, alcohol, tobacco and other kinds of addictive components is a major reason why a brain loses its functionality.

Exercise helps in the protection as well as the recovery from addiction. Exercise promotes the release of dopamine in your brain. Dopamine is a reward or pleasure hormone that is released due to drugs, sugary foods, alcohol, sex, and exercise. So, your brain gradually de-prioritizes addictive components and gains its sense of reward through workout sessions.

The high alcohol content in your body can disrupt your sleeping habits. Not being able to sleep or wake up from the sleep prevents your brain from resting. Exercise is the solution to this too. A good workout session promotes the sense of rest, which lets you attain a sound sleep without having alcohol.

## 7. Attaining a relaxed mental state

As you already know, a relaxed mind is necessary to attain the alpha state of mind to learn efficiently. In addition, workout sessions at a moderate intensity can help you achieve that. Sound sleep and relaxed muscles are the reasons you feel comfortable. This happens after 1 to 3 hours of working out. Regular workout sessions, however, tend to make you feel relaxed immediately when you sit after an exercise session.

## 8. Feeling inspired and creative

An inspired and creative mindset is how you can ace accelerated learning. These two factors are probably the most important in memory improvement. So, you have to train your brain in every possible way to feel creative and inspired. Moreover, exercising is one of those ways for sure.

Workout sessions create sync between your mind and body. You get better control over how your body and mind feel. Furthermore, a well-synced mind leads to inspirations and creativity.

# The Golden Combination of Physical and Mental Exercise

To maximize brain training, you can choose physical exercises that target brain function. Though all activities are beneficial for your brainpower, some forms such as ballroom or ballet dancing require more mental involvement. Similarly, it is better to cycle than run to involve more cognitive functions in your workout sessions.

Therefore, the goal should be choosing workout types that include the brain's sense of rhythm, coordination, and strategy.

Every aerobic exercise is beneficial for your body and mind. Aerobic exercises provide increased oxygen, making your brain cells healthier.

If you exercise first thing in the morning, before work or college, it keeps you relaxed all day long. You get a better perspective, and your decision-making capacity stays at its peak for the whole day.

## The 4 Types of Workouts That Offer Brain Health

### 1. Cardio

Cardiovascular exercises are also known as aerobic exercises. You can choose a low-intensity workout such as dancing, or a high-intensity workout such as fast cycling. The intensity of cardio exercises stays flexible, so you can increase or decrease as per your choice.

These exercise types tend to elevate heart rate up to 50 to 80 percent of the maximum. Generally, people are advised to indulge in 30-40 minutes of low-intensity cardio 5 times every week. Or, you can indulge in high-intensity cardio for about 20 minutes or so, 3 times every week.

You can choose cardio exercises such as jogging, cycling, treadmill, dancing, or aerobic sessions. If you want to work on your physical health faster, high-intensity cardio works better. You can start with low-intensity and gradually increase to higher levels. This is an excellent approach to improving your brain function as well.

## 2. *Weightlifting*

Weightlifting is effective in reaching peak physical levels and improving your brain function. Lifting weights increases the heart rate, enhances muscle and makes your bones stronger. While the first benefit helps your brain get sufficient oxygen, the other two give you a physical shape you desire.

Weightlifting programs differ regarding current body weight, body weight goals, age, gender, and diet. But, generally, you can rely on moderate weights and medium-intensity exercises. This way, you can save yourself from feeling exhausted and maximize the mental and physical benefits of weight training.

A great advantage of weight training is that you can focus on specific muscles at a time. When you work on certain muscles, and they improve, it gives a sense of confidence and reward as well. This way, your brain starts believing in the process of working and getting results. That mentality promotes accelerated learning as well.

## 3. *Endurance exercises*

Endurance exercises are usually a combination of cardio, weightlifting and other forms of exercise. Such combinations let you work on your overall physical health. These exercises require greater mental involvement during the sessions.

The goal of endurance exercises is to keep pushing your limits every time you exercise. For instance, you can feel exhausted after working out for about 15 to 20 minutes constantly. But, regular exercise tends to increase endurance, and you can push your limits to 30, 40, 50 minutes and so on.

Depending on your physical state, you can choose a suitable combination of cardio, weightlifting and other forms of exercise.

## *4. Having some leisure time and resting*

When you are disciplined about your other exercises, leisure and resting become a kind of exercise for your body. Meaning, the rest and leisure activities also help your body and brain improve regarding performance.

Leisure time means activities that you enjoy doing, such as going to events, meeting your friends, visiting a local park or any other. An activity you like is a great way to relax your mind and reenergize. However, remember that you need a disciplined rotation of exercising and leisure time during the week.

Along with leisure activities, taking breaks is as important as working out. Intense exercise without stopping can make you addicted to working out as well. Though not as dangerous as consuming alcohol, not resting can make you crave for more and more exercises. So, you can easily cross the limitation of healthy exercising.

Every time you indulge in an exercise session, it tears your muscle fibers, especially during weightlifting. Your immune system needs some time to work on the torn muscle fibers and repair them. If you do not give breaks to your muscles, the immune system keeps on working and repairing. It reaches a level when keeping up with the repair demand becomes impossible and that causes injuries. That is why experts suggest a cycle of exercising and taking breaks to promote steady and useful growth of muscles.

Over-exercising leads to over physical and brain training, which is not good at all. You can feel restless and lose the quality of sleep. Your heart beats at an increased rate most of the time, which does not allow you to relax. This affects your ability to sleep at night. In addition, if you cannot sleep properly, your brain can't function properly during the day.

Therefore, breaks are as important as working out to maximize your physical and mental abilities safely.

Use physical fitness to increase your energy level, confidence and focus. Enjoy a healthy lifestyle to improve brain function for memory improvement. No need to dive into intense workout sessions. You should initiate your work light and gradually increase it towards intense levels. Moreover, keep yourself balanced regarding diet, workout, and breaks.

# Chapter 8: The Importance and Influence of Sleep

Just like your body needs rest from time to time, your brain requires rest too.

Why?

Your brain works every single second, no matter whether you are sleeping or awake. But the level of activity reduces to minimal when you are sleeping. Otherwise, you keep on thinking all the time, which requires your brain to work.

Every second, your brain remembers a million things such as memories, breathing, walking, talking, and so on. It all requires constant control of communication between brain cells. On average, your brain can use 400 to 2000 calories on an average every day. This energy is utilized to manage body functions and memories.

Imagine yourself walking for 100 miles without stopping. What if you do not allow your leg muscles to rest even after that? The same can be said for why the brain requires rest after conducting all the tasks every day.

Optimal rest is key to keeping your brain's performance. Without optimal sleep:

## Your memories start overlapping with each other

There are three areas in your brain that work on memories - the hippocampus, prefrontal cortex, and the parietal lobe.

These areas work on neural networks of memories when you sleep. So, sleeping strengthens your memories.

If you do not get optimal sleep, your brain does not get enough relaxed time to work on these neural networks. Most of the time, the brain has to focus on informational pieces you see around you. This starts overlapping one information with the other. You either forget things or remember it in a wrong way due to this.

## Your brain decreases in size

Not enough research available, but experts believe that lack of sleep can reduce the size of the brain. Most affected areas include frontal, parietal and temporal lobes. They become smaller in size, which eventually impacts your brain function and other physical functions as you age.

## You lose control over emotions and feelings

When you do not get enough sleep, your brain can't figure out what's going in the surroundings — the evaluation and analysis capacity decreases, which results in the misinterpretation of situations. So, even a minor issue becomes a mountain of problems, and you react irrationally.

You lose control over your anger and sadness. The brain lets you feel aggressive frequently, which can even lead to consequences you might regret after coming to your senses.

Sleep hygiene tips for quality sleep regularly

After knowing the importance of optimal sleep, you would want to ensure a good night's sleep. For that, you can focus on building a hygiene routine.

# Sleep hygiene involves all kinds of behaviors you follow to get quality sleep every night.

### *Decide a fixed sleep routine*

First and foremost, you need a fixed time when you go to bed and a fixed time when you leave your bed. This routine is a must if you want to subconsciously prepare your mind and body to sleep every night.

Initially, it would seem uncomfortable not being able to go to sleep right away. But you should keep going to bed at the same time every night. Eventually, your mind will start adjusting to the signs, and you will get the feeling of going to bed at the same time every night.

## *Avoid naps during the day*

If you have napped for 15 to 20 minutes or longer during the day, it can affect your ability to sleep at night. Mostly, because your brain feels a false sense of relaxation. You can surely rest and relax, but avoid taking any naps during the day.

The naps also break the cycle of sleep routine you are trying to develop at night. Your brain does not know when to sleep if you keep having naps during the day. The initiation of quality sleep at night is easier if you avoid sleeping during the day.

## *Do not sit awake in bed*

If you go to bed and stay awake for 10 to 20 minutes, it works against quality sleep. But this is pretty common among people. Mostly, we all tend to fall into the cycle of thoughts that happen during that day. Or, our concerns, worries, insecurities and other emotions get a chance to appear on the surface of consciousness.

In such conditions, you should not stay in bed. Otherwise, your brain will start associating the bed with worries, thought processing and information analysis. You do not want that! So, get out and take a walk in your living area, sit on a couch or a chair as long as you do not feel the need to sleep. Make sure you do not give yourself any sort of entertainment through television, mobile phone, or other gadgets. Be with your thoughts as long as they do not indulge you to choose a negative path.

## Do not use your bed to watch television, reading or work

If you use your bed for activities such as watching TV, reading or working at night, it loses the impact on your brain. So, even when you do want to sleep and go to bed, your brain does not feel cozy enough.

Associate your bed with sleeping only to set the mood right.

## Avoid substances that counter sleep

Sleep fragmentation does not let you get enough rest periods. Your brain does not reach a state of deep sleep due to substances such as alcohol, cigarettes and certain medications. So, you need to stay as far away from them as possible.

## Develop an exercise routine

You have already understood the importance of exercising in a balanced manner. Regular exercise also improves your ability to have quality sleep. The increased quantity of endorphins in your body helps in the initiation of sleep when you go to bed.

## Create a comfortable and quiet bedroom

The atmosphere and feeling of your bedroom matter a lot to get quality sleep. Generally, there are two major aspects you need to consider- comfort and quietness.

To create a comfortable environment, you can work on the temperature first. Make sure the room's thermostat creates a convenient temperature in the room. Try aiming for a cooler atmosphere instead of making it warmer.

Along with the temperature, you can switch off all the bright lights and make it darker. Bright lights are not helpful in the bedroom at night. If you do not feel comfortable about complete darkness, you can keep a dim bulb on for the night. Also, choose a comfortable mattress to give your body proper comfort to promote sleep.

To ensure quietness, you need to switch off the television, if you have one in the bedroom. Also, put your phone in silent mode, so the unwanted notifications do not bother you at night. At the same time, try making your bedroom doors and windows partially soundproof. If there are pets that make noises, keep them out of your bedroom at night.

## *Practice yoga and deep breathing before going to bed*

One good habit you can develop is meditating before going to bed at night. Just for 10 to 15 minutes, you can relax and remove all thoughts from your mind and focus on deep breathing. Inhale through your nose and exhale through your mouth. This will relax your mind and prepare for a wonderful sleep every night.

## *Have a warm shower*

If it suits you, a warm shower before bed also relaxes and promotes sleep. You can make it a habit and push yourself initially to the shower. After a few days, your body will ask for a shower every night before bed.

## *Have caffeine with caution*

In this same book, you have read how caffeine alerts your brain and increases your mental attention. However, these things are not effective when you are trying to sleep at night.

The fact that caffeine stays in your system for a few hours makes it important to drink it with caution. If you drink too much coffee or sugary soda drinks a few hours before going to bed, it interrupts sleep initiation.

In the short-term, caffeine works as a stimulator for your central nervous system. You feel alert within 10 to 20 minutes of having caffeine, depending on the quantity. Its effect stays for about 6 or more hours.

Suppose, you drink a cup of coffee, containing 200 mg of caffeine at 6 p.m. Then, at 11 p.m., your body will still have about 100 mg of caffeine in the system. This is a big reason why coffee drinkers fail to get quality sleep at night.

Moderate caffeine amount during the early hours of the day is beneficial. Your mind can encode short-term memories more efficiently due to the increased alertness boosted due to adrenaline — the heart rate increases, which sends more oxygen to your brain allowing enhanced productivity. But in the long-term, high caffeine consumption leads to a lack of sleep or lack of quality sleep. You lose the ability to go to deep sleep at night, which does not allow your mind to relax effectively.

The best thing you can do is choose the right quantity and time to have coffee and other beverages that contain caffeine. Always restrict your coffee consumption after 2 p.m. This way, the caffeine will fade away in your system by the time you reach your bed. Also, keep the amount moderate up to 1 to 2 cups only.

## Myths about Sleep and Memory

Now, let's debunk some common myths people have about sleep and memory.

### *Myth #1 - Memories do not go anywhere just because you do not sleep.*

This is probably the biggest myth out there among common people. Most people do not find any logic between memories and sleeping. How can staying awake make your long-term memories go away? But that happens. Consistent cases of insomnia can lead to the shrinkage of the hippocampus and other areas of your brain.

Your brain loses the ability to study the surroundings properly, which influences memory encoding. The wrong information encoding in the first place does not allow your brain to think rationally or make correct neural networks. So, you either cannot memorize or memorize things incorrectly.

Plus, the level of toxins such as cortisol increases, which leads to other health issues too. So, not sleeping can impact your ability to make short-term and long-term memories.

## Myth #2 - My optimal sleep period is 6 hours only.

Generally, the optimal sleep period is 7 to 8 hours for most people. Only a few people have different biological conditions that allow them to get all the health benefits with less sleep.

However, most people these days sleep less and think that they are sleeping enough. This happens due to the conditioning of our brain with time. People tend to sleep for about 6 hours or less and feel normal because of the adaptation of their mental state. But it still damages your brain all the time.

Just because you wake up using an alarm and drink a coffee, it does not compensate for the lack of sleep you get. Such people perform their everyday tasks in a reduced mental state, which keeps on declining mental performance.

## Myth #3 - I can complete my sleep at the end of the week.

Many people go to bed late and wake up early for 4 to 5 days of the week. Moreover, they think that the lack of sleep is coverable during the weekends. But sleeping does not work that way! Our body and mind require a consistent routine of sleeping and staying awake to feel fresh. Otherwise, we tend to feel tired all the time.

Plus, people, who change their sleeping patterns during weekdays and weekends, experience a kind of jet-lag experience. Their body and brain become confused about the time zones, which increases memory issues, irrational thinking, and tiredness.

Sleeping a little longer during weekends is fine, but you can't expect it to cover the deprivation caused due to the long-term habit of early mornings and late nights.

## **Myth #4 - I can always have a sleeping pill to get good quality sleep.**

Not at all. People think about why to bother with sleep hygiene when you can have one pill and sleep for the whole night.

That does not happen. Sure, people look asleep after taking a sleeping pill. But that sleep is not natural. Using a sleeping pill does not allow your brainwaves to reach the level of deep sleep. You simply stay sedated for the whole night without getting the real benefits of deep sleep.

That is why sleep induction with medication is not a healthy solution. Some studies suggest that sleeping pills negatively impact the connections between brain cells. Hence, you gradually lose learning ability and memory holding capacity.

# Chapter 9: Studying Hard Is Old School, Study Smart for Exams

If you are a dedicated student, 24 hours in a day do not seem enough to manage everything. You have assignments, projects, and classes to cover. Between all that, you have to find time to effectively prepare for exams. Then, there is your social life, commitments, and other activities.

Studying hard for exams has always been a common concept. However, you can study SMART by understanding your brain and utilizing that knowledge in your study patterns.

This chapter will tell you how concentration and focus are achievable conveniently if you target studying strategically. A strategy that does not just appeal to your syllabus, but also to your brain's ability to perform.

## Find different ways to learn one topic

Your brain has different kinds of sensitivities. Different forms of information source stimulate different sections of your brain. So, it seems logical that you can understand a topic more effectively if you consume it through different modes.

The modern-education system allows you to obtain the same study material in the text, audio, video, and other forms. So, you can study one topic in different modes to create a strong map of information in your mind. Furthermore, you can increase knowledge retention by talking about a topic. Helping your friend understand a topic can also help you strengthen that information in your brain.

One important thing to remember is the distribution of different learning modes. Do not sit down to complete all the workloads in one go. Divide the process for a distributed time period and consume one-by-one for better results.

## Pick multiple different subjects every day

If you take one subject and take a deep dive in a single day, that is not a smart move. Similar information going in your brain can easily overlap with each other and make incorrect memories.

To save yourself from misinterpretation, you need to choose multiple different subjects to study on a daily basis. You can pick suitable sections, which you can cover easily and do them one-by-one.

Also, try to pick very different topics together such as physics, history, and literature. This way, you will be able to avoid information overlap in your brain.

## Follow a periodic schedule of reviewing

You have seen in this book how reviewing is a great tool to help your brain strengthen a memory. You can apply that to your exam preparations as well. Periodic and distributed revision is effective to retain the learned topics.

You need to develop a distributed reviewing schedule for every topic you study. This way, you can transfer it to the level of long-term memory.

Commonly, you can select 5 reviews after studying a topic. Divide those reviews into intervals such as 1 day, 3 days, 7 days, 30 days, and 45 days.

## Minimize distractions

If your mind is focused (or not so focused) on two or more things at once, the productivity reduces. There is no such thing as multitasking. In theory, multitasking means focusing your brain in doing two things. This is not impossible but it does not help when you need to concentrate on one thing. For instance, you can walk, read and listen to music at once, but that just distracts you from grasping the details of the content you're reading.

Solving mathematical problems while watching TV, answering messages on your phone and checking your social media profiles. This is not the way to study smarter.

You need to create a comfortable environment for studying by minimizing distractions. So, your phone needs to go on silent mode, if not switching it off. You can at least turn off the access to the internet for the time being.

When working on a computer, keep the tabs minimal. Keep books and notes that you need in front of you at that moment. The less clutter, the better.

# Connect new information with existing memories and learnings

This is the biggest approach to improve your ability to learn and retain knowledge. New concepts are easier to learn when you connect them to existing memory.

For instance, your existing knowledge of water current can help you understand the concepts of electricity. Battery works as a water pump, water current is the electric current, and voltage can replace the water pressure.

Similarly, you can understand the antibodies of the human body with the concept of war. Just like soldiers, antibodies in our body fight alien particles to keep the body protected from diseases.

This is a great way of learning concretely and developing memory connections that last for a long time.

# Use your eyes and voice when reading

When you read, seeing the text just stimulates one memory sensitivity of your brain. You can double the impact by including your auditory sensibility.

Read notes aloud once and keep highlighting important statements.

Then, you can go through the highlighted portions once again, reading them out loud. This will allow your brain to grasp the important information properly.

# Take a break once in a while

You need breaks from your studies. No matter how vast your syllabus seems, you can fit in regular breaks with a well-established system. Breaks will allow your brain to relax, which improves focus and enhances the clarity of thoughts.

Instead of studying for hours, give yourself small breaks of 5-10 minutes, after every 45 to 60 minutes of studying. This sense of break can also become a distraction if you keep looking at the clock to reach your 10-minute break. So, use a stopwatch for this purpose.

Another important thing is how you utilize your break. Picking up your smartphone or using a computer will not help you relax at all. The purpose is giving your mind some time to relax. So, you need to stay away from any device. You can sit with your thoughts or walk.

# Set positive rewards for a good study session

Before you begin your daily study session, decide a reward in your mind. A positive reward such as eating healthy food you like, playing your favorite musical instrument, going out for skateboarding or anything else.

This will become a positive reinforcement for your brain to concentrate. The sense of reward is a big deal for your brain and it enhances productivity.

After completing a study session, you can enjoy that pre-decided reward. This will relax your mind and motivate you for the next day as well.

## Believe the process

Let us get it out there - the difference between average students and successful students.

An average student decides his or her performance goals. But students that find success in their education usually tend to focus on learning goals.

This small diversion from performance to learning makes a big difference.

You concentrate more on learning important concepts rather than thinking about obtaining 98% on your upcoming math test. You give yourself daily learning tasks and master problem-solving ability. So, high scores come along automatically.

It is true that most education centers give importance to exam scores. Nevertheless, as a student, you need to define your learning path. If successful, you will not have to worry about exam scores.

When preparing for exams, have faith in a disciplined process of learning. Follow your approach and work on weak and strong subjects from time to time. Embrace more challenges and push yourself to improve.

# Designate a fixed learning space

You have to have a fixed study area at home — a place where you only go to study your subjects. Studying anywhere or everywhere works fine, but it does not allow your brain to feel organized.

On the other hand, having a single place for studying allows your brain to get into the learning zone immediately. One organized study area also automatically becomes a memory palace in your mind. Your brain creates a mind map of that study area and keeps all the valuable studied material there. This way, you can memorize faster and keep those memories in the long-term memory zone.

# Chapter 10: Bring Your A-game at Work

If you are a professional, your office is the one place where you are supposed to be sharp, concentrated and productive.

But the workplace is also a place packed with distracting activities. So, it creates a contradicting scenario for people who want to bring their A-game and perform.

Staying focused and sharp at work is about working on your memory and brain function. You want to reduce the stress levels so that your work does not become a pile of mess for you.

At the same time, you want to improve your memory and remember important information, names, dates, passwords and other things. This will surely reduce stress and save time when working. Feeling positive and thinking faster can also make a huge difference in your workplace productivity.

All these enhancements can improve self-confidence. In addition, guess what! It is all possible with some easy changes.

# How to keep your mind sharp at work?

## *Switch tasks*

You already know how memories are divided into short-term and long-term. So, use that knowledge and trigger both kinds of memories when working.

You usually focus on your long-term memories by following the same procedures at work. How about switching tasks to activate short-term memories more often. You can pair a task that you do daily with a task you have not done ever.

This will give a sort of challenge to your brain and activate most neural networks. You will be learning and using your existing skills at the same time.

A flexible approach to work keeps our mood fresh. Our brain can focus on different things one after another and concentrate better. So, you can feel on top of your game all day long.

## *Find new social groups to hang out with*

Do you go out with your office friends only? If all your buddies belong to the same profession, you are limiting your social mingling opportunities. People who share the same profession tend to have a similar broad point of view. Your mind needs to feel challenged to evolve and get sharper.

For that, you need to find new social groups to hang out with. Make friends who do not have the same profession as yours. Interacting with new people will give you new perspectives. Your mind will have to find different assumptions, blind spots of thoughts and biases.

This way, you can enhance your viewpoint and discover new ways to see opportunities and solutions for the same problems. Not just at work, but also in life!

## Find your best work hours

We all are different concerning productivity and concentration. Some people feel at their best in the morning, while others need a few hours of steady pace to pick up. You need to find out what sort of performance you have regarding productivity.

Then, you can choose your peak productivity hours for the important tasks of the day. This will give you a chance to utilize the best work hours without stressing too much. You can schedule important meetings and discussions during peak performance hours for maximum results.

### *Take a break*

Just like students, professionals also need breaks after consistent working periods. This can depend on your mindset, stress levels and work in hand. No need to make a set routine, but it is important to make sure that you do not overwork. Whenever possible, give yourself 15-20 minutes of free time. You can relax with a cup of coffee, talk to your colleagues, or go out of the office for a walk.

Even if work is too much and you cannot go out for 20 minutes, simply stand up and stretch your body. This would not take more than 1 to 2 minutes. You will surely feel refreshed and ready to finish that work in hand.

## *Pick one task at a time*

Instead of multitasking, you should approach work with monotasking. No matter how packed your day seems, quality, productive results are possible only with monotasking. You can make things more organized by making a list of tasks and creating a mental strategy of how you can do it all.

## *Eat tangy fruits*

Tangy fruits such as oranges contain vitamin C, which has plenty of health benefits. But the citrus taste of such fruits also allows your brain to feel alert immediately. You can have a glass of orange juice if you are particularly feeling out of focus at work.

## *Watch a funny video*

Of course, you do not want to waste your precious time at work. But a single video of a funny cat or dog can cheer you up. Then, you can double your focus level and work more productively.

Sometimes, constant work leads to boredom. You start resenting the work which you love doing. That is why you need a mood booster to energize your brain for another session of productive work. Watching a funny video for even 5 to 10 minutes can give that boost and help you up to your game again.

## *Utilize 20-20-20 method*

This method is a quick solution to reduce overstimulation and overstressed scenarios at work. Most people can't take long breaks when the workload is too much. In such situations, you can utilize this method to reduce stress levels.

The method involves staring at an object, which is 20 feet away from your desk. Stare at the object for 20 seconds. You have to do this after every 20 minutes of consistent work. Hence, it is called the 20-20-20 method.

This is a great exercise to keep your eyes and brain away from the computer for a while.

## *Schedule meetings after 1 pm*

If a meeting is important, you have to prepare in advance for that. Early-morning appointments and meetings seem to begin a day with high-stress levels. You feel hurried during the morning period, which makes you feel stressed during that whole day.

To save yourself from the morning stress, always try to set your important meetings after 1 pm. This will give you enough time to prepare and keep your mind calm.

## Consider deep breathing

Deep breathing works on your mind and body together. You can use this exercise whenever you feel stress on your mind and increased heart rate. Give good 5 minutes of inhaling and exhaling air.

Inhale through your nose and exhale through your mouth. Do it slowly and repeat by focusing only on your breathing. After a few breaths, your mind will start getting the rhythm and focusing on the air going in and coming out. The heart rate will calm down, and your mind will feel relaxed.

And when you feel relaxed, you can get more work done productively.

## Stop notifications

One sound of "bling" on your phone can bring you back from a focused mindset. Looking at notifications on your phone can't keep you productive. But you can't put your phone on silent mode like a student. Important people call you during office hours.

So, you need to smartly minimize the distracting notifications. For instance, log out from all the social media profiles or put their notifications on silent to avoid unnecessary alerts. This way, you can avoid the temptation of looking at your phone constantly every few minutes. You stay aware of the work in hand, which enhances your productivity.

## *Spend 10 minutes every morning strategizing*

A rough strategy in your mind can give you a plan for the day. Our brain likes to work strategically. People, who sit and start typing buttons on their computer right away, tend to work less productively. Smart people sit and give 10 minutes to overviewing every task first, then, choose a sequence of doing those tasks.

You can do this and become more efficient at work without putting too much pressure. At the end of one task, your mind can smoothly switch to another. Hence, you can make your office hours smooth and productive, without putting too much pressure on your mind.

## *Go home with no work*

These days, people have forgotten the difference between home and office. Laptops and smartphones allow you to work 24 hours. But you have to pay the price regarding your mental productivity. Your mind has its limits, so you can't work beyond 8 hours. Plus, your home should be a place where you feel relaxed. If the stress of work comes to your home as well, your mind won't feel calm anywhere.

That is why you need to leave your work at an office, whenever you stand up to go back home. Sure, some exceptions are possible. But you should try never to bring work back home.

## *Practice eating with chopsticks*

Eating with chopsticks is not an easy task, especially for beginners. It takes your mental alertness and complete focus initially to pick food with two chopsticks and eat. You can dedicate one meal to this method of eating. This will become a fun exercise for your brain to learn alertness and improve concentration.

If you already feel comfortable about chopsticks, use your non-dominant hand for the same activity. The left side of the brain controls the right side of the body and vice versa. Using your non-dominant hand will further activate your brain function.

## *Use new routes to your workplace*

When you follow the same route and commute for years, it puts your brain on an autopilot mode. The brain does not have to do much to take you to your workplace and bring back.

How about you give a little stimulation to your brain first thing in the morning! Leave home early enough and pick a new, unfamiliar route to your office. This will activate the hippocampus and cortex areas because your brain will start encoding the new visible information.

Along with the route, you can also change the mode of commute. Try switching from cars to bikes and even walking if possible. Designate a day of the week when you take public transportation to reach the office and come back.

These new changes to your routes and commute will make you feel more focused and alert.

## *Learn and practice cooking*

People do not look at it that way, but cooking is a great exercise for your brain.

When cooking, all your senses become alert. You see and touch ingredients, hear the sound of cooking food, smell its aroma and taste from time to time. Moreover, every ingredient has to go in the right amount. So, your brain keeps on analyzing and evaluating the quantities. All this makes cooking a comprehensive mental exercise. In addition, the amazing part is that most people feel good about cooking once or twice a week.

You can choose cooking as a weekend hobby and indulge in making new dishes to stimulate all memory sensitivities of your brain.

## *Pick low-tech days*

If you can face a tsunami, a swimming pool can never make you afraid. Meaning, you can upgrade your mental capacity picking hard things and doing them successfully.

We all rely on technology in one way or the other to manage our life and work. So that becomes the best thing to challenge yourself. You can choose one suitable day during weekends as your low-tech day. If you need to reach out to your friends, you can go directly to them, or memorize their phone numbers and call via public telephone booths.

Similarly, you can find your ways without using a GPS. Grab a map or ask locals to reach an address. See how many tasks you can do with minimal use of technology. This will make you confident and improve your mind's capacity to resolve problems faster.

Other important habits you already know about:

- You need to get enough sleep to keep your brain at its maximum capacity.
- Keep yourself physically active throughout the day to ensure mental activity.
- Avoid bad habits such as smoking and limit your consumption of alcohol and caffeine.
- Develop the best-suited diet for your body and mind.

As a student, you keep learning new things, but this newness in learning reduces as you move to professional life. Sometimes, you need to make proactive efforts to challenge yourself. You need to find new things that can help you activate your short-term memory senses. Volunteering, working on a new skill and choosing new projects to work on. New learning is always a reliable method of keeping your brain sharp.

Along with that, you should try and involve most of your senses when working. The more senses involved, the better your brain can create long-lasting memories with them. Do not just see things, allow your brain to use the sense of smell, touch, taste and hear whenever possible. Of course, this is not possible when you are working in front of a computer. That is why a hobby matters, with which you can utilize all your senses. Playing golf, going to dance classes, and other hobbies can help activate your brain's maximum performance.

Many people start forgetting things because they believe in

forgetting. If you have faith that you will forget things because you are aging, it will happen. You have to have a different kind of faith that you can keep your brain function in top-notch condition. Your memory preservation capacity stays secure if you keep learning and follow a healthy lifestyle. Along with that, a positive mindset is also important to keep your cognitive functions to its optimal state.

To improve your memory holding capacity, you can apply repeating tasks. A task or information, which is completely new, requires repetition. Say information out loud three times to memorize and do a task 3 times during different times of a day. Repeat to create a strong memory of doing something, until your brain attains an autopilot mode.

When repeating something, try to distribute it in a long period. Repeating in a short period will not do any good if you want to memorize a method of using new software - space out the practice time. Practice once, then, repeat every day once only to get in the zone of basic usability. After attaining enough confidence, you will become ready to use that software for your daily tasks.

# Chapter 11: Mistakes and Learning: How to Get Fastest Results

There are two ways to learn something:

Either you make no mistake and aim for perfectionism.

Or, you make mistakes and learn in the process.

So, which one would be the best pathway to learning most efficiently?

Believe or not, perfectionism can become a self-defeating approach in a learning process.

Look at it this way - the existence of life is about surviving by adapting and being flexible with the external scenarios. That is how human species have survived and evolved. But what does perfectionism do? It contradicts the concept of survival by making rigidifying expectations.

Perfectionism is usually a result of the social surroundings and expectations of others. What begins as tiny expectations for parents, tend to destroy abilities if your brain gets hardwired to aim for perfection.

To understand this better, you should know what perfectionism is.

Perfectionism is a type of personality that seeks the highest performance standards and absolute flawlessness. Anything less than perfect is not acceptable by such personalities. Such people tend to become more critical about their performance and other people's performance as well. They constantly stay in an evaluation mode. It all seems fine until it doesn't!

Perfectionism has its serious side effects that can stop you from learning new things in the first place.

## Even tiny mistakes cause unbearable stress

A perfectionist personality cannot handle mistakes. Even small mistakes impact them hard and put them in a stressed mode. The brain easily loses the broad picture and starts focusing on that one mistake only. Mostly, such people divert from their goals and stay focused on resolving unnecessary mistakes. This increases the time of learning things.

## Wasting time becomes unavoidable

A perfectionist person is unlikely to move ahead without resolving all the problems present currently. This is harmful when you have a set deadline to learn something or complete a project. Absolute perfection is almost impossible in most things we do in our lives. So, such people waste a lot of time without considering the importance of time efficiency.

## Procrastination comes along

You might not suspect a perfectionist to delay his processes, but it happens very often mostly because a perfectionist looks for the best resources, time, place and conditions to start something. This regressively opens the gates of procrastination and do not allow the initiation of a learning process.

## Slow development of self-loathing

It is common for perfectionists to not feel good enough and self-criticize. The person finds imperfections in his or her work. Those imperfections keep on coming repeatedly, which instills a belief of limited abilities. The person starts thinking that he or she can't ever achieve the perfect results. This belief in failure sets the path to not being able to learn anything.

## Perfectionism and Psychological Distress

If perfectionism becomes a part of the psyche, you tend to develop a pervasive approach to learning. Trying new things becomes a daunting task because you assume that you are going to fail. Your unachievable expectations do not allow you to take new challenges. So, your hidden abilities stay hidden.

Self-focused understanding is another issue with perfectionism. You think about your performance all the time. Which is why new learning opportunities come and go without gaining any of your attention. With that, you keep on losing your ability to innovate, create new things and adapt to the growing world around you.

Moreover, perfectionism can become a continuous source of unwanted emotions. Staring at your report card for hours or thinking about one remark made by a senior at work all day long. All these things make you feel anxious, depressed and frustrated. And none of it is helpful in learning new things.

Every mistake becomes equivalent to failing. You believe that you are losing respect due to your mistakes, even when the errors are not so big in the first place. Personal standards become so high that you lose the hope of ever achieving them. You doubt every decision, every step you take towards your goal. And that does not let you stay productive or efficient.

Setting high standards is not perfectionism. Most successful people start by setting a high standard where they want to reach. The self-destructive nature of perfectionism lies in the concern you feel about your mistakes. High standards are supposed to keep you motivated and take you to the desired success. But some people feel so worried about mistakes that they tend to punish themselves with concerns and doubts. Because a perfectionist becomes a self-critic, he or she assumes that other people are also thinking the same. This gradually makes that person reluctant towards new activities, projects, and opportunities.

Perfectionism gives a bad feeling about mistakes, which interrupts the gradual process of learning. All sorts of learnings in life involve mistakes. Seeking excellence is about enjoying the mistakes along with the learning process until you reach the desired goals. But perfectionism does not let you have that enjoyment. You forget about 100 things you are doing right and find one or more mistakes somehow to loathe yourself.

For example, if a perfectionist student moves from a grade C to grade B, he will not feel good about it because he wanted Grade A in the first place. For him, the goal is to get grade A, no matter if he can retain the learned knowledge or not. That is the problem with perfectionism! They forget about the real value of learning new things.

This is why perfectionists conceal most of their mistakes from people, who can give genuine feedback. They do not let their mistakes come out, which does not allow them to gain crucial insights. If a student of literature avoids showing written work to teachers, he or she can't improve. Hence, the performance in exams keeps on going down. The same goes for people working in an office and hiding mistakes from their seniors.

## How to Use Mistakes When Learning

Instead of being a perfectionist, you should think about being a high achiever. Do not be afraid of the mistakes, use them!

Just like a small mistake haunts a perfectionist, the same mistake becomes a learning tool for a high achiever.

To acquire that approach, you need to pass the feeling of panic, inconvenience, and embarrassment. Everyone is making mistakes, and everyone is fine. Do not stress over a mistake because it happened. Learn why it happened, and do not let it happen again. That is how you can utilize mistakes in your learning process.

A mistake is not equivalent to failing. You fail when you waste your time in the wrong ways of doing things. A mistake is just a single wrong action. So, you can shift your path to the right ways and obtain success in learning.

How to do it?

## *Take the ownership of your mistakes*

First, you need to own the mistakes you have made. Owning is about accepting the mistake to yourself first. Then, you need to make sure that everyone who needs to know about it knows. Be proactive and tell every relevant person about the mistakes you have made. Do not put excuses in it, simply acknowledge the mistake and apologize. Also, convey that you are working to resolve the problem.

If a mistake does not concern anyone except you, no need to tell anybody, in fact, you should not even think about what other people "may be" thinking.

In your mind, or to others, never try to blame your mistake on others. Accepting your mistakes is a sign of integrity and courage. Even if other people around you do not think so, you should have faith in the power of accepting mistakes. When you attain your goal and resolve the mistake, people will remember you for your integrity and courage.

If you keep ignoring your mistakes, you can't work on them ever. So, accept your mistakes if you want to learn something, anything!

## *Learn to reframe your mistakes*

It is common for all of us to feel a little shocked or embarrassed about a mistake at first. But this negative light should shine for an initial period only. Otherwise, you will start self-loathing like a perfectionist.

What you need to learn is the ability to reframe the way you look at your mistakes. Instead of evaluating yourself, start evaluating the reasons why that mistake occurred. Try to remove the emotional aspect of this evaluation. Treat your mistake as a conclusion of certain actions. Your job is to analyze those actions to discover the real problem.

This approach will increase your knowledge and bring you closer to your learning goals. At the same time, you will feel motivated to resolve the problems and move forward.

For example, suppose you were working on a project, and the results are full of mistakes. In that case, you can go through the process you used and find the loopholes. Maybe you did not invest time in the on-going testing of the project. So, the solution would be the introduction of a planned testing method. You can also include a checklist of every step to monitor the progress of your project.

The idea is to lean towards your productive side no matter what mistakes you make in the process. Every situation, positive or negative, can benefit you one or the other if you have the right approach. Unfortunately, the opposite version is also true. You can destroy a good or bad situation without your negative approach.

It is all about your mind-set towards mistakes. They happen, and they will happen! All you can do is keep a productive mindset. So, whenever a mistake appears, you can productively go through it without stopping at all.

But remember, you can't be too OK about making mistakes. You are supposed to have a positive approach, not a careless approach. Take the mistakes responsibly and learn from it.

## *Analyze mistakes objectively*

In the previous point, you got a glimpse of how to look at the objective side of mistakes. Here is how you can do it:

- Think about the objectives you wanted to achieve.
- Note the wrong actions you made in the process.
- Find out the time when it all went wrong.
- Make a list of reasons why you made mistakes.

Again, it is important to stay on the objective side of this analysis. Asking yourself "why" can easily take you to the emotional lane of making mistakes. Do not let it happen. Be honest and choose the objective side of every reason behind the mistakes.

## *Put your conclusions into practice*

If you analyze and do nothing, it will not help. There is always a feeling that pulls us back to the regular, habitual tasks. Resist that and work on the conclusions you attain after analyzing your mistakes. This is a key step to learn something and memory improvement. If you quit, you break the process of growing your mental capacity and skills.

Most of the time, the necessary steps involve changes in your habits or surroundings. You need motivation and self-discipline to make those changes, or it all goes to the self-sabotaging mode. The benefits of mistakes require these changes if you do not want to get stuck with limited knowledge or skills.

Moving forward, you need to find out the resources, knowledge, skills or tools required to avoid those mistakes this time. Do not seek quick fixes as they do not last. Think about finding a permanent solution so that you never make that mistake again. If you have to commit to a new habit forever, do it in the name of disciplined learning.

When learning, most mistakes are personal ones. This enhances the importance of giving a deadline to yourself to implement the required changes. You can't take forever in fixing one mistake. Decide a fixed timescale and be disciplined enough to follow that timescale.

The type of tools will depend on the mistakes and their causes. For example, if your mistakes were a result of forgetfulness, you need to work on your memory by using accelerated learning tools and techniques. Giving importance to details need to become a part of your habit. Plus, you need to become more organized to remember things. For that, you will require handy pre-planned strategies to work with.

Similarly, if you are constantly failing to deliver quality work to your clients, you and your team have to work on improving communication channels. Some mistakes are organizational rather than personal. But they can equally impact your ability to learn new skills. You have to become more creative about such mistakes. Try including other people associated with that mistake and find creative personal ways of conquering it at the same time.

Making a small or big change is a required action to resolve mistakes. These changes are important, so you have to be willing to adapt. Also, do not feel scared to ask for help. If you have people who can help in the process, always approach them. Most people feel good about helping others. But you have to be ready to take the ultimate steps. Others can only provide tools or encourage you; the ultimate change has to come from you.

### *Monitor your progress*

It is "monitor" your progress, not "feel worried" about it. A successful upgrade after a mistake allows you to prevent the old mistakes at least. The goal is surely to make minimal mistakes, which is why you should monitor your progress regularly. Find out if the implemented actions are working in your favor or not. Evaluate to ensure that you aren't making the same kinds of mistakes. If possible, you can also choose a reliable person to keep an eye on your actions and mistakes. This will help in staying committed to the task of learning.

## Key takeaways

Making mistakes is a common habit. Punishing yourself for mistakes is not a solution. Perfectionism can lead to the wrong way of learning. It does not allow you to learn, as you keep thinking about the negative emotions cultivated due to impossible expectations.

Owning your mistakes and working on them objectively is the fastest way to learn anything. You save yourself from the negative emotions and stress and allow your brain to learn skills, resources, knowledge, and tools.

So, aim not to repeat the same mistakes. Try and become a higher achiever instead of being a perfectionist.

# Chapter 12: What You May Not Be Aware Of

Have you ever marched into a room full of confidence and all of a sudden forgot why you came in there in the first place? If so, you will understand that human memory is full of marvel. We often forget the very important information and yet we remember millions of useless details we will never even need. Why is it so? Here are 7 of the most surprising and strangest facts about human memory. Let's have a look at all these in detail:

## There is essentially no limit to the amount of info that you can remember.

Considering how much we tend to forget on a daily basis, it may come out as strange. However, it is true that our mind has a virtually unlimited 'storage capacity' to learn. A rough calculation done by Paul Reber, the Professor of Psychology at Northwest University indicates that the brain can store about 2.5 petabytes of data, which is 2,500,000 GB or say, 300 years' worth of television.

"The brain consists of around 1 billion neurons. Every neuron makes about a thousand links to the other neurons, which amounts to above a trillion links. The neurons come together so that each one of them can aid in some memories at one time, exponentially enhancing the memory storage capacity of the brain to something closer to about 2.5 Petabytes."

Hence, if we have an essentially unlimited storage capacity, why do we still obliterate so much? This is a huge topic, which is worthy of its post. However, a lot of pieces of evidence suggest that we are more likely to commemorate something if we make an active and bustling effort of understanding it and if we come across it on a regular basis - as this strengthens the links between the neurons in the brain & makes information simpler to recall.

# Nonetheless, we can only learn and memorize only a handful of things in our 'short-term' memory

A huge part of the reason that we seem to forget a lot of things may well be that, even though our long-term memory is essentially limitless, our short-term 'working' memory has a very small capacity. The initial research into short-term memory suggests that we can only remember five to nine pieces of information there at a given time. Nonetheless, some more recent experiments have suggested that it may even be as low as just four!

Still not convinced?

You can try it out yourself with a quick experiment. Given below is a list of words, which you need to study for two minutes. Then, write down as many words as you remember from the list, without looking.

- Nine
- Plugs
- Army
- Clock

- Desk
- Swap
- Lamp
- Bank
- Horse
- Hold
- Cell
- Apple
- Fire
- Color
- Find
- Ring
- Table
- Hold
- Baby
- Bird
- Lust
- Sway
- Worm
- Sword
- Rock

This confinement on the short-term memory explains why 'sloshing' the information just before an examination does not work very well. Hence, one clear strategy of remembering more of what you learn is to "space out" your studying. By this, more information is moved from your 'short-term' to your 'long-term' memory.

## Studying or acquiring new information makes physical modifications in the structure of your brain.

It is quite easy to think of the brain as a magical box in which your memories, emotions, and thoughts are stored. However, when it comes down to it, the brain is just a part of your body like your muscles and your heart. Exercising your brain in particular ways, whether it is learning some new skills like a musical instrument or some new language, or simply just learning the things from any book produces the physical changes in the structure of the brain.

Thanks to the contemporary imaging techniques like MRI, i.e. Magnetic Resonance Imaging, scientists are able to see these modifications before and after the learning takes place. Additionally, they have found not just the major enhancements in the activity (which is measured by the blood flow) in the particular areas of the brain linked with the activities, but also the long-lasting structural modifications concerning grey and white matter.

## Being able to approach the information quickly on the internet makes you less in favor of remembering it.

It is always better to access any information in just a few seconds and resources like Google, YouTube and Wikipedia have been the major parts of an insurgency in how we find the information. However, studies have suggested that there is an interesting adverse effect of being able to access the information in such a convenient way. If your brain is aware that it can simply re-access it in this easy manner, it is less likely even to bother to remember the info itself!

We do not try to store the information in our memory to the same level that we have always used to. It is because now we know that the internet knows almost everything. Anyone can contemplate that this limits the personal memories. Constantly looking at this vast world through the lens of our smartphone cameras can result in us believing our smartphones to store our memories for us. In this way, we are paying less attention to life itself and are becoming even worse at remembering the events from our own lives.

This phenomenon is now called 'The Google Effect' and has become part of a continuous debate as to whether the internet is making us dull and dumb.

# We are capable of remembering things, which did not even take place.

As time passes, it can become difficult to know how precise our memories of any event are. Certainly, for a lot of our childhood memories, it can be a little hard to know for sure whether we are remembering the director, the primary event itself, or are just recalling some story which our parents told us or from the home videos or from photos from that time.

However, this concept has a much scarier connection, which has been studied by psychologists. In one experiment, interviewers were able to persuade seventy percent of the people that they had committed a crime when in actuality they had not.

This has very big implications for the legal system, and on the way, the eyewitness testimony is used in the court. It provides other amazing insights into how human brains work.

# Testing oneself on the information is better than just re-reading or rehearsing it.

The term 'test' is as the case may be, up there with the 'public speaking,' regarding its ability to certainly terrify the people. Nobody likes tests, and even the educational professionals argue that people are 'tested' away too much and apparently, it is getting in the way of the 'real' education. Of course, there is an often-cited quote in the education circles, which goes something like this-

"You do not fatten a pig by continually weighing it."

Along with the amount of compulsory national tests, which the students are expected to take in today's time, it is hard to argue with. Nonetheless, research shows that consistent 'low-stakes' tests can be immensely advantageous in the whole learning process. Instead of constantly being pampered and catered to the information by re-reading it in the same book, testing charges us confront the gaps in the knowledge, and makes our brains work harder for retrieving any information. In doing so, it also strengthens the neuronal links & makes it simpler to retrieve in the future. The brain, in this way, is just like any muscles in the body: you have to exercise for it to remain stronger.

There are some reasons to begin testing yourself on what all you have learned right away!

# (Nearly) Forgetting Something Makes It More Likely To Be Remembered.

Partially forgetting something & then striving to remember it is an essential part of the process of memory formation. When we struggle to remember things, we are exercising our brain & telling it that 'This information is critical, store it somewhere very safe and easily available.' This is the main concept behind the 'spaced repetition' approach.

The information is re-visited in set intervals for strengthening the memory of it in this study technique. The concept is that you re-visit any information when you have almost forgotten it, and thereby bringing it back to the interior of the mind. This process is used in many systems including SuperMemo, Anki, and Synap.

# Conclusion – Final Words

### *The Tip of the tongue phenomenon*

Have you ever been asked anything that you know the answer to but you still find yourself struggling to think of the exact right word? "Oh I know this one!" you may say, "I know that it begins with a J."

We are all familiar with this kind of sensation. This common state has a name. It is called 'lethologica' or the 'tip of the tongue phenomenon.' The psychologists define this as a feeling, which accompanies comes with the temporary inefficacy of retrieving the information from memory. Although you are aware that you know the answer, the ambiguous information just seems to be out of your mental reach. This kind of feeling can be very annoying when you experience it. However, one of the pros of lethologica is that it lets the researchers analyze various aspects of the memory.

Some of the amusing things which the researchers have discovered about it are:

1. It is universal.
2. The surveys have suggested that about 90% of the speakers in various languages from all across the globe report to have experienced the moments where the memories seem to be momentarily inaccessible.
3. These kinds of moments occur many times and the frequency increases with age.
4. The young people generally have 'tip-of-the-tongue' moments about once in a week, whereas the older adults find that they may have it at least once every day.
5. People generally remember partial information in bits and pieces.

For instance, they might remember the letter of the word that they are looking for begins with or the no. of syllables of the word.

## What's the reason behind this phenomenon?

How do the researchers analyze and clarify lethologica? Language is an immensely complicated process. Most of the time, this course takes place so smoothly that we barely even notice or realize it. We think of something, and the brain gives words to show these abstract ideas, and we then speak out what is on our minds. However, since this process is so complicated, several types of things can go wrong, inclusive of the tip-of-the-tongue moments.

When that happens, you may feel that the info is there just outside of your hold. You know that you know it, but it seems temporarily secured and sealed behind some mental brick wall. The moment something finally does bring about the retrieval of the memory, or when somebody else gives the missing info, the relief of those frustrating feelings is tangible.

## *Why does this happen, though?*

Researchers believe that many factors can play a role. However, the exact processes are not completely clear. These events are more apparent to happen when people are just tired. For instance, even though the other feature of the memory like how well the info can be encoded & the presence of any meddling memories can also have access.

The metacognitive clarifications for this phenomenon suggest that the tip-of-the-tongue state acts as a kind of alarm. Like a cautionary signal in your car, these can alert to any hidden issues, which need to be looked at.

As per such theories, these moments are not in & of themselves an issue. Instead, they serve for alerting you that something is going on with the retrieval system & it lets you correct the problem. In case you find yourself having this kind of experience constantly before any important presentation or exam, you would then know that you may need to study more for that it remains in the memory for long and deep.

## *Are there any preventive measures for it?*

Some researchers have found that this state can play an adaptive role in the learning and memorizing process. Some of the studies have found that the more time people spend on attending to any of this experience, the better their memory and learning of that material becomes in the future. This implies that these moments may result in the stronger encoding of memory, and hence making the retrieval much simpler in the end.

Nonetheless, some other researchers have found out that spending the time in trying to recall the information, which seems to be on the tip of the tongue can be problematic. Even though it may be tempting to spend some time in struggling to find the solution, psychologists Amy Beth Warriner and Karin Humphries suggest that the more time you put in trying to remember one word on the tip of your tongue, there's more likeliness that you will struggle with this word again in future.

What they came to realize is that once people enter this state, it becomes more possible for that state to occur again whenever the person tried to remember that word. Instead of learning the right word, it seems that people learn to go into an incorrect state when they try to get back the word again.

In this study, the researchers displayed thirty participants' questions that they knew, didn't know, or had answers on the tip of their tongues. For the latter-kind answers, the participants were then haphazardly assigned to the groups, which had either ten or thirty seconds to come up with any response. The method was then repeated 2 days later.

The longer the participants spend in that state, the more likely they were to have a similar experience the next time they came across that word. The additional time that the people spend in trying to unearth the word is what the researchers call as the 'incorrect practice' time. Rather than learning the right word, people learn the mistake itself.

In a study done in the year 2015, it was found that this re-occurrence of this phenomenon is possibly a consequence of constant or contained learning, which involves learning of complicated info in incidental ways without any knowledge or understanding that it is learned.

## *Meaning of the Research*

The study has critical applications for educators and students. At the time of the next study session, aim at looking up the right answers instead of trying to recall the information. For the teachers, the study implies that it is more advantageous to give students the correct answer instead of letting them struggle in recalling it on their own.

What are the ways of preventing future issues following a tip-of-the-tongue event? The best way of breaking the cycle is to repeat that word to you, either aloud or silently. This step created another procedural memory, which aids in minimizing the negative impact of the prior wrong practice.

The good news is that even though these states generally tend to reoccur and are learned, the wrong learning can be corrected either by resolving the issue spontaneously or by using bits of help for triggering the information retrieval. In case you have ever had that evasive answer pop into your head all of a sudden, often when you were not even trying to think about it, then you have experienced the impulsive settlement of Lethologica.

## *Last Tip for Tip-Of-The-Tongue Phenomenon*

The tip-of-the-tongue phenomenon can be a feeling of discontent, but it might just be reassuring to know that it is not compulsorily a sign that your memory is declining. These kinds of experiences are common and are, in most cases, just a source of annoyance and disappointment. By all means, they can sometimes be very serious in case you experience these at the time of your critical exams or between any important presentations.

The research has suggested that the roots of this phenomenon may be intricate and connected to various causes. You may be more likely to experience it when you are exhausted and tired, or maybe your memory of information was just weak at best. It does not matter what the cause may be, struggling to remember the evasive and ambiguous piece of information may make recalling harder in the future. Rather than struggling to bring forth the memory, only looking up the answer can be more advantageous in resolving your next tip-of-the-tongue experience.

## *Improving the Memory*

A strong memory relies on the vitality and health of your brain. Whether you are a student preparing for your final exams, a working professional concerned about doing all you need to remain mentally sharp, or any senior looking to enhance and preserve your grey matter as you age, there are many things you can do which can improve your mental performance along with your memory.

## *Final Tips*

1. Do not skip your physical exercise - Do not give up on simple aerobics.
2. Exercise your brain - Memory is just like muscles—use it or lose it. Always remember this.
3. Get your Zzz's (sleep well) - Follow your regular sleep schedule.
4. Try to remain stress-free - Take breaks.
5. Make time for your friends - Healthy relationships are the ultimate brain boosters.
6. Eat brain-boosting diets - cut back on caffeine.
7. Laugh - because it is the best medicine.
8. Take practical steps of supporting memory and learning.
9. Treat and identify your health issues.

# Part 3: Masculine Emotional Intelligence

*The 30 Day EI Mastery Program for a Healthy Relationship with Yourself, Your Partner, Friends, and Colleagues*

# Introduction

Hello and thank you for choosing my book as your guide into the realm of masculine emotional intelligence. If you are curious about emotional intelligence but still not sure about what it is, means, or looks like, then hold onto your hat because after this guide is through you will be able to understand what your emotional intelligence is and how to develop it.

Through the years, the importance of emotional intelligence has been widely recognized. In fact, one of the most famous books regarding emotional intelligence was published in 1995 by a man named Daniel Goleman. His book sought to help others understand what emotional intelligence (EQ) is. Goleman's work was largely influenced by the article that two psychologists published in an academic journal back in 1990. John Mayer and Peter Salovey laid the groundwork for what would lead to some of Goleman's greatest work.

It was not too long after this that emotional intelligence overtook the world and made its way into things such as children's toy advertisements and other conventional trade items. Since the days of Daniel Goleman's book, he has been impressed with how quickly emotional intelligence has been embraced by the general public as well as scholars.

So, what exactly is emotional intelligence and how does it affect you? The shorthand for emotional intelligence is EQ, and it stands for emotional quotient. Emotional quotient is just another name for emotional intelligence, so don't worry too much as the terms are interchangeable. You should get really familiar with this shorthand because we are going to delve deep into the world of emotional intelligence. There are varying definitions explaining the boundaries and limits of EQ, but to put it in layman's terms, EQ is your ability to clearly distinguish and monitor your own personal emotions and the emotions of those that are around you. However, it is not this simple. Like everything in life, there are layers to your emotional intelligence.

Along with being able to control and realize your own emotions and the emotions of others, EQ involves the ability to identify the different types of emotions and accurately depict them. Per Goleman's description in his famous book, your EQ is also defined by the way that you process the information you have about emotions and use this emotional information to help guide the choices that you make, your own personal behavior, and how you influence others.

You might be wondering why EQ is so important. I am sure that all your life the importance of having a high IQ has been driven into your mind. But let's be honest. Success is more than just a high intelligence quotient. Having a high EQ is vital to your ability to succeed in life - in fact, the two go hand in hand with one another.

The list of reasons for why EQ is so pivotal to your success can span miles long, but to sum it up into two short and sweet points: your EQ relates to your own self-awareness and your social awareness. These two categories can make or break a venture, and between you and me, I am sure you would rather be on the positive spectrum of this equation.

The main difference is that your IQ measures your cognitive intelligence. Your IQ is pretty easily measured through standardized testing. However, times have certainly changed in the last century and your IQ is not the only thing that matters anymore. With the understanding we have gathered on EQ, we now have several different branches of intelligence that go beyond the scope of the cognitive abilities we possess. For example, you might find that social intelligence overlaps a lot with emotional intelligence. Yet, it is extremely important to remember that they are two completely separate areas of intelligence and should not be interchanged with one another.

A growing number of businesses and employers are valuing EQ higher than they are IQ. Don't get me wrong, IQ is still a great thing to have and take pride in if you have a high one, but it is not a substitute for EQ. The game is changing. It has changed, and we were all asleep as EQ took over the world overnight.

In the job field, an overwhelming 71 percent of employers look at high EQ numbers versus high IQ numbers. Emotional intelligence is taking over the workforce at an alarming rate, and there is a reason why. Those who have higher levels of EQ are reported to have increased job performance as well. This is why the mindset around EQ is shifting.

When surveyed in 2011, one in three managers reported that they would rather promote or hire a candidate that had higher EQ levels than one with higher IQ levels. The proof is in their work statistics. If a hiring manager thinks that your emotional intelligence is low, then they are far less likely to hire or promote you. According to 59 percent of managers that make the hiring decisions for their companies, low EQ means you're out.

In fact, if you are looking to move up into a position of leadership, then working on your emotional intelligence is the single best thing you can do to make sure that you stand out from your competitors. Why? It has been proven through research that managers with high EQ values have a significant decrease in team grievances - about an average of a twenty percent decrease! This is because they are able to read, understand, and adapt actions based on what they know about emotions. A boss or manager will look for all the qualities that signal someone is in tune with their emotional intelligence. They are watching to see if you can understand what emotions are on display, interpret them, and then react and respond accordingly. Nobody wins when there is a hothead in the office, or just an obtuse manager who will never understand why their staff is falling like flies.

The same can be said for relationships. When you bring high EQ values into a relationship, there is a larger chance for its success. That is because relationships are all about emotions! There are about 80,000 emotional calls that your partner sends out to you through the course of a forty-year relationship. Being able to interpret and appropriately answer those emotional calls spells the difference between a relationship that is healthy and lasts and a relationship that fails.

If you find that you have problems in your career or your relationship, then you might want to examine your emotional intelligence before you do anything else. Regardless of how well you think you are doing, it is always a good idea to stop, take a breather, and figure out where your emotional intelligence lies.

I get it, I have been where you are too. Being reluctant is just a step in the process, but don't shelter yourself from information that can change your life. As men, we are often recalcitrant to make changes or to admit to the flaws that need to be worked on. But I am here to tell you that we can do better, and there is better for us. It just involves a little bit of self-work.

There are several reasons you might have picked this book up. Perhaps you wanted to learn more about emotional intelligence, or maybe you realized that you are lacking and need to get your emotional intelligence buffed up and ready for use. Whatever the reasoning, you need to know that you are not the only one of your kind - otherwise there would be no need for this book, now would there?

Your main problem is that you struggle to interpret the emotions of those around you and use them to help you navigate through work and love life situations. That stops today. I am looking forward to journeying through these next few chapters with you so that you can see what emotional intelligence is all about and how you can change your life with it.

If you have ever been passed up for a promotion or job that you felt you deserved, then delve right in. If you have been on the receiving end of a loved one telling you that you "just don't get it," then come on and start reading, because there will never be a better time than right now. Don't let another relationship or job pass you by before you decide to do something about it.

Being a man does not equate to having low emotional intelligence. Drive that line into your mind right now, because it is the truth. There are many powerful, successful men out there who are walking around in tune with their emotional intelligence. You could be one of them. Yes, being a man and conditioned to the world we live in, you might have to work a little harder to get your emotional intelligence to where you want it to be, but a little hard work never killed anyone.

You don't have to lack emotional intelligence. You don't have to lose relationships. You don't have to give up jobs and promotions. You can be your best self by simply understanding how your emotional intelligence works. I will be there with you through every step!

So, let us start by jumping headfirst into this problem, shall we? The first chapter is going to be all about emotions! We need to learn about them and talk about them if we are going to understand them. The next time your partner tells you that you "just don't understand," you'll be able to tell them that you do and safely navigate the emotional waters into your favor. If you are ready for your overall quality of life to improve, then what are you waiting for? Let's go find out more from those pesky emotions that constantly seem to elude us at our better moments.

# Chapter 1: Human Emotions

"There is no greater agony than bearing an untold story inside you."
- Maya Angelou

Emotions can be difficult to understand and interpret, especially when the world we live in has left us without a base to understand them. Our emotions impact the way that we live, how we interact with those around us, what course of action we choose to take, as well as our understanding of our environment. So, where do we go in order to understand more about the emotions that seem to elude us? The main goal of this guide is to ensure you are able to master your masculine emotional intelligence. However, how can you reach that goal if you still don't understand what makes your EQ?

Luckily for us, the psychologists of our world have identified and landed on a basic set of emotions from which all other emotions build. While there are many different ideas and theories regarding emotions, there is still a base set of emotions from which the others are formed. This means that in order to begin understanding your EQ, you need to understand the emotions that you feel and that all others stem from.

It began with Paul Eckman who was a psychologist in the 1970s that decided upon and identified six "basic emotions" that everyone experienced through every culture. The basic emotions he coined were sadness, happiness, fear, surprise, disgust, and anger. While this list did later grow in order to include other feelings like shame, excitement, pride, and embarrassment, it is still agreed upon today that Eckman's base emotions are the foundation of other emotions.

However, the study of emotions did not stop with Eckman, and soon another psychologist named Robert Plutchik was giving his input about the world of emotions. In fact, Plutchik created the idea of a "wheel of emotions." This wheel was supposed to be just like the color wheel that we use. The emotions were combined or mixed to create other feelings. See? Just like you would mix green and yellow to get blue, you could mix anger and surprise to get another emotion. Eckman laid down the foundation for our basic emotions, but Plutchik brought forward the idea of combining these emotions into more complex emotions. It is important to remember, though, that all complex emotions stem from our list of basic emotions. They are the roots.

We have come a long way since the 1970s, and while Eckman's work is important for our foundation of understanding emotions, our understanding has grown far beyond what we knew in the 1970s. In 2017, a new study was released that showed that there are a lot more basic emotions than we first believed. The researchers published their work in the Proceedings of the National Academy of Sciences and indicated that they have found a total of twenty-seven other emotions. All these emotions occur on a scale, and rather than being distinct in their own right, each emotion is experienced on a gradient. They overlap with one another. However, in order to understand the gradient of emotions, we do need to take a more in-depth look at the basic emotions that we will continue to build on for the rest of this guide.

# Happiness

Happiness is one of the most common emotions that people want to experience. I mean, who does not want to be happy all the time? Or, perhaps, at least most of the time. The reason that happiness is such a sought after the emotion is that it creates an emotional state that is pleasant for the person. We could all enjoy raised levels of contentment, satisfaction, gratification, and joy that promotes an overall healthier state of being. In fact, happiness is such an important emotional state that we humans try to achieve that the research rate has increased tenfold on it. From the 1960s and into today, a lot of branches within psychology study happiness and how to obtain it. One of the biggest areas of study within the happiness emotional state is "what does happy look like?"

I know that we all want to achieve happiness. We go to work, we live our lives, and maybe we start a family. But what does happiness look like within our ordinary lives? Happiness is expressed in several different ways that are crucial to look for in expanding your emotional intelligence (these will be further expanded on throughout the guide):

- Body language is key to understanding emotion. You will see most likely a relaxed position in the body.
- Facial expressions indicate emotional states first. Look for smiling and a relaxed face.
- The tone of voice can also indicate what emotional state a person is in. Happiness reflects in the voice in a normally upbeat tone.

Happiness does not look the same for everyone everywhere. This is important to remember, as cultural differences can severely impact what happiness looks like for someone. The different types of cultural experiences that a person subscribes to will influence what they stake as the parameters for their happiness. For example, in American pop culture today, it is believed that the path to happiness is paved with a house, a well-paying job, a marriage, and maybe a child or two. However, not all paths follow those directions to happiness. It is so important when you are considering emotional intelligence to understand that happiness impacts everyone differently. Happiness is a highly individualized emotion that does not always subscribe to what the next person thinks is happiness.

While happiness is a basic emotion, there is a strong correlation between happiness and physical health. It is no surprise that happiness is connected to mental health, but it can also impact how long your life is as well as any satisfaction or joy that is derived within a partnership (be that a friendship or a more intimate relationship). If happiness is linked to health, then being in a perpetual state of unhappiness is also linked to bad health. Diagnoses like depression, anxiety, and stress are highly linked to unhappy individuals. Understanding this is the key to understanding how to heighten your emotional intelligence.

## Sadness

Another basic emotion is sadness. Sadness is normally characterized by feelings of disinterest, a low mood, and even grief. Sadness is a part of life, and as you know it is completely normal for people to experience sadness at intervals in life. When we miss a shot on a goal or lose a game we were trying hard to win, it can feel defeating. It is important to be able to balance emotions. After all, we cannot be happy all the time.

A prolonged period of sadness can be debilitating and result in depression for the person who is experiencing sadness. When you are looking for signs of sadness, you are normally looking for:

- A quietness within the subject
- Extreme lethargy; energy levels are below what they normally are
- If their mood seems sad, or upset
- If they begin to withdraw from everyone around them
- Tears and crying over the event that is causing sadness

Sadness occurs on a gradient, like all other emotions. Depending on what causes the sadness and how long the sadness goes on for, the severity of a bout of sadness can be debilitating. You want to be able to tell when sadness is triggering unhealthy behaviors in yourself and those around you. This way you can learn how to adapt and correct behavior. You want to repeat a positive series of actions to negate the feelings of sadness. This is not to say that you should try and never feel sad, but that you want to find healthy ways to cope with sadness experienced by you and others.

# Fear

Fear is another basic emotion, but it plays a significant role in our lives — especially considering how powerful of an emotion fear is. So, why is fear so important? Throughout our lives, we are going to be faced with a lot of different scenarios. Some of them are going to be ones that involve putting ourselves in danger or may even be life or death.

Fear results in what is known as the "flight or fight response." When you experience the fight or flight response, what happens is that your muscles will tense up and your breathing rate will increase. You might feel like your heart is pounding in your chest as well, but this is only as a result of an increased heart rate. Your mind will jump into overdrive as you examine every little thing in the scenario that has invoked fear within you. In these moments the fear is driving your mind to decide whether it wants to stay and fight the perceived danger, or whether you need to run as far away from the situation as possible. This response system is critical to your being able to decide how to manage threats that you feel. When trying to deduce what fear looks like you will see:

- eyes that widen, the chin being pulled back and other facial expressions pulled tight
- rapid breathing, an increased heart rate
- avoidance of the threat

Fear manifests differently in everyone. There are those of us who are more susceptible to fear and others who are harder to trigger. There are specific images and situations that can act as trigger warnings for us, and that manifests as the beginning of fear.

When presented with anything that your mind perceives as a threat, fear is going to be the first basic emotional response that is called to your body. As mentioned earlier, a gradient is a plane on which these basic emotions occur and then expand into several other emotions. Why does this matter with fear? Well, fear can manifest in some particular detrimental behaviors when it exceeds the higher end of the fear gradient. For example, anxiety could be generated from the constant fear of perpetuated in a person's mind. They then develop unhealthy fight or flight responses as a result of their anxiety.

Most people avoid situations that instill fear in them, however, there are people that live off the adrenaline rush. These people seek out thrills that bring the rush of the flight or fight response. While fear can present as anxiety, it can also be adrenaline and create excitement within the body.

## Disgust

In Eckman's first basic emotions that he laid as the foundation, disgust was amongst the others. Disgust is the repulsion that a person feels toward another person, situation, or even an object. When you are looking for disgust as an emotion in either you or someone else, then you need to be watching the way that:

- their facial expressions manifest; they might wrinkle their nose or suppress the lines of their lips in disgust
- they turn away from what is causing disgust
- they physically react to the object of disgust; this might be vomiting or heaving in disgust

Disgust can be a direct result of multiple things, and as it occurs on a spectrum, like fear, disgust can be different for every person. A simple sight, smell, sound, or even taste could end up being the trigger for a person. Throughout history, it is believed that this emotion developed as a reaction to stay away from bad or dangerous foods and situations. However, as time has progressed, so has the scale of disgust.

## Anger

Anger is among the basic six emotions that all other emotions were founded on. It is a powerful emotion, one that is based on frustration, hostility, and agitation. Anger is normally manifested from an act or event, and can even be the result of a perceived threat. We all react differently to various stimuli, so what might strike fear in one man strikes anger in another. When you are looking for signs of anger, look for:

- yelling or harsh tones in their voice
- frowning of the lips, glaring, or hard glaring with the eyes
- strong body language closed off stance or even moving away from a person
- behavior that is physically aggressive where there are broken objects, hitting, or even kicking of objects
- turning red in the face, sweating from stress and anger

Anger is normally termed as a negative feeling or emotion, however, when let off in the right way it can be a healthy and constructive emotion. I am sure you have heard the term "blow off some steam." That is normally used when expressing the need to let some anger out in a healthy manner. The reason it is important to let your anger out in a healthy manner is that it can afford you some clarity that you need to navigate relationships and carry out certain actions.

Like all things, anger can become a detrimental emotional problem. If a person does not learn how to control their anger using healthy outlets, then their behavior can become abusive and dangerous to those in relationships with them or to those who just so happen to find themselves in the angry person's path on a bad day. Because anger is such a delicate emotion when not handled correctly, it can spiral into a huge problem that creates both physical and mental consequences for all those involved. When your anger controls you, there is very little control that you have over making sound decisions.

## Surprise

The final emotion that forms the foundation of the basic six emotions is a surprise! If you have ever had a present, a birthday, or lived long enough on this planet to cognitively process information, then you have most likely dealt with the emotion of surprise. The surprise is an emotion that is never long term, but rather brief in nature.

Surprise is one of the basic emotions that can take hold in several different ways. It does not have to be positive every time or negative every time. Surprise can manifest either positively or negatively depending on how a person has received the information regarding the surprise. For example, a good surprise for some of us might be getting new golf clubs on our birthdays — or even just because. A bad surprise might be finding out that the leftovers you were looking forward to eating all night were cleared out before you managed to even have another bite. When trying to identify what surprise looks like, look out for:

- any physical response such as jumping, hand clapping, or shaking.

- subtle or not so subtle facial expressions such as widened eyes, a gasping mouth, and even raised brows.

- any verbal response that includes screaming, yelling, or even a gasp

Similar to fear and anger, your fight or flight response can be triggered when you are placed in an emotional state of surprise. This is because you can become startled and the adrenaline associated with the fight or flight response is generated within your body. Surprise can be used when we are making quick and minute responses to stimuli in our environment.

So, that is the breakdown of what the six basic emotions are, what to look out for in order to discern them from one another, and how they can affect the body and mind. Humans are emotional creatures. As much as the world would like to discount the emotions of men, we too are emotional beings. While we might like to think that all of our decisions are based on facts and logic, that is not true. In fact, it is farthest from the truth. Our every decision is based on the emotions that we feel and experience. These emotional triggers become the way that we process our actions and decisions. Our bodies end up building a standard set of reactions that we revert to when exposed to those emotions.

When I was younger and still learning a lot about emotional intelligence, I did not realize just how important my emotions were in every fundamental decision I ever made. One of the most distinct memories I have is when I got incredibly angry at a slight that I believed a friend had done against me. This friend we will call Mark. After fifteen years of friendship, going through the ups and downs, we had a disagreement at lunch over a topic that I hold near and dear to my heart. Because this topic meant so much to me, my judgment was clouded and I was closed off to all other perspectives that did not align with mine.

Yes, I had research, facts, and figures to back up my position. I thought I was entirely logical in my thought responses. I got so angry that I shut him off and I turned away from the friendship. Out of anger. I let my anger control my decision and I made a very rash choice in the heat of the moment. Of course, I soon realized that I was not being logical in the decision to end the friendship. I have learned a lot about emotional intelligence through the years and I have expanded on my own levels of EQ. Because of this, I am able to better control my actions in every single one of my emotionally charged states.

## More on Emotions

It became very clear that more than just the six basic emotions existed. When Eckman first began his research, he classified that the six emotions he laid as the foundation to all other emotions were experienced by all humans across all cultures. However, these theories adapt and change as we learn new information and are provided with new facts. Eckman added a series of other emotions to his foundational list as he continued to study emotions more in-depth throughout the rest of his career.

There is a key difference in the following emotions that Eckman added on versus his original six basic emotions. His basic emotions relied on tell-tale physical and facial cues to interpret, however, these newly added emotions were not necessarily given away by any facial cues or physical actions. These new emotions that Eckman expanded his list with were:

- Excitement
- Relief
- Contentment
- Amusement
- Satisfaction
- Guilt
- Pride
- Embarrassment
- Shame

Now, remember that there are many great minds in this world, and not all great minds think alike or agree on theories - particularly those theories that are based on emotion. Eckman's research was groundbreaking and important to the study of emotions, but it is important to know that not all theories and psychologists agreed with Eckman's classifications of emotions. There are many other theories out there regarding how our emotional state affects our human experience.

These theories are as vastly different as they are numerous in quantity. There are theorists who believe that only three basic emotions exist to make up the foundation for all other emotions. Some researchers believe that emotions occur in the form of hierarchy. Your top emotions would be those such as love, anger, sadness, joy, and surprise. Secondary emotions are broken down from the top emotions experienced. For example, from love, we can then get affection and tenderness. It does not stop here though, as they continue to break down these secondary emotions into a third tier. So, you might have love first, then you have affection and tenderness, and from that, you find emotions like compassion and care for others.

As I mentioned above, the latest research that is most widely believed across the psychological field is that twenty-seven different emotions exist and connect to one another on a gradient.

The researchers that tested these emotions used a group of 800 men to study and control. They had these 800 men watch over 2,000 videos — each video designed to prompt an emotional response from the viewer. The researchers examined and notated every single emotional response that these men had to the stimuli presented toward them. This was largely in an effort to understand how each emotion related to the other.

Dacher Keltner was the senior researcher for this study. He works for the Greater Good Science Center as their faculty director. However, it was not just him alone. A team of researchers came together and found that they could identify twenty-seven emotions that were distinct from one another in the responses given by the men.

So, based on this new information that they compiled from the men, it was easy to deduce that emotions are not singular feelings that happen one at a time per the stimuli presented, but that they can occur on a gradient. Each emotion that was felt was connected to the next, rather than separated as was first suggested back in the 1960s.

Emotions are important to study because they not only affect our moods, but they affect our behaviors, our physical conditions, and our mental states. In fact, it is heavily emphasized that the more we can identify our emotions, the easier we make the research for everyone invested in understanding, not just the human mind and psyche but also the human body.

Your emotions influence your everyday life, whether you are ready to admit it yet or not. We are not beings that run on logic and operate from learned placed. Instead, we are governed by our emotions in everything that we do. The way that we interact with others and our environment are all pre-determined by our emotions. You want to be able to understand these emotions that you are experiencing because the direct result will be that you will have gained deeper insight and control over your actions.

Your emotions are as complicated as you are as a person — and if you want to say that you are not complicated, let me get ahead of you right here. Humans are all complex creatures. Every single one of us has a complex body with an even harder to understand mind to accompany it. We are confusing creatures at the best of times. However, this does not mean that you do not have a chance at understanding and controlling that complexity. All of your emotions work together on a gradient to express your feelings about the stimuli in your environment, and when you can understand that, then you are already halfway to understanding how to have greater control over your emotional responses and actions.

Your emotions are divided into two very distinct groups that have survived for decades — basic emotions and complex emotions. Your basic emotions are standard emotions that can be foundational for other emotions and are easy to identify as they have set appearances and facial expressions to accompany each feeling. You already know that sadness, happiness, fear, anger, disgust, and surprise comprise some of the basic emotions we experience. So, it becomes easy to tell when someone is happy because they are smiling happily and their stance is open and receptive throughout the communication.

Complex emotions can be harder to read because their cues can be made up of several components that are interchangeable amongst other emotions. Yes, while the basic emotions are usually a lot easier to tell apart from one another, the lines between them can also become blurred. This is because a person's body language or facial cues are not always accurate representations of the emotion that they are feeling. We have learned and adapted to not always show our true emotions on our faces. Why? Because there are moments when we want to hide our true feelings from those around use for a myriad of reasons. For example, if you are having a family dinner but received particularly unsettling news right before dinner, you might still put a smile on your face and be perceived as cheerful. You do this for several reasons, but in the end, you have managed to mask your true emotional response to your stimuli.

However, there are also times when your emotional response might not be easily understood even when you want it to be. This is because emotions can manifest themselves in several ways across a person's body and face. For example, when a person is depressed, their face might take on the cues that are more closely associated with anger. A regular feeling of sadness will be quite distinct from the facial cues that are seen with depression. Do you see how this can become tricky?

Remember, just because we call it a basic emotion does not mean that emotion cannot be broken down into more categories. Earlier I mentioned how surprise can manifest both as a negative or positive emotion. It is key to understanding your EQ to also understand that even basic emotions can be complex when we are learning about them. Basic simply means the foundation or the first, not basic in terms of simplicity.

Emotions can vary depending on the person that is expressing them. This is because across different cultures and experiences, there are different ways that people learn to use their emotions in response to their environment. For example, everyone goes through and processes their grief in a different way. For some people, anger is a completely normal stage to grief. They might find that they need to let their anger about the loss out before they can move on and experience a different range of emotions. For others, anger might never come into play with their loss.

Grief is one of those complex emotions that we keep talking about. There is still an argument about all the different emotions that are comprised within grief, but the general consensus agrees that surprise, fear, anger, denial, sadness, and acceptance are all components within grief. While they are separate emotions, a person will go through each one on a gradient and each emotion will be connected to the last in order to form the complex emotion of grief. There is no one simple way to understand these emotions, because like I keep saying they vary from person to person. This is important to your EQ because you need to learn to understand your emotions and your response to situations. Then you need to always remember that not everyone is going to have the same response that you do to your environment.

Your emotions can begin to affect your health and your personality when they are sustained over a long period of time. Let us continue examining grief for this example. Since grief is made up of many different emotions that are experienced over a period of time, the emotional stage of grief can last for some time. When we experience a certain emotion for a prolonged period we then find that we have changes in our thought processes and our behaviors.

## *Why Do We Have Emotions?*

So, now that you understand more about the basic components of emotions, how emotions function, and where they come from, why do we have them? Your emotions are a necessary part of your everyday life. They help you navigate the different situations that you encounter. This is why EQ has become so prevalent and overtaken the importance of IQ because your EQ gives you the ability to understand what emotional response and action is appropriate at the moment.

Psychological issues and mental illness are the direct results of an overflow of emotion. I am not just talking about the big disorders like depression, but also the lesser publicized problems like phobias, obsessive disorders, anxiety, borderline personality disorder, substance abuse, and traumas (PTSD included). On the spectrum of emotions, as humans, we feel everything. Sometimes this can feel like a real kick in the butt to have to constantly deal with our emotions, but there is a power to it once you understand how to handle your emotions.

Emotions are the reason for our survival. If it wasn't for our emotions, our bodies would be at a loss about how to respond to situations and environmental stimuli. For example, if we did not have the emotion of fear, we would probably fail at recognizing when we need to flee a dangerous situation. If you were to ever come face to face with a polar bear and your emotional fear system did not respond, you would most likely end up mauled before you had a chance to logically process the situation. Your emotions are akin to your first system of response.

You could make the argument that there are many natural things that exist in this world that do not rely on emotion. So, again, why do humans have such an intrinsic emotional response built into our systems? It exceeds our need to survive in the world. If we only needed to survive, then all we would need are emotions that bring our adrenaline up and our fight or flight response to the table. The reality is that humans are complex and emotional creatures. Our lives revolve around more than just instinct, and we live for more than just the need to survive. Our basic emotions help us navigate and survive the world, but our more complex emotions allow us the ability to interact with and envision our world or our place in the world.

As the world has modernized and changed, so too have our emotions adapted to assist us in living and dealing with the new stimuli that we face every day. A roaming polar bear is less of a fear, but impending debt, a new job interview, or even that first date could be enough to jerk our fight or flight response into high gear. I mentioned before that mental illness is an excess of emotion within a person that goes uncontrolled. This is true, and it can have devastating effects on the way that a person acts and the choices that they make with their environment.

In short, our emotions are very important to our daily functioning, our reasoning, as well as our relationships — this includes work and intimate relationships. However, when emotion plays such a large role in our daily lives, it becomes hard to discern when we are doing a good job at controlling it or not, particularly when a certain emotion becomes excessively felt and displayed. For example, when we live in a constant state of fear that turns into an anxiety that we live with, this can hinder our work life and our romantic life. So, therapy emerges with different tactics and procedures that one can implement in their lives to try and regain and maintain balance in their emotional life. The use of therapy assists us with making sure that we can step back from our overwhelming emotions and rationalize them so that we can make the right decisions.

In today's function, emotion serves the purpose of helping us relate to the community around us and to continue to build a farther-reaching community. Nobody wants to be closed off or uncaring about the world around them, and if you find yourself in that position, then you likely have an unbalanced emotional feeling within you. Life is hard, and it can be harder when we are faced with navigating through different relationships with people. At our core, it is our emotions that allow us to connect to our world, and we should never take that for granted. In the next few sections, we are going to take a closer look at emotions and list all the ways that they help us, as this is ultimately why we need emotions.

- Emotions enable us to avoid dangerous situations as well as thrive in our environment. The study of emotions can date back to the time of Charles Darwin, who believed that in order to survive, our emotions are an adaptation that came around. Our emotions adapted from a need that humans were lacking, and now they have response systems to stimuli in their environment that help them navigate the world's sticky situations. They help us learn what we want to positively seek out and what we want to avoid. Our avoidance would be for negative experiences. So, when faced with a lion, we might change paths and run away, but when faced with the prospect of feeling cared for in a prospective mate, our positive emotional experience will allow us to connect with the other person.
- Emotions are decision-makers. Every choice that we make, every fork that we choose to go down in life, is fueled by emotion. In fact, even the decisions you might think have no emotion behind them are fueled by emotion — a decision as small as what to have for breakfast. I promise you that even the most logical man has his emotions fuel his decisions. If you are shaking your head no to my previous statement right now -

that's an emotional response.

- Our emotions allow us to connect with others and allow others to understand us better. It can be hard for other people to see into our lives and our minds sometimes, and that is where emotions play another major role. The emotions that we express give the people we are interacting with insight into our feelings and emotional state of mind. Through our facial expressions and our body language, we give off cues about our emotions to others. Sometimes we are experts at masking our true feelings, but we can also allow others insight into our feelings. We can verbally communicate to others what we are feeling by directly telling them. They use this information in order to make their decisions on how to interact with us.

- Emotions also allow us to understand the emotional state of those that we are interacting with. That's the great thing about emotions; they are not just a one-way street. We can read their emotions and interpret them, the same way that we allow them to do for us. When we take a moment to examine the world around us, we are able to gather information about our social standing with others as well as their emotions. Understanding how to appropriately navigate social communication impacts the way that we communicate with others and how successful we are at it. Responding in the right way to other people is essential because it is the pathway to building deeper relationships, strengthening existing relationships, and connecting with others on an emotional and social level. A connection is the greatest tool that we have in our human arsenal, and we should take every advantage that we can in order to use it for our benefit. The other benefit of being able to read and interpret emotions and social communication is that we benefit from it in the workplace.

From this chapter, you should now really understand why we need emotions to function and why they are so important to us as humans. Emotions were not given to us by a happy accident, but they are a necessary adaptation that we need in order to survive. With that being said, emotions are still complex ideas that we need to try our best to understand in order to navigate their waters accurately.

Emotions are tools that we need to know how to handle, because like other weapons and tools when we do not know how to control them, they can become dangerous. But they bridge divides between people, between nations, and even between cultures. Emotions are the epitome of human communication.

## *How Do Emotions Fool Us As Men?*

If emotions are the epitome of human communication, what does that mean for us as men? You have probably grown up your entire life being told that you are not a good emotional communicator, or that you should even mask your emotions because feeling and displaying emotions as a man was not an appropriate response.

It's not surprising that there are a host of men out there that exist who have trouble explaining or expressing their feelings to those around them, particularly when they enter into romantic and personal relationships. Emotions can be tricky fields for men to navigate because we have been taught that we should not feel, that part of our manly existence is to be nonchalant about what happens to us and around us. Raising our EQ is fundamental to our success as men in any part of our life.

As a man, you need to work to break the boundaries that have been imposed on you and that you have been raised with. You need to destroy the stereotype of the emotionless man that society has tried to put on you over the course of your entire life. This will take active work by you in order to make sure that you are constantly and consistently expressing your emotions to the ones that you care about. Being vulnerable with your emotions is not something that you should be afraid of. Instead, it should be something that you embrace. When you accept your emotions and become ready to share them, you begin to raise your EQ.

The first step can just be admitting your emotions to yourself. Sometimes, this is the hardest. Nobody wants to admit when their feelings overwhelm them or when they are feeling an emotion that strays away from the "macho" emotions that are considered appropriate to show. It can help to take small steps. When you wake up in the morning, repeat a mantra to yourself in the mirror or even have it written on notes hung around your house. It should be a mantra that is about your emotions, a positive admission of how you are feeling and that you are entitled to that feeling. It can be as simple as "Today I am angry" or "Today I feel sad." Your emotions are your power, and you should not be afraid to express the way that you feel.

Emotions are tricky for men because we shut them off for so long that we forget what to look for when others are exhibiting concerning emotions. We lose our ability to properly react to their responses. We need to accept what we feel like men in order to embrace the emotions of others and have others embrace our emotions.

There are two main emotions that men experience. These are happiness and anger (I promise you being horny is not an emotional state, so don't try to add that one in, it will not garner as much sympathy as you think). I myself have had problems embracing my own emotions. This is because of the way that society has drilled into me that as a man, I should have none.

When I came to realize that I was avoiding all of my emotions that I thought were not "macho" enough, it was the first step that I needed to start accepting every single one of my emotions. Anger can be a hard emotion for men to master because of the unhealthy relationship that we have with it. We have been taught that anger is the only safe, rational emotion for a man and that it is normal to find ourselves angry. We are also taught that there is a delicate balance with angry, and being too angry and too emotional is a bad thing as well.

When we respond to our emotions, we are succumbing to one of two possible response types. There is the primary response and the secondary response. Your primary emotion is simply your first emotional response, the one that you automatically feel when stimuli in your environment affects you.

The secondary emotion is our second round of emotional response. This occurs when we are hard on our emotions and the way that we feel about things. Instead of our primary response to the stimuli, we hide our feelings and mask it with our secondary emotional response. This can cause issues and a lack of comfort for the person who is masking their true feelings.

It can be very difficult trying to reprogram the way that you have been brought up to hide and destroy your primary emotional response. I had a friend whose childhood and adolescence was especially hard on him. His family never accepted when he was sad, and anytime he displayed the emotion he was promptly chastised and ignored. In fact, he was told to "be a man about it" and "man up" when it came to his emotions. So, whenever he felt sad or an emotion that his family deemed was not manly, he learned to replace it with anger to hide his vulnerability and protect himself.

This hindered his future relationships because when my friend finally got married, his partner was quickly fed up with his anger and his bluntness that was a result of his anger. His marriage suffered pretty quickly because he was unable to display any affection that was not seen as manly, or at least that he did not perceive as manly. My friend constantly complained that his marriage made him feel angry and that it was in a bad state, but he had no idea how to change the state of his marriage.

At first, I did not think much of this, but after a while of him telling me about his anger I asked him if he ever felt sad about his marriage. He broke down eventually and described his emotional turmoil that he kept hidden inside and masked so that he never displayed weakness. It was not long before my friend shut himself down and admonished himself for being open and vulnerable. His anger came back out and kicked the sadness to the curb.

This inability to connect with his sadness stemmed from the way that his parents brought him up and drilled within him that he could never feel anything that was not appropriate for a "man" to feel. But, his admission of sadness was the step in the right direction. Slowly and surely his wife began to understand him a little bit more.

You see, our responses to anger are designed so that we can protect ourselves from feeling any other emotion that might hurt or damage us. The object is to avoid pain and to let the anger take control.

So, why is it so hard to put aside our secondary emotional response and allow our real emotion to show through? The reason is that it can be scary to open yourself up raw to a partner and trust them not to pick apart at your delicate emotions. The problem begins when we continually shield our true emotions with anger. We become the root cause of all emotional distance within a relationship. We would rather yell and get mad because this is deemed as the correct male response than cry or admit vulnerability in our emotions. Nobody wants to be seen as weak, so we will curl away from emotions that we have been taught are weak emotions. In this regard, society and our upbringing have really let us down.

To be truly strong, you need to be able to fully express your emotions. This includes the full range of your emotional capabilities and not just the emotions that are seen as "macho" or strong. As soon as my friend admitted to himself and his wife how much time and energy he spent trying to mask his emotions, they began to see a real change in their relationship. He began to open himself up to his wife and allow her to see parts of him that he had never shown her before.

Your emotions have a direct correlation with your partnership and how happy both you and your partner will be due to your feelings. When you hide them, you are effectively shutting your partner out and creating a wall that exists between the two of you.

Childhood behaviors can be hard to break or shake as we grow older. This is because it is like a bone that has grown out of shape and needs constant work to slowly pull it back into the correct place.

Behaviors are not easy to change once they are set in, however, we should always try and make positive changes when it comes to our emotions. The benefits you get when you embrace your emotions will be immediate and you will forever be grateful. If you want to connect with those around you, then you need to be able to be open about your emotions.

In intimate relationships, being honest about your feelings is the only true way to make the relationship real and to make it work. When in a fight with your partner, instead of being angry or using your anger as a deflection for your other emotions, be honest. Tell your partner "This is hurting me, I am sad" or even "Us fighting like this disappoints me." You will be able to reach them on a similar emotional level, you will meet each other halfway, and the fight will soon be a distant memory as you guys work together through your emotions to fix the problem. Your anger does nothing but escalates an already tense situation, especially when pride comes into the picture. Put these weapons down when communicating through tense situations. They don't help your progress the same way that emotional honesty will.

I know it can be tempting to fall into the stereotype of the man who feels nothing, but you will harm every relationship that you ever have with this train of thought. Despite our best attempts as labeling men as unfeeling, this is not true. We are human beings. We feel every range of emotion that our opposite gender feels. We have just been systematically brought up to repress those feelings. So, instead of being in tune with how we feel, our emotions are foreigners to us and they trick us because we do not get to know them. Our society has left men at a distinct disadvantage as it has undermined our ability to feel and embrace our emotions. This is a disadvantage that I seek to correct!

Whoever said that you cannot teach an old dog new tricks has never tried to show a man how to access his true emotions. It is entirely possible for you — no matter what your age is — to tap into the emotions that you have locked away. Hopefully, by correcting this problem now, we can spare an entire generation of men from having to battle with embracing their emotions.

Yes, men might have a harder time because of societal norms expressing how they truly feel. However, this does not mean that they do not feel their emotions. They do, and they feel them deeply. They are just forced to suppress these emotions and because of that, their emotions become strangers to them. They are unsure of how they feel and why, and they revert to the automatic response of anger.

Emotions that men feel may be mistaken for others. When we feel sad or even vulnerable we will override them with pride and anger in an attempt to seem "macho." Do you see how this macho man stereotype is doing a disservice to our entire gender? We need to throw aside the antiquated societal conventions about men and their emotions and learn what our emotions are really telling us and how they are making us feel.

There are so many instances in your life as a man that will require you to rely on your emotions — the emotions that don't include anger or pride. You will likely take on the roles of a colleague, lover, partner, husband, dad, grandad, and so on. All of these roles will at some stage require you to tap into what you are truly feeling in order to make real connections and progression.

I had a friend named Jim, and he came to me with a serious problem. His youngest daughter had been seriously and physically harmed by a boyfriend of hers. His reaction to the event alienated both his wife and his daughter, as he only let his anger surface and he focused on wanting to hurt the boyfriend. His family was in serious distress over his words and they were fearful that if he carried out his threat that he would find himself arrested. Jim's anger was a cover-up for how he truly felt, but he was unable to understand or work through his real emotions, so he expressed himself in anger.

Together, Jim and I got him some help and we talked through his emotions. We found that at the root of his feelings he was deeply sad and tormented that he could not help his daughter's pain. He felt like he was at fault for all that his daughter had gone through, that he had somehow fundamentally failed her. Here is the turning point in Jim's story. He was finally able to confront his true emotions and be honest with himself and his family. He did not need to exact revenge on the boyfriend, but to be honest with his family and himself and help his daughter heal and move forward.

This is not an isolated story, either. There are thousands upon thousands of men out in the world today who struggle with the same concept of being true with their feelings. They are fearful of society's backlash if they express their true emotions, and therefore they leave themselves at a large disadvantage.

We need to change society's perception of men dealing with their emotions in healthy and positive ways. We can not expect men to do better and show emotion when we are systematically cutting them down for doing that very same thing.

We deserve the same chance and ability as women have at understanding and embracing our emotions. Emotions should not be foreigners to us that end up tricking us or fooling us into situations that are far worse than if we had just been honest about our true emotions in the first place. Now, more than ever, when EQ is such an important value in the workplace and at home, it is essential that we educate and help other men around us boost their EQ and understand that their emotions are not something to be afraid of expressing.

I could give you an endless amount of examples where men have struggled to express themselves with the people in their lives. There are also often defining moments when their emotions come to the surface and shock those around them because it is unusual for them to fully express themselves. Men experience emotions on the same intensity that women do, we have just failed men by not equipping them with the same practice and expertise that women have in dealing with emotions. Their only options are to bury their emotions deeper and overlap them with macho emotions like anger and pride.

It is easy to see that men are not creatures that do not feel and have no emotion. Rather, they are humans who society has trapped in a shell where they are unable to be hurt, cry, or be sad because then they are too effeminate and not manly enough if they actually express these emotions. That shell needs to be broken, and that is what we are going to work on through this guide.

# Chapter 2: The EQ Models

"Human behavior flows from three sources: desire, emotion, and knowledge." - Plato

There have been so many researchers that have studied emotional intelligence, from Peter Salovey and John Mayer to David Goleman and even more recent researchers who understand the importance of EQ. Through their research, they have come up with three models that are used in the field of understanding and representing emotional intelligence. The models that are widely used are:

- The Trait Model
- The Ability Model
- The Mixed Model

The model that we will refer to in this guide is David Goleman's mixed model, as it is the most universally used model. But, we will also expand on and explain the other models that we will use or reference in this guide.

## The Ability Model

The ability model was created by Peter Salovey and John Mayer. It was the first of the models to be created and used to understand EQ. The Ability Model follows the following outline:

- Perceiving emotions: this is where we can understand nonverbal communication and signals such as body language and facial expressions.
- Reasoning with emotions: this is where we use our emotions

- in positive ways to conduct our thinking and our decision making processes. Our cognitive activity is used during this step.
- Understanding emotions: we need to understand and interpret the emotions of those that are around us. When we can tell if people are angry, sad, or hurt and what is causing their emotions i.e.: are you the cause or is a particular situation the cause of their emotions?
- Managing emotions: the final process of the ability model includes the ability to regulate and control your emotions and respond with the appropriate emotions to situations every single time.

## The Mixed Model

David Goleman makes use of what he calls "The Five Components" in his mixed model. His attempt to describe emotional intelligence makes use of the components in his model below:

- Self-Awareness includes your confidence and the ability to recognize feelings.
- Self-regulation includes your ability to control your emotions, you're trusting of your emotions and your adaptability.
- Motivation is your drive, commitment, optimism, and initiative
- Empathy is your ability to understand the feelings that others have, your attention to diversity and even your political awareness.

- Social skills are the final arc in this model where your leadership skills, conflict management, and communication skills are on display.

## The Trait Model

The trait model was created by Konstantin Vasily Petrides, and he himself called the trait model a constellation in which your emotional perceptions of yourself are found at the lowest levels of personality. His description of emotional intelligence involves two points:

- Your understanding and perception of your own emotions
- Using the framework of your personality to understand and investigate emotional intelligence based on personality traits.

## Five Components of Emotional Intelligence

Emotions come in a gradient where there is a wide variety of different emotions that a person can feel at any point in time. The great thing about emotions is that normally there are behaviors exhibited when a person is feeling a certain emotion that can be observed and recorded. Your emotions include your behavior (like body language and facial expressions), the feelings that you express, and any changes in your state of mind. Each individual will feel their emotions differently, and the way that we express them is what gives our personalities their individuality. Intelligence comes into play with our emotions by the way that we can learn about emotions and then apply that learned behavior. Essentially, emotional intelligence is just your ability to manage other people successfully based on what you know about their emotions. You do need to understand your own feelings first in order to understand those of other people that you interact with. Daniel Goleman has already given us the five components that make up emotional intelligence. To go over them once more, they are:

- Self-Awareness
- Self-Regulation
- Motivation
- Empathy
- Social Skills

## *Self-Awareness*

Self-awareness if your ability to first realize your own emotions, motivations, and then abilities. After you realize these, you also need to be able to understand them. It includes not just understanding your moods but also understanding how your moods affect those that are around you. Goleman believes that when you are in a place of total self-awareness, you are controlling your emotional state and identifying every emotion that you feel. These are the traits you can work on and look for in others to see if they are mature enough emotionally to be self-aware:

- the ability to laugh at your own mistakes or goofs
- confidence in yourself
- being aware of how others see you

## *Self-Regulation*

Being able to control your actions and first-hand impulses are incredibly important when you are dealing with emotions. Often, we want to lash out with the first emotion we feel, but if we are truly self-aware then we are able to process these emotions and identify the appropriate emotion to react with. In essence, this is your ability to think before you react or say anything about a situation. Through self-regulation, you are emotionally mature when you are able to:

- be responsible for your own actions
- adapt to changes in the environment
- respond correctly to the irrational behaviors or emotional displays of others

That last one can be very hard to do, especially in an emotionally charged situation. For example, when someone is yelling and screaming at you, it can be tempting to yell and scream back. But being emotionally mature means that you are able to stop, interpret what they are truly mad at, and then approach the situation with the right emotion. A person who self-regulates well would not feel the need to yell back automatically.

## *Motivation*

Your motivation is actually one of the most, if not the most, crucial components in emotional intelligence. Motivation is how interested you are in learning about emotions and your own self-improvement. You need to be motivated to jump over the hurdles and obstacles you will face or you will get nowhere if you have no drive. When you are motivated, you will set goals for yourself and you will follow through and hold yourself accountable for them (yes, this does also tie into self-regulation). The traits you display when you are motivated are:

- taking initiative
- showing commitment to the completion of a task
- persevering even when adversity is mounting high against you

Feeling motivated all the time can be hard to accomplish and frustrating when you feel like you fell short of your goals. Keep in mind that you do not have to be 100 percent successful all of the time. For example, when you choose to motivate yourself with smaller goals that are meant to help you become a better person or a more knowledgeable person, then you are practicing internal motivation and that is a sign of being emotionally mature. Exterior motivations are where you seek to attain riches and wealth or a position of power for the benefit of looking good to those around you - this is emotionally immature behavior and not a good basis for motivating yourself.

## *Empathy*

Empathy is your ability to interpret the emotions and reactions of other people around you. You are not going to succeed at being empathetic if you are not self-aware. All of these components interconnect with one another, and you cannot achieve high emotional intelligence without each component. Goleman's belief is that you need to have a fundamental understanding of yourself and your emotions before you can try and understand others. When you emulate empathy while being emotionally mature it looks like:

- being perceptive of others' feelings and actions
- having a true interest in the problems and concerns of other people
- having the ability to understand and anticipate another person's emotions regarding a situation or problem
- being aware and understanding societal norms and the actions of people.

For example, when you are truly empathetic, you can understand the feelings that someone else is going through, particularly feelings of sadness or hurt. You do need to understand yourself completely and have a good grasp of your own feelings before you can understand people who differ from you and your experiences.

## *Social Skills*

The final component is your social skills. Social skills include a vast range of abilities and interactions but they are mainly your ability to understand sarcasm, jokes, and innuendos around you, your customer service, and your ability to hold on to and maintain both intimate relationships and friendships. You also need to be able to search for and find common ground with people that are different than you or those that you are in disagreement with. When you are emotionally mature, your social skills and abilities include:

- having great communication skills
- managing time efficiently and effectively
- your ability to lead and manage others

- your ability to resolve conflicts and difficult situations by means of negotiation and persuasion.

All of these models are important in understanding EQ and how to be emotionally mature. We will constantly refer back to Danial Goleman's model — the mixed trait model — and his five components when we are exploring how to increase our emotional intelligence. Now that you have a basic understanding of emotional intelligence, the components of being emotionally mature, and what it looks like to have high emotional intelligence, we are going to focus on what it means to be self-aware in the next chapter.

# Chapter 3: Be Aware of Yourself

"To be yourself in a world that is constantly trying to make you something else is the greatest accomplishment." - Ralph Waldo Emerson

I have devoted an entire chapter to be aware of yourself simply because this is the most important component of being emotionally mature. Without self-awareness, you have no place to begin in the journey to increasing your emotional intelligence. It really is as simple as that. Every journey or path needs a first step, and being self-aware is your first step towards being the master of your emotional intelligence.

Emotional self-awareness is where you have the skill to interpret your own emotions and how they affect your actions, your decisions, and even your performance on a particular task or job. When you are emotionally self-aware you know exactly what emotion you are feeling, when you are feeling it, and why you are feeling it. This is so much more important than I could ever stress. When you can understand the rationale behind your emotions, you are able to see how your emotions are helping or hurting you in a particular situation. Here's the thing: in social situations, when you are equipped with self-awareness, you can gain insight into how other people perceive you and you can then direct your actions and choices to either fit their idea of you or to change their idea of you.

Instead of basing your self-confidence on arbitrary and immaterial matters, you can base your self-confidence on the real understanding of emotional competence because you know that you can navigate a social situation properly. You know what your strengths are, you know how the other party feels, and that puts you in a spot of advantage. You are also able to clearly establish your own values, morals, and personal goals and purpose. It is crucial to have this quality as a leader so that you have the ability to make the tough calls, speak with authority, and implement your vision in a way that will be well-received by others.

It happens often in the workplace where those around you are not adept at performing in social interactions, and so their job performance suffers as a whole. I once worked in an office where the main office leader struggled with how he spoke to people in the workplace. Many of the other office employees called our leader a bully and had little respect for his authority. While the leader was great at the specifics of his job, he had very few people skills and so his management suffered due to this. He never listened to their ideas, he never opened the floor for everyone to feel comfortable, and he often played favorites which created a toxic work environment.

This office lead did not last very long as an office lead, because soon the whole office was turned against him. No one wanted to work for him, with him, or even under him. All interactions with him were unpleasant, and finally, when the risk of losing an entire office staff came to the higher-ups' attention, they had to look for the common denominator. The office leader ruled his office with anger and pride every day, and he lacked the emotional self-awareness to relate to his staff and see how they perceived him. He was put at a severe disadvantage in the workforce.

When you are in a position of leadership and you use it to torment others, or you have extreme arrogance and stubbornness, then you are most likely viewed as incompetent amongst your peers. Those are not the assets of a good leader. In fact, the antiquated times that correlated a loud voice and large presence with success are gone, and so you should hang that outfit up. Better yet, throw that particular outfit away as you get ready to step into your emotionally self-aware suit.

There was a research group that took a bunch of leaders who had strengths that spanned several different trait areas in the emotional self-awareness category and did a study on them. The Korn Ferry Hay Group was in charge of this research, and their results showed that an astonishing ninety-two percent of the teams with strengths in emotional self-awareness were the teams who had the highest energy levels and the best performance statistics. The reason for this is because leaders who are able to create positive emotional environments are ones that have higher self-awareness. They do better at motivating groups of people. In stark contrast to those results, the group who had leaders that were particularly low in the self-awareness department created toxic environments seventy-eight percent of the time. That is a lot of upset teams.

There is a reason that emotional self-awareness is the foundation for all the other components — even though it is the hardest component to track and see visible progress. Unfortunately, you cannot simply strive to be emotionally self-aware and then never think about it again. Unlike a car that you buy once and then you are set for life, your emotional self-awareness needs to be constantly tended to — like a garden. In every moment that you feel an emotion, you need to be practicing your self-awareness so that you can continue to make accurate predictions about how you are feeling and then exhibit rational responses based on those feelings. Self-awareness does become easier the more that you use the tool, and it can become almost like second nature. A good way to practice this is to make sure that you remind yourself to mentally check in on your emotions and see what they are telling you. Do this several times a day. It will help you realize whether your behavior or actions are on the right track or if you need to make a shift in order to achieve the goals you want. Remember that these goals can be long term goals or even short term goals that exist solely for the basis of a conversation that you are partaking in during any moment. Sometimes when your emotions get overwhelming you might feel like you need to separate yourself. A stressful or sad situation can make you want to hide in bed and not come out from under the covers for a week. Unfortunately, in a professional environment, you cannot exactly wig out or go and hide under your bed. You need to be able to act appropriately and manage your emotions. That is why it is important to check in with your emotions every day. Keep in mind that while you may not be free to choose the situations that you are placed in, you are always free to choose how you will react.

Let us start by analyzing the negative emotions that you most commonly experience at work. This way we can help you come up with a plan to strategize your behaviors and reactions when faced with these emotions. It only takes a brief moment of being self-aware to gather how you are truly feeling. The difference between being a good leader and a bad leader is how you handle these negative emotions. Do you work through it and make the best choice for you and your team? Or do you let the negative emotions overwhelm you and spill into how you treat your colleagues?

A 1997 study by Cynthia Fisher revealed the most common types of negative emotions that people feel when they are at work. The list includes:

- Frustration
- Dislike
- Unhappiness
- Irritation
- Aggravation
- Anger
- Disappointment

If you work in any type of professional environment, then you are bound to have experienced any one of these emotions at any given time. But there are strategies that you can use in order to help you overcome those negative emotions so that you benefit, your team benefits and your work performance benefits. Below I have grouped some of the common behaviors together because they overlap one another in similarities.

## Frustration and Irritation

Frustration is not a new emotion, and I promise you that everyone feels this at some stage in their life. Whether it is professionally or privately, frustration can easily creep in on us and before we know it, we are acting out. Normally, you would feel frustrated when you feel like you are trapped or stuck in a situation with no sign of a way out. Sometimes just the lack of forwarding mobility can cause frustration as well. This can be because you are not seeing eye to eye with a colleague on a project's direction, you feel like you don't know where to take your project, you are suffering from dealing with a difficult boss, and even something as simple as your day not going according to schedule.

These feelings crop up for all kinds of reasons and at the most inopportune of times; the trick, however, is to find them and nip the feelings in the bud as soon as they begin. Frustration and irritation are emotions that can get out of control very quickly and become negative feelings like anger. You don't want your emotions to escalate negatively like that, so let us take a look at some ways to manage your frustration.

- Stop and take a look around. Sometimes you really need to take time out and think about your situation. Stop the rising panic of frustration in your chest and get to the root. Ask yourself, "Why am I feeling frustrated right now?" If it helps you to write it down then do so. Just make sure you are being specific about what is irritating you. Once you have done this, take a positive look at the situation you are in. Focus on a positive, because there always is one. For example, if you have a meeting set with a colleague and they show up ten minutes late, take that extra ten minutes to prepare for the meeting and go over what you would like to talk about. Better yet, take that ten minutes and relax. Don't let it bother you.
- Finding a positive in the frustrating situation makes all the difference. Thinking positively when you start to get

frustrated can honestly make all the difference that you need in your day. It may seem like a small change, but it can have big impacts on your levels of frustration. You are choosing not to let the little things or the irritating things get to you, but rather to move past them and work with what is positive. Remember, not everything that frustrates you is done to frustrate you.

- Think about what happened when you were last frustrated or irritated. Sometimes it helps to ground ourselves. Take a look at the last time you got frustrated about a situation. More than likely the situation resolved itself and it worked out alright for all parties involved. Being frustrated is not going to help you come to any solutions. It is not worth wasting time on it when you can practice letting it all go and be positive.

## Nervousness and Worrying

Work can be a daunting place. Depending on what you do, your work environment, and the stress that you experience, you might find that your fear and anxiety are causing you to be nervous at work and worry about things that are beyond your control. When you worry overtly about what happens at the workplace, you risk your mental health with the negative emotions that you allow to take control. Sometimes it helps to try some of the tips below:

- Do not allow your environment to be filled with worry. This means that if you find your colleagues are surrounded in one spot and gossiping about the latest wave of layoffs or changes in company policy, then you should make a conscious effort to avoid that area. You do not need to add additional worry to your plate. I am sure it is full enough already.

- Practice deep breathing. There are apps out for this nowadays, or you can even simply time yourself with your watch. The purpose of taking in slow and deliberate deep breaths is to slow down your heart rate. When you feel your heart pounding with worry, stop and breathe in for five seconds. Then, breathe out for the other five seconds. The only thing that you should be focused on accomplishing during this time is your breathing. Do not worry about what is stressing you, the conversation behind you, or even the next project on your plate. Just take three minutes and take at least three to five deep breaths.
- Find ways to make the situation better. If you are afraid that something negative is going to happen, then you should not just sit and wait for the shoe to drop. Think of ways that you can get ahead of the problem and make it better. Turn the negative situation into a positive one.
- Keep a journal handy and write down your anxieties and fears. Writing can be therapeutic. When you write down everything that bothers you or causes you to worry, you have a list that you can work on clearing out. You need to make time to deal with each situation that is causing you anxiety.

# Anger and Aggravation

I guarantee you that if you let your anger get to you and control your behavior that it will be one of the most destructive things you do for your image in the workplace. It can be a very harmful emotion to the harbor when you are at work, and honestly, when it is not handled well, anger can cause you a lot more problems than it ever solved. You want to keep a lid on your anger, but in a way that is healthy and lets you express your true emotions.

- Keep your eyes peeled for any early signals that you are feeling angry. When you practice self-awareness you are able to identify when your anger or aggravation is mounting. The earlier you recognize the feeling, the sooner that you can nip it in the bud. The sooner you get ahead of this emotion, the better for everyone involved. You can choose the way that you react to every situation—this is emotional intelligence. I get that you may be angry, but that does not mean you have to act on emotion. You can choose to act appropriately.
- When anger rises, stop immediately. Sometimes it builds up fast and comes out all at once. Just stop whatever it is that you are doing and close your eyes. Start your deep breathing to try and get yourself to calm down. Remember to focus on just your breathing so that your angry ideas and words are cut off.
- Think about what you look like when you are aggravated or angry. Do you think that you like the picture of your behavior? Are your actions something to be proud of when you are angry? You don't want to convey the wrong image of yourself to those around you, so you might want to think about what you look like when you start to get upset. Seeing someone else be angry can be scary. Do you want to be scary? I am betting the answer to that is probably no.

# Dislike

New policies, new colleagues, new rules, change in management, and all other changes can be an area that causes you to dislike. In fact, I bet you have had to deal with someone or something that you dislike in the workplace. The important part is to remain professional, even when you feel dislike towards a person or thing.

- Maintain respect. You will not always get to work with people you like or in environments that you like, but you would still want to be respected. Sometimes you need to put your ego to the side when you find you are having a hard time liking someone. Be courteous and respectful as you interact with them. Even if they do not give you the same courteous treatment, make sure that you maintain a level of professionalism.
- Use your assertive voice. Sometimes you do need to be firm and assertive - this does not mean be rude. If the person you are interacting with is being unprofessional, then just exit the situation until you can be calm and assertive but maintain your respectfulness. You want to be the example that they look up to, not the other way around.

# Unhappiness and Disappointment

Life can be tough, and the workplace does not always take it easy on us. It is no surprise that there are times when disappointment and even unhappiness can crop up in our lives and spill out into our work. These emotions are difficult to handle because they affect the way that we are productive when we work. Disappointment and unhappiness can correlate with our energy levels and our enthusiasm. When we let these emotions take effect in our work, then we are holding ourselves back from truly achieving our full potential. By being self-aware you need to:

- Accept your current mindset. If you are feeling disappointed then acknowledge it, accept it, and make a positive change. Just because you know why you are disappointed, that does not mean that you have to continue to be disappointed. You can begin to change your mindset. For example, start to make changes in your path and get excited about those new prospects.
- Adjusts any goals you have. Sometimes we fall short of a goal we intended and that causes disappointment. Just re-evaluate your goal and adjust it so that it is more attainable. These can be small or big adjustments. Life won't always go the way we plan it to. Don't let a setback destroy your outlook.
- Journal about your feelings and thoughts. It can help to write out exactly how you are feeling in your moments of unhappiness and what the root causes are. When you are able to pin down the source or sources of your unhappiness, then you can draw a roadmap towards actual happiness. You don't have to let the unhappiness define your every thought and feeling, but you can let it propel you into a plan of action.
- Keep a smile on your face. Sometimes, amongst the greatest adversities, disappointments, and unhappiness, the best thing that you can possibly do for yourself is to smile.

These are some ways that self-awareness can help you navigate your emotions while you are at work. The potential of being emotionally self-aware definitely does not stop here, and in fact, the possibilities are truly endless.

# Chapter 4: Regulate Yourself

"When you control your thoughts and emotions, you control everything." - Marshall Sylver

No day will pass by without you feeling some type of emotion. They are vital, necessary, and mandatory aspects of our lives. It can be as simple as enjoying the company of a loved one or getting annoyed at a fly that won't leave you alone. Every emotion you experience, whether it is positive or negative, impacts your emotional, mental, and physical health.

The other thing about emotions is that depending on how you act, you affect your image in other people's eyes. You want to make sure that your reactions match the best and appropriate response for every social situation that you find yourself in. This is important, because imagine if you are sitting in an important meeting and you inappropriately burst out in laughter. That was not the right response when you are in a business-like setting. You might want to be taken seriously and have people listen to your ideas, but you will not if your actions don't match up with the image you want. This is where regulating your emotions really come into play. Once you have laid the foundation for recognizing your own emotions and being self-aware, then you can build on that with self-regulation.

Like with most other theories and studies that regard the psyche, there is a debate within the field that studies emotions as well. Because emotions are complicated parts of our psyche to understand, there is going to be conflicting evidence and debate amongst the scientific community. With every new year, there is more learned about the human mind and our emotional regulation than ever before. Strides are being made in the emotional field, and while psychologists might not always agree with one another, they do agree that our emotions make up every interaction that we have each day.

In 2001, a model for capturing how and when emotions are created was proposed by James Gross. He created a model made up of four stages named the "modal" model. In the modal model, he uses a situation to grab the attention of a person. Then he measures how they react to the situation and what emotional response stems from their reaction.

Emotional regulation can be tricky, but it can also be very simple. Sometimes, especially when you are experiencing a positive emotion, you simply need to let your emotional response continue. For example, if you are happy that something worked out, be happy and express that happiness. You do not always need to temper your reactions; it is perfectly alright to shout out in glee at the appropriate moment. Emotional regulation is all about the right reaction for the right situation. If you know that you get frustrated, annoyed, and angry easily, then you need to offset that with techniques to calm you down. Being outraged is not always the best reaction to small inconveniences in your life. Excessive negative emotions like these could result in the loss of relationships, friendships, and even your job.

When you are unable to regulate your emotions, then you are more likely to have any number of psychological disorders. For example, depression and borderline personality disorder are both disorders that share common qualities with unregulated emotions. This is why educating yourself about emotional intelligence is so important. Most people can regulate their emotions fairly well - they simply choose not to. However, if you find that you cannot regulate your emotions no matter how hard you try on your own, then it is time to seek out help (there is no shame in this).

When you are regulating your overwhelming emotions, the best techniques to try are :

- Don't suppress your emotions every time. Regulating your emotions is not always about suppressing what you are feeling at the moment. Sometimes that can be more harmful than good. There are healthy ways for you to handle and deal with negative emotions or even overwhelming emotions. For example, when you feel like you are becoming angry at a situation and you want to let out some steam, go out and take a walk. Clear your head. Kick a small rock if you have to. But work on calming yourself down before you carry on with your day or rejoin the situation that frustrates you.
- Adapt to how you handle situations. You need to be able to adapt or modify the scenario that you are in. Adapt your expectations and you should be able to easily deal with disappointment and other negative emotions. It can be hard trying to manage your negative emotions in a healthy way, but there are many methods that you can use. The most important thing to remember is that your negative emotion does not have to control you or your response. You are in charge, so when you think that you are setting your expectations too high, bring your goals down and meet those

first before jumping higher hurdles.

- Shift your attention elsewhere. Disappointment can be a heavy emotion to experience, and one that is not pleasant for anyone involved in the aftermath. If you are having a hard time with your expectations of yourself, set your goals lower. Sometimes we look at those in the environment around us and judge our own success off of their work. If you find yourself doing this, don't focus on the people who are succeeding the best but focus on those who are trying their best and along the same path that you are on. This helps keep you more motivated toward achieving your goals.

- Modify your thinking and your inner monologue. When you change the way that you think or what you are thinking about, then you are able to change the way that you perceive a situation. For example, if you are mad at work because you feel like someone is outshining you and that they are talking down to you, as a result, shifting your mindset can make you see this scenario in an entirely different light. Instead of being the victim in this, you might change your thinking to believe that your co-worker is only trying to help your output match theirs and that they are motivating you. This does not change the situation you were in before, but it gives you an entirely new perspective on how the situation affects you. This helps you manage your own reaction and also motivates you to push yourself to do better.

- Change the way you respond. Let's say that you are unable to avoid the situation, modify your thoughts, or shift your focus away from what was bothering you. All of your emotion is now brimming on the surface and it wants to come out. You now need to use your emotional regulation in order to get yourself under control and out with the right response. For example. if your heart is racing due to a rising emotion, just breathe. Take thirty seconds to close your eyes and focus on your breathing. Then, once you feel calmer, think about how you want to respond and carry out the correct response to the situation.

The above steps can be used to help you adapt in most social situations when your emotions are needing regulation. They mainly revolve around knowing and identifying your own emotional triggers and avoiding them. The ability to change how you are thinking and correct your behavior with rational thought is also a huge part of regulating emotions.

There is a driving force behind emotional regulation, and that is motivation. Without motivation, we would not feel propelled toward our goals. According to Danial Goleman, there are four elements that comprise motivation:

- personal drive
- commitment to our goals
- initiative/readiness to take opportunities
- optimism/resilience

These elements all work together in order to help you become a more successful and motivated person when it comes to your emotional self-awareness and your self-regulation. In any career that you take part in, you are going to need more than just "smarts" to make it. In fact, you are going to need to be motivated so that the quality of work that you are delivering every time is exceptional and at your full capability.

This really comes into play when you are loving what you are doing for work. Sometimes you don't even have to love what you are doing, but you need to at least enjoy the work that you are doing. Why? Research has proven that when you enjoy your work, you are a more productive person and your output results are greater.

Intrinsic motivation is a motivation that is fueled by you from the inside with your own personal desire to overcome challenges and adversity. You desire to give high-quality results at work and to be liked and trusted by your workmates.

There is also extrinsic motivation in which factors that are external are your champions. When you look at the factors of extrinsic motivation they can include (but are definitely not limited to): pay raises bonus checks, time off, the potential threat of earning no money or job loss. These are some pretty motivating factors to do your best at the job that you find yourself in.

Both intrinsic and extrinsic modes of motivation are one hundred percent okay to be fueled by; the important part is just to identify which motivation you respond to best so that you can use these methods in the future to motivate yourself when you are having a hard time. Normally, you want to be able to relax a little in the job that you work in. By relax, I mean to have the ability to look around and feel content because you love what you are doing. Motivation comes naturally when that is the case.

Do you think that you are motivated in life and at your job? Most studies do show that those who are motivated are able to quickly and easily adapt and more often than not they have bright attitudes when at work. Who doesn't love working with happy souls all day? Much better than working with grumpy ones! Most employers want motivated individuals because this means that their own reputation gets boosted by having a positive employee. There are also a lot fewer call outs when people enjoy coming in to work. Both methods of motivation are fine, however being intrinsically motivated reaps rewards personally and professionally a lot faster. This is why you see so many jobs trying to focus on promoting a healthy work culture.

Take a moment and think about those people in your life. I am sure there is at least one person that you look at in awe because no matter what the social situation is, tense, awkward, funny, etc., they always handle it well and appropriately. This is merely emotional intelligence on display, and you can manage to boost your own, too.

I don't need to beat a dead horse by repeating to you what emotional intelligence is, but I do want to add that there is no debate amongst the experts about how important it is. There is a general consensus that your EQ plays a major role in your success in all areas of your life. Gone are the days when IQ was the sole driving force of the smart, but now without EQ, you do not fall into those same categories of intelligence. This is because your EQ drives not just your intellectual performance but also all other emotion-based decisions that you make.

Every day we are led by our emotions, whether that is in joyful situations or even painful situations. When we feel excited at new opportunities we take chances to make them work, when we are hurt we will cry, and when we love we sacrifice for what we love. If you try and state that your emotions play no part in any decision that you make then you are not giving them enough credit and you are definitely hindering your ability to truly become in touch with your emotions. There is nothing to be gained from acting like the "macho man."

Navigating your emotions is a delicate balancing act at the end of each day. This is because you want to make sure that you are balanced and not lacking or in excess of any particular emotion. This is why being able to express your emotions in a positive and healthy manner is prize one because you are able to control your emotional response to external stimuli.

Our negative emotions are particularly susceptible to occurring in excess or being hard to control and navigate. This is especially true in the heat of the moment when a person might be feeling overwhelmed by their emotional response. If negative emotions such as rage, bitterness, and even envy are allowed to take root and fester within a person's mind, then there are some detrimental effects that can affect the quality of life that you have. This can look like someone who is always angry or a person who is constantly sad. These aren't ways that we are born, but the consequences of emotions that were allowed to build until that is all that was left. We want to feel our negative emotions, but in a healthy and positive way, not in a way that is allowed to fester within our minds. There are six steps that can be practiced in order to make sure that you control your emotional response, make sure your decisions are made with rational reasoning, and manage emotionally challenging situations:

- Never react at first. When you first feel an emotional response rise up you need to recognize it before merely acting on impulse. This is particularly true with negative emotions because you do not want to say or do something which will bring you to regret or shame later. Take a breath, steady yourself, and think about your response and make sure that it is rational. Don't answer when your heart is racing or you are in fight or flight mode.
- Rely on and ask for guidance. You can ask for guidance from those around you or even seek guidance within a faith. It does not matter what faith you decide to rely on, as long as you are able to ask for help and wisdom in combating the obstacles that stand in your emotional intelligence journey.
- Look for or create a healthy way to express yourself. When you have learned how to control your emotions, you need to also find ways to let out any emotions you are feeling in a healthy way. You do not want to repress your emotions, bottle them up, or avoid them until they get so big that they explode. This can take form in many different ways. For some, they just need a trusted person to vent to, and a call or a text can often be the perfect solution. Others find hobbies like painting, writing, or even running to express the negative emotions that they are feeling. Meditation, physical activity, journaling, etc. are all just healthy ways of expressing your emotions and letting them out. As long as it is helping you, do it.
- Take a look at the bigger picture. Sometimes we focus so much on the here and now that we forget there is a bigger picture to look at and live by. Everything that we do serves a

purpose towards an ultimate goal. Simply because you don't understand why something is happening at the moment does not mean that it does not have a purpose. Understand and trust that there are factors outside of your control and that there is always a bigger purpose in this life.

- Change your thinking. When you experience constant negative thoughts, then you are allowing yourself to enter a negative cycle. When you feel like an emotion is cropping up that is leaving you disheartened or is draining you because of its negative pattern, then you need to work to change it. Engage in an activity or even merely focus on the positives in your life to drive out the negative thought processes. Replace these negative thoughts with happier thoughts.

- Be forgiving to yourself for your triggers. Sometimes triggers are great - when we get happy or excited at the moment and express that towards our loved ones. And other times, triggers are not so great - when we feel angry and we become outwardly upset or frustrated. You want to be able to make sure that your emotional triggers work, but that you temper them with rational thought before responding. At the same time, forgive yourself. Don't be hard on yourself when you feel irritated because the same commercial played on television five times in a row. Allow the irritation to pass, then forgive yourself. Don't dwell on it and do not beat yourself up about it. Forgiving yourself allows you to detach yourself from the negative emotions.

I cannot stress enough how much humans rely on emotions for their everyday interactions and functions. We are emotional beings - and that one hundred percent includes us, men. There will forever be moments where emotions crop up, we feel certain things, and we want to react in ways out of impulse. Take a time out when you feel your emotions become overwhelming. You will thank yourself when you do. Sometimes, all you need is a moment of clarity to master your emotions.

# Chapter 5: Recognizing Emotions

"Emotions are the most powerful things to recognize and honor. Don't discourage your feelings." - Bindu Lamba

Most people have trouble identifying their own emotions, much less the emotions that those around them are feeling. However, it is an important skill and when it comes to emotional intelligence, it is a skill that you cannot move forward without. This is worth investing time into so that you can learn how to perceive your own emotions and also the emotions of those around you.

If you seem to have trouble right now recognizing or identifying what you are feeling at any given point, take a look at some of the tips below and apply them to your own life. Maybe take a moment now to analyze how you are feeling by using this list!

Firstly, look at your physical response. The first place your emotions are most likely to manifest is within your body, and you can tell by your body's impulse reaction to your emotion. For example, you want to look out for:

- Pain or tightness in the stomach: could indicate sadness, distrust, betrayal
- Blush spreading across face and neck: could indicate happiness or even embarrassment
- Tightness in the chest or tensing of muscles: could indicate fear or anxiety

Your physical reactions might very well be different from the ones described above, and that is okay. Your job is to become familiar with what your physical responses are. When you feel yourself having a physical response to an emotion, simply stop and ask yourself why you would be acting that way.

Secondly, you need to try and identify what you are feeling. I know this might sound easier said than done, but you want to put the work in here. If you need to, draw or download a chart of feelings or even a wheel (if you want to make it a fun game) and use this to pinpoint and identify what emotion relates to the feelings and thoughts that you are having at a particular moment.

Thirdly, you need to avoid judging yourself or your emotions. Embrace the emotions that you experience. They are a part of you. Not a part that needs to be hidden away, or a part that you need to be embarrassed about. Everyone feels. As a man, I know it can be hard to express those feelings because we have been taught that it somehow makes us less than other men, but it does not. When you confront and accept your feelings head-on then you are less likely to have emotional outbursts from repressing or judging them.

My fourth point to you is that sometimes you just need to stay still. It can be easy to move quickly and cycle through emotions just as fast as our movements, especially when we want to get over the negative emotions we are experiencing. However, sometimes you need to sit with your emotions, see how you are feeling, and address them. Meditation helps with this, but if you just want to go ahead and spend ten minutes in peace where you are not fighting your emotions then that works, too.

Writing is an amazing outlet, and that brings us to our fifth area to work on when trying to recognize our emotions. There are therapeutic qualities to writing, and when you are able to get your thoughts, ideas, and emotions onto paper, that is a whole lot less left to jumble around in your mind. Try writing a stream of consciousness (this is where you do not stop to think about what you are writing, you just write, write, write continuously for ten or fifteen minutes).

When you are overwhelmed or trying to process emotion, you should lean into someone. Talking to someone is my sixth tip for you, and one that you should not undervalue. This does not have to be in the form of a therapist, and sometimes meeting with a friend for coffee and explaining how you are feeling can give you some clarity. There is nothing bad about showing vulnerability to your loved ones. In fact, only good can come from that.

On another note, music has been an excellent escape for many. Whether you play music or you listen to music you can find a way to let out exactly what you are feeling. There are millions of songs out there that are devised to help us pour our emotions out. You might just try finding a quiet spot and listening to some music that suits your mood.

Finally, you should take some time before you go to sleep every single day and you should reflect on what happened during your day. This daily reflection can help you sort through the different emotions that you encountered as you lived your day. Sometimes you can record this in a journal, or if you prefer to internalize it in a monologue that is okay, too. As long as you are sorting through the emotions you felt, then you are actively working to identify and recognize your own emotions and how they affect you.

"Let's not forget that the little emotions are the great captains of our lives and we obey them without realizing it." – Vincent Van Gogh

Those are some wise words by Vincent Van Gogh, but accurate words as well. Our smallest feelings can impact us in great ways and we should always pay attention to all our feelings; even if we are tempted to ignore them as inconsequential emotions.

Learning how to recognize these emotions is the first step to helping us regulate and manage our emotions. Ignoring your emotions will only create a build-up or pent up and unexpressed emotion, which can cause a scene when it all comes crashing out of you all at once. Make sure that you give yourself time to analyze and interpret your emotions before you move past them and onto the next thing. When you finally are able to interpret your emotions, that is the beginning of your healthy decisions. You do need to be honest with yourself, and this can be a scary thought at times. Take comfort in knowing that you are not the only man out there with feelings and that your honesty will only take you further along your journey to mastering your emotional intelligence.

## Recognizing Emotions

Marsha Linehan, who is the doctor that created a therapy known as Dialectical Behavior Therapy (DBT), has created a process that involves six steps towards recognizing your own emotions. You need to put in the work, but the process goes as follows:

1 - What happened?

During this step, you write down or describe in full detail the emotional issue that is plaguing you. Don't get caught up in he said/she said and write down just the facts of the event.

2 - Why do you think that this event happened?

In this part, you want to identify the reasoning you believed caused the emotional situation to arise. It is important to think about the why because this will allow you to easily identify what social interaction garnered a response from you and then how you could best approach that interaction in the future. Correcting your negative emotional behavior with rational thought is super helpful in your future interactions and can prevent emotional events from happening in the future.

3 - How did this event make you feel both emotionally and physically?

Now you want to make sure that you record both your first emotional responses and your secondary emotional responses to the situation. Also, note down how your body physically reacted to your emotions. Did your jaw tighten? Did you clench your fists? Did you pout or cry? All of these are important in understanding and defining your emotional outputs.

4 - What did you want to do because of your emotions?

When you think about this question, be honest with your answer. You need to think about and identify your emotional urges to your feelings. Sometimes it is hard or it can even hurt when we admit the actions we want to take when we were in the heat of the moment. But it is important to take stock of what you wanted to say or do so that you can be aware of your emotional response and know-how and where to rationalize your behavior in the future. Simply because it was an urge that you had, that does not mean you have to act upon it. There are ways to control your urges when you are in the middle of an emotional battle.

5 - What did you do and say?

You need to identify how your emotions led you into certain behavior. Even if the behavior you displayed was less than favorable, you still need to be honest about the way that you handled the event so that you can make corrective behavior changes in the future.

6 - How did your emotions and actions later affect you?

Finally, you need to list what the long term ramifications for your actions were. Did your words or reactions leave an effect on your life or someone else's life? Did you handle your emotions well or do you have regrets about what you said or did? You want to hold yourself responsible for the way that you act, what you do, and what you say. We are free to make our own choices and conduct our own behaviors, but we are not free from those consequences.

As you find yourself in another emotional event, take a moment to really rationalize your behavior. Use this list to analyze what the real problem is, what the root of your emotions are, and then how to proceed forward in the best possible manner.

# Body Language

I have spoken a lot about body language in passing, and now I want to really focus more in-depth on it because when you are trying to understand and recognize the emotions of others, body language is going to be your best friend.

Body language includes the non-verbal signals that we use when we communicate. Most of our communication is actually non-verbal through every single interaction that we have. This can be from facial expressions, body movements, the space our body takes up, and even lack body movement. All of the things that we do with our body communicates how we are feeling. In fact, your daily communication is about seventy percent body language! That is a huge chunk of communication that is not coming from your words. This is why you want to focus on two things: What your body language is telling others, and what others are telling you with their body language.

## *Facial Expressions*

A picture tells a thousand words, and that is mainly because we interpret body language when looking at pictures. Our facial expressions can give away a lot of what we are thinking and feeling. A simple smile can convey happiness, while a frown can signal unhappiness. A raised eyebrow might show interest or surprise and an open mouth could indicate shock. Even if you tell someone that you are fine, they can often scan your face and see how you really are faring. In fact, a few of the emotions that can be read from facial expressions are:

- Happiness
- Fear
- Anger

- Sadness
- Excitement
- Surprise
- Desire
- Disgust
- Confusion
- Contempt

When we are analyzing a person's facial expressions we make split-second decisions on whether to believe what they are telling us or whether they are lying. When it comes to a universal language, facial expressions make it into the top ten because many of the basic expressions such as anger, sadness, and happiness are expressed through the same facial patterns throughout the world.

Facial expressions are so important in our interactions with other people. In fact, studies have shown that we make judgments about the intelligence of other people based solely on their facial expressions and the look of their faces. Someone with a more prominent nose accompanied by a narrow face was perceived as an intelligent person. Likewise, those who had a smile and expressed joy with their facial expressions were believed to be more intelligent than those who demonstrated angry expressions. Below, I am going to outline several areas of the face and how they are used for expression and communication.

## *Your Eyes*

I am sure you have heard the eyes called "windows to the soul." This is because they are able to show others a lot about what you are thinking or feeling. When you talk to someone else and stay engaged with the conversation, focus on their eye movements. They say that maintaining eye contact is an important part of communication and here's why:

When someone is avoiding your gaze, blinking too much or their pupils dilate, then you are getting a lot of information about their emotional state. Each eye signal tells you what the person might be feeling, and that allows you to react in a way that might best fit the outcome for the conversation that you are looking for.

Eye gaze is important. If a person is maintaining eye contact with you and looking in your eyes, it means that they take an interest in what you are saying. You know that they are paying attention to you. However, this can take a turn when the eye contact becomes prolonged, as it can appear threatening when coupled with a dark glare. If a person constantly breaks your eye contact or looks away from you a lot, it might mean that they are uncomfortable in the conversation, distracted, and even possibly trying to hide their true emotions at the moment.

Blinking is a natural part of providing your eyes with lubrication. However, sometimes you can tell if a person blinks way too fast or way too slow. In a distressed situation or a situation where the other party is uncomfortable, they may appear to blink a lot faster. If they blink slowly or infrequently then that is a sign that the person is intentionally trying to control what their eyes are telling you by controlling all movements.

The size of a person's pupils is the most subtle non-verbal form of communication that comes from the eyes. Light levels can impact pupil size, but so can emotions. For example, if you are talking to someone and their pupils become highly dilated, then they are most likely interested in you or aroused by your presence/what you are saying.

## *Your Mouth*

Your mouth tells a lot about what you are thinking and feeling, even when you do not want it to. It can be as subtle as chewing on your lip in public subconsciously, but that automatically conveys to others that you are experiencing either anxiety or worrying about something. Sometimes in public people will cover their mouths in conversations. This is a polite effort if you are going to yawn or cough, however, it can also be used to hide a frown or disapproving twist of the mouth. Even your smile can be read in more than one way, and it does not always express feelings of happiness. A smile can be sarcastic, happy, and even sinister in nature.

Pursed lips appear in the tightening of a person's mouth. This shows distaste and disapproval, and at times it can also be an indicator that the person thinks you are acting or being distasteful.

When you bite your lip it can indicate that you are worried, stressed, and even anxious about something.

Covering the mouth is mainly used in conversation when people are trying to mask their true emotional reactions. For example, if they smirk at something you said but don't want to offend you then they might cover their mouth.

If your mouth is turned up or down it can indicate a lot about how you are feeling. Slight changes in the mouth's curves can mean a lot. For example, a curve upward normally indicates happiness and optimism, while a turndown of the mouth's curves can show sadness, disapproval, or even a grimace of disgust or anger.

## *Your Gestures*

Gestures are direct signs of body language that are easy to interpret and are almost always going on when in conversation with someone. There is a large amount of movement that is classified under gestures but they do include waving, pointing, and even simply using your hands to articulate a point. Gestures can be some of the most direct and obvious body language signals. It is important to note that not all gestures are the same culturally and they do vary by culture, so make sure that you are familiar with the gestures of the culture you are interacting with. Here are some of the more common gestures:

A closed or clenched fist illustrates anger, but depending on the context it can also mean that you stand in solidarity with others.

When you give a thumbs up or down to someone you are normally communicating that you either approve or disapprove of something.

When you touch your thumb and your index finger together to form circle gestures that everything is "okay." This is mainly in mainstream American culture and I would be careful using it in other cultures as it might not imply the same connotation of being all right.

In many countries when you hold up your index and middle finger to make a V shape it is indicative that you are throwing up a peace sign. Again, this is not how it is seen in all countries, so unless you are familiar with the gestures of that country you should refrain from making this sign.

## *Your Arms and Legs*

Your arms and legs say a lot that your words might not be saying. You can cross your arms in a defensive manner, or you can even move your legs away from someone in a signal that you are not comfortable with that person. There are a lot of subtle ways that our bodies communicate even when we are not speaking or engaged in conversation. For example, take a look at what you might be saying with your arms and legs:

Crossing your arms signals that you are feeling defensive or that you are closed-off and not receptive to advances. It can also mean that you are protecting yourself.

If you place your hands on your hips it might show that you are in control of what is going on. Alternatively, it is also a sign that you are upset or aggressive.

You might clasp your hands together behind your back every now and then, but it normally indicates that you are either bored or anxious about something.

An impatient, frustrated, and even bored person might tap their fingers on a desk or object, and even fidget a lot to show how they are feeling.

When you cross your legs you are also indicating that you are closed off. It can also signify that you want to be left alone or given privacy.

## *Posture*

Posture is an important part of how we hold our bodies in relation to the space around us. It is also an indicator for others to read our body language. When you are observing someone, their posture can tell you a lot about what they are feeling; but it doesn't end there, because posture can also relay a lot of information about their personalities. If you're trying to figure out whether someone is receptive to you, confident in their abilities, submissive to those around them, and even closed off to advances, you can look at their posture and make an informed decision based on their body language.

For example, when someone sits up straight, this shows that they are being attentive to the area around them or a particular scene. Now, if that same person is sitting up but hunched over their posture is telling us that they are bored with the scene in front of them.

As you are practicing your skills at reading body language, pay attention to what a person's posture is indicating to you:

- Open posture is where their upper body will be exposed. That means they won't have their hands crossed across their chests or stomach. When a person has a posture that is open, that means they are open to friendly advances, and willing to listen to or go along with suggestions.
- Closed posture is where you see that the person is closing or hiding their upper body. They can either hunch over or cross

their arms around their body or cross their legs. When a person exhibits a closed posture this means that they aren't open to advances, they could have anxiety, and it could even be a display of hostility.

## *Your Personal Space*

If you have never said that you just need your personal space, then I am sure that you have at least heard someone tell you they need personal space. If you have felt a need for personal space, you might become uncomfortable when a person stands too close to you or hovers over you.

Edward T. Hall, an anthropologist, created four different levels of social distance when he created the idea of proxemics. Proxemics is merely the distance that exists between people who are interacting.

Intimate Distance is a space of 6-18 inches. When you are this close to one another it normally signals that you have a close relationship with the person you are interacting with and there is a comfort that exists in the space between you.

Personal Distance is a space of 1.5-4 feet. This level of physical distance occurs normally between family members and close friends. You can tell the level of intimacy in a relationship by whether they maintain personal or intimate distance.

Social distance is a space of 4-12 feet. Normally this level of distance happens between people who are acquaintances. Meaning that you know them, but you are not familiar enough with them to feel comfortable standing or interacting in a space closer than this.

Public distance is a space of 12-25 feet. At this level, you are normally in a public setting with people you don't know. You might be giving a public presentation or teaching a class.

While the level of space a person wants and feels comfortable at can vary depending on their culture, you should still try and respect the personal space that a person creates between you and them. When you have a stronger grasp on body language and what it is telling you, you will pick up on these subtle social cues a lot faster. It will also make your interactions a lot more pleasant.

Remember that you don't want to analyze every minute body language or facial expression on its own, but as a whole together. Often a smile on its own does not tell us as much as the posture of the shoulders, body placement, eye expression, and an eyebrow raise might tell us when combined with that smile.

# Chapter 6: Social Skills

"Communication - the human connection - is the key to personal and career success" - Paul Meyer

Empathy is simply a person's ability to recognize and share the emotions that someone else is experiencing. This could be a real person or even a fictional person. When a person is truly empathetic they can see a situation from the other party's perspective as well as share the emotions and distress that a person is feeling.

Sometimes people can confuse demonstrating empathy with having pity, sympathy, or even compassion. While these are similar to one another, they focus more on the plight of others while empathy focuses on a shared experience. For example, pity is when you feel uncomfortable over someone else's behavior or feelings and you use a condescending or paternalistic tone to convey your pity. When pity is dealt out, it is being said that the object of the pity does not deserve what is happening to them and that they are unable to change their own fortune around. When you pity someone you do not engage with them on the same level that you would when you empathize with them.

When you display sympathy you are showing that you care and have concern for someone that is close to you. Normally, when you sympathize with someone you want to see them happier, or even just doing better than they are doing currently. Sympathy does connect more on a shared level of experience with the other person, but it does not involve you sharing their perspective or their emotions.

Compassion is considered akin to being right alongside another person. It is more engaged with the individual than empathy is, and normally the goal of feeling compassionate is to alleviate the stress of the other person. Empathy is where you can share a person's emotions, but compassion goes a step further and builds on empathy.

Sometimes even when you have empathy, it can be hard to know what to do or what to say in a social situation. You feel with the person that you are talking to, but you have a hard time finding the right words because it seems like nothing you say can affect the moment. This happens all the time. Simply because you can empathize does not mean that you magically know all the right things to say and do. This is why empathy is made up of a component of skills that you can use to your benefit to help you navigate sticky social situations. We will cover ways to offer help, control your own emotions, take action, learn when not to act, and following up with the person.

## *Responding With Empathy*

1 - Offer your help. Not everyone that you come across will need or want your help. Sometimes they do want help, but your help is not the help that they are after. This can be hard for some people to get over, but the truth is that when you are empathizing you need to respect their wishes. Practicing empathy is not about your innate need to feel better or help, but rather the person that you are connecting with. Talk to them and find out what the best way to help would be. They might want your advice, a shoulder to cry on, help to and from work, and they might not even want your help.

When you see someone in need and you feel their need, offer to help and then respect their decision to accept or reject that help.

2 - Control your emotions. Emotion contagion is how you are able to feel the emotion that another person is experiencing. Feeling what the other person feels is a necessary part of empathy, but if you let it overwhelm you then you might not be able to help the person you are empathizing with.

3 - Take action. If a person wants your help, then get into gear and get moving. It can be hard to know whether you are taking the right action or not, but your empathy will help drive you toward the right decision. A good way to help if they do not indicate a specific way that they need help would be to ask yourself what you would want to be done if you were in their shoes.

4 - Know when to withhold action. Not everyone will want your help. In fact, some people just want to be left to their own devices in their own space. They could want that for a variety of reasons that include simply needing their time to sort out their emotions. It might be that they don't feel completely comfortable with you just yet. It is just as important to know when not to do anything as it is to know when to do something. Even if you want to help with every fiber of your being, you still need to remove your own wishes and respect the wishes of the person that is in need.

5 - Follow up. You might have helped the person, or you might have done nothing per their wishes. The important part is that no matter what you chose to do, you follow up. You don't just walk away and fail to follow through. When you leave people alone when you feel like they are no longer in a tough spot, they might find themselves

isolated and alone. It is always a good idea just to check in on them and let them know that you are there.

The other thing you should keep in mind is that suffering does not go away overnight. If you knew that someone had an issue, don't assume it went away just because they no longer talk about it. Reach out to them and check in on them - you don't have to talk about their problem necessarily. Make sure that you keep the lines of communication open to them. These techniques are devised to help you maneuver a situation in which you need to practice your empathy. Contrary to the world's popular belief, not every problem needs a solution. Sometimes all a person needs is someone who understands why they feel the way they do.

## *Dealing with Negative Emotions*

Positive and negative emotions are both a standard part of life. Without one we cannot have the other. Sometimes, though, we struggle to appropriately express our negative emotions and they can build up and cause some serious issues and harm to our health if we do not know how to handle them. While it is an easy fix to lash out when you are feeling sad, angry, and even fearful, this won't help you deal with your real emotions or the event that brought up the emotions. Emotions that do not get dealt with can end up being managed in harmful ways such as:

Denial: A person will refuse to accept that something is wrong or that they need help. People often deny that they have any negative emotions or feelings that are causing problems. These bottled up and pent up feelings end up exploding at some point and can cause harm to the person in denial and those within the firing range.

Withdrawal: a person might not want to be around anyone or hang out and participate in activities that they once liked. There is a pivotal difference between wanting your solitude every now and then and withdrawing yourself from social interaction consistently. Withdrawal is one of the first signs of depression, and can also be an indication that the person is ashamed about something that they have done or are feeling.

Bullying: a person that threatens, forces others to do their will and ridicules in order to possess power is bullying those around them. When a person bullies another it is indicative that they have shortcomings (or perceived shortcomings) in their own selves and so they lash out at others. The object of bullying is to feel better about oneself by putting down those around them.

Self-harm: is a serious and dangerous result of unregulated negative emotions. This can take the form of cutting, starving, binge eating and purging, and any other behavior that leads to physical, mental, or even emotional harm. Those who self-harm often feel like it is a reprieve from the emotional distress that they are in.

Substance use: when a person uses alcohol or drugs in an inappropriate manner in order to feel numb to the world and their emotions, they are participating in substance abuse. This form of abuse can have serious effects on their brain, causing damage and in cases of overuse of alcohol and drugs, it can even cause death. When using substances that are addictive and mind-numbing, it can increase the likelihood that the person will have suicidal thoughts or create a lifelong addiction. If this is ever a concern for you or someone that you know, find ways to get help. Speak to someone. Involve other people that are going to be objective.

This is why I stress the importance of being able to regulate and express all of your emotions, even the negative ones. I want you to have healthy and balanced emotional health. A good way to deal with your negative emotions can be to practice PATH:

- Pause
- Acknowledge
- Think
- Help

Pause: this is step one and it involves you stopping instead of immediately reacting to your feelings. When you stop and think about things you gain a new perspective. So take a deep breath and count to 100 if you need to. The point is that you need to truly pause.

Acknowledge: step two is where you acknowledge whatever emotion you are feeling and know that it is completely okay to feel that way. You can feel however you want and are entitled to that.

Think: by step three you have now thought about your emotions and acknowledged that you have a right to feel them. But in step three you need to think about what the right response is to the situation that you are in. This means thinking about what you are feeling and what will make them feel better.

Help: step four is your time to take action and put into motion the plan that you came up with in step three.

## *Different Ways to Help Yourself Express Emotions*

Sometimes we need a little help figuring out constructive ways to express our emotions. So, I want to give you a list to work with. This can help you become more comfortable expressing your full range of emotions if you are not there just yet.

Boost your Mood:

- Read a story of a person that you admire
- Play with an animal
- Clean up your space or reorganize your space
- Create a travel list
- Watch a program that offers comedic relief

Cater to your Basic Needs

- Drink some water
- Take a hot shower or even a relaxing bath
- Take a nap if you need one
- Eat a healthy meal or snack

Process your Feelings

- Punch a punching bag (a pillow works too)
- Scream to let out frustration
- Cry if you need to (because it's completely okay to do so)
- Rip up paper
- Draw or write about how you are feeling
- Write out a list of things you are grateful for

Never underestimate the power of a good venting session. This is not where you are asking for help, but rather where you use someone as a sounding board for your feelings. Sometimes all you need is to say how you are feeling out loud without being judged. Sometimes writing a letter that you never send helps you vent without needing to talk to anyone. I advise you to partake in whatever methods help you vent safely. My only caution is to avoid social media, as people can misconstrue your venting and this can lead to more negative feelings.

If you feel overwhelmed by your problems, write every single problem down in a list. Then, with the help of a friend or even family, find solutions to some of those problems, and take it one small step at a time.

You are a person of strength as well. When we experience negative emotions we can forget that fact. Write down what your strengths are on a list and appreciate that sometimes you simply are just amazing.

Practice Acts of Kindness

- Help out a stranger
- Volunteer at a cause you care about
- Do something selfless for a friend or family

Stress Relievers and Hobbies

- Play a game that you love
- Start a garden, get the material and learn to plant something new

- Write a story, or express your feelings on paper
- Create a craft project that allows you to immerse yourself

There are a myriad of ways that you can help yourself or things that can fit your needs in order to express your emotions in a truly healthy way. You might find that none of these techniques are helping you.

I strongly advise that if you find yourself recurrently struggling with expressing your negative emotions in a healthy way that you seek out professional help. You don't want to suffer silently with anxiety or depression.

There are online websites such as mhascreening.org that you can go to for help in regards to taking free screening tests or even looking for resources for your next steps or where to seek help. My only goal is that you find a way to get in touch with your emotions and that you find healthy ways to express them.

Yes, you are a man. And men feel, too.

# Chapter 7: 30 Day Emotional Intelligence Booster Program

This is probably the most important part of this guide that you have been waiting for - a thirty-day guide to boosting your emotional intelligence. Don't get me wrong, the first half of this book provides you with invaluable information about understanding emotional intelligence, the components of emotional intelligence, and what you can do in order to help yourself be more self-aware, self-regulated, motivated, empathetic, and socially aware. However, now we are going to practice everything that you learned and you will have thirty days to boost your EQ.

I will be with you through every step of this journey. Don't worry, it is going to be practical, easy to follow and understand, and I will have a wealth of resources and examples for you to lean on as you battle your way into a higher state of emotional intelligence over the next month. You will need to keep yourself motivated and on task, though. It is helpful if you get a journal that you can write within each day and tackle your emotions and problems so that you can continue to progress. Every single day for the next thirty days needs to be started and finished with you being consciously aware of your emotions.

At the end of every day, you need to set aside time and analyze what happened in your day, how you responded to each situation, and if that was the appropriate response. It is important to write down and evaluate your day every day over these next thirty days in order for the program to work. Trust me, you will be excited to come in at the end of the day and see how you did and how you are improving in your EQ skills.

# Days 1-5: Getting to Know Yourself

## Day One

"Knowing yourself is the beginning of all wisdom." - Aristotle

Today is day one of your journey into boosting your EQ. I am going to start by saying congratulations on starting! This is a big step as a man to decide to break societal conventions and for the sake of your emotional health take learning into your own hands. Every day for the next five days we are going to practice getting to know yourself better. This is the first step towards self-awareness. If you want to brush up some more on the reasons why self-awareness is so important, go back to Daniel Goleman's model of the mixed model in chapter two and give yourself a refresher. This journey is going to be broken into his five main components so that you can focus on yourself, then others as you learn to navigate the emotional minefield.

In a separate journal I want you to document each day what happened, how things happened, and your response. However, we are going to take it one step further than this.

On the first day of your journal I want you to write down your goal. For the first five days we are going to aim to recognize when we are feeling the basic six emotions that we went over in chapter one:

- anger

- disgust
- happiness
- sadness
- surprise
- fear

Once you recognize when you are feeling each emotion, your goal is to identify the emotion and your choices that stem from it. For day one, however, we will simply focus on recognizing emotions.

At the beginning of today, write down how you currently identify and label emotions or feelings that you go through in your day. I also want you to write down each of the six basic emotions and how you think you would typically feel when you are experiencing these emotions. For example, you can write down: "When I feel sad, my body seems to slow down and I don't seem to function quite as quickly as is normal for me. My body feels weighed down by sadness." You don't have to go in-depth with the answer unless you want to. You can keep it short and sweet.

Then, go live your day. Go about your day as you would normally. If you can pay extra attention to your emotions and what you are feeling in an attempt to identify them then great! If not, that's okay. The point of today is to get you comfortable with your emotions and to start you on your goals.

At the end of the day, take some time on your own and get your journal out. On this page of your journal I want you to write out every emotion that you can recall feeling today. Leave some space by each emotion because we are going to go back in and fill in some information about the feeling you felt. Now that you have established the emotions you recognized, go back and write down what you believe triggered every emotion.

For example, if you wrote down that you felt happy you also need to write down what event or person made you feel that way. And how did you react as a result of this emotion? Do you think that you reacted in the appropriate manner for the emotion?

If you felt a positive emotion, I want you to write down if it helped solve any problems or situations that you faced. Vice versa, if you felt a negative emotion I want you to write down how that emotion influenced the situation you were in. Then reflect on each emotion and congratulate yourself again. You managed to go through your first day of navigating emotions. If you are feeling discouraged by the end of day one, give yourself a break. Understand that this is a thirty-day process and it will take time before you show progress in boosting your EQ.

## Day Two - Four

"Honesty and transparency make you vulnerable. Be honest and transparent anyway." - Mother Teresa

Days two, three, and four will follow the same patterns and exercises as one another. The reason is that the goal of these days is to get you comfortable with recognizing emotions. You should see your abilities at feeling and recognizing your emotions improve with each day that passes. These days I want you to remember the words from the quote above. There is nothing wrong with vulnerability, despite what the world tells you as a man. You need to be honest with yourself for this process to work. You need to stop masking your emotions under anger and pride. Do not be afraid to truly feel your emotions.

Your Exercise:

For each of the next three days, you are going to pause throughout your day. If you can manage to pause every hour from when you wake up to when you get home that is the most ideal. Set a timer on your phone if you have to remind yourself to pause. Then, with each pause, focus on identifying the emotion that you are currently experiencing. Write the emotion down in your journal or someplace that you can later transfer to your journal when you get ready to do your journaling. It is possible to feel more than one emotion at a time. If you find yourself in this situation, simply write down every single emotion that you are feeling.

This exercise is extremely important to your success. It might seem repetitive, but it is helping you learn to use muscles that you are not accustomed to using. Your mental muscles are getting exercise when you name each emotion while you feel them through your body. When you name the emotions and write them down, then you are forcing yourself to physically think about your emotions as well, not just simply react to how you are feeling without thought.

I want to stress a point about your emotions. While men do use anger and pride as a mask for their other emotions, that does not mean that these are not healthy or valid emotions to experience. You are perfectly valid if you do feel angry, however, you need to be able to control your response and express this anger in a healthy and mature way. Emotions like anger can be turned into a positive emotion and do not always have to be a negative emotion.

Remember, every emotion we feel is an emotion that has been developed for a reason.

## *Day Five*

"Learn to know yourself... to search realistically and regularly the processes of your own mind and feelings." - Nelson Mandela

On day five, I want you to keep your exercise in mind and still work on that today. Don't drop the ball now that you are getting the hang of it. You should still be journaling at least once a day, but preferably twice a day. The optimal way to journal would be to wake up in the morning, write down what your goals for the day are, then at the end of the day I want you to record the emotions that you felt, the way you handled the emotions, and how you reacted to the situations you were placed in. You need to always keep in mind that while you cannot control your impulse emotion, you can always control how you react and what you do after you feel the emotion arise.

Day five is really where you should be comfortable with identifying your emotions — even if it is just privately for right now. There is no requirement that you have to be open to everyone yet. It is a big step just to admit to yourself that yes, you do feel something other than anger and pride.

You can record all sorts of interactions that you have and how you handled them. I did this program myself as I was testing it out before implementing it in this guide, so I am going to share an excerpt from my own journal at each step. This is what my journal looked like on day five:

"Today's goals are:

- recognize and notate what emotions I feel every few hours and in situations that stir up emotion
- regulate my responses as best I can for my emotions
- be honest with myself about the emotions that I am feeling

The emotions I felt today were:

- Anger - I was running late for work because I snoozed my alarm once and then the second time I accidentally turned it off instead of snoozing it. This made me feel aggravated. I could feel my frustration stir up inside every muscle in my body and so before I walked out of the door of the house I stopped, breathed, and I felt a little better.
- happiness - I was happy for the most part. It was Friday today which means I have the whole weekend to look forward to as relaxation away from work. I felt like I was productive at work as well since I finished a big project.
- Sadness - I had been looking forward to some leftovers but they had gone off by the time I had come home. I felt sad and was able to cheer myself up by whipping up an equally delicious meal for dinner.
- Interactions that I had:
- My wife and I spoke about the kids' school schedules this morning and how best to navigate our different schedules with their extra-curricular activities. I was feeling frustrated because I was running late by this point, and it spilled into the conversation, but I apologized, took a moment, and we were back on track in a healthy conversation.

- At work, I had a colleague critique some of my research and I felt hurt. I wanted to shut down but I asked about their opinions, forced myself to be objective about their input, and then gave my research a second glance. They were right about a few things and I took the opportunity to thank them and expand my research which benefited my team in the long run."

Now, your journal might look completely different from my entry, but its main goal is to track your progress. Be honest about your successes as well as your failures. There is always a chance to improve on what you did the day before, so do not beat yourself up about not being where you want to be just yet. Focus on your goals and be diligent with your journaling so you can track your progress.

# Days 6-15: Improving Yourself

### *Day Six*

"Change is your friend, not your foe, change is a brilliant opportunity to grow." - Simon T. Bailey

We keep the ball rolling on day six and we take it one step further. We are going to go one step further than being self-aware; we are now going to focus on self-regulation and improving our actions. If this sounds like a lot, it is because it can be.

Self-regulation is not without its challenges, but I promise you that your improvements will be the best thing you could do for yourself. Change truly is an opportunity that you need to learn to embrace. The sooner you accept and move toward change, the easier being in tune with your emotional intelligence will be for you.

Your daily goal is still going to be recognizing your emotions, but you are going to take it one step further, Now, I want you to consciously adjust your behavior and actions by placing rational thinking behind your emotions. For example, in a moment that you feel anger, stop and recognize it, but then make sure that your actions are appropriate for the situation. You might be angry, but there is no reason to yell or break things.

Being able to recognize your emotions and then regulate them is what will separate you from the millions of other people out there. While emotions are important to us, nobody wants to be ruled by emotions. You want rational thinking to remain in control here.

Today, I want you to write your goals down in your journal and then go through your day trying to recognize your emotions. When you do, I want you to write down your response to each emotion that you felt and then explain whether you thought it was the right way to react. Don't get too upset if you struggle today. In the next few days, you're going to keep working at it and on an exercise that will help you regulate your emotions.

## *Day Seven to Fourteen*

"The final forming of a person's character lies in their own hands." - Anne Frank

This next week is going to be full of you using your skills to regulate your behavior. If you struggled with this on day one, then don't worry about it. I will be here to give you some more structure over this next week. As you journal and write down your interactions and your successful and unsuccessful regulation attempts, I also want you to take a look at the emotions you are experiencing. Don't be so focused on regulating them that you become out of touch with your emotions and what they mean to you.

Your goal with regulating your emotions is to be able to respond in the best way in any situation you find yourself in. This could be at work, in an intimate relationship, and even with a friend. You do not want to let your emotions get out of control and then you lose control of a problem. Don't get me wrong, I am not telling you to repress your emotions or hide from them, but rather listen to them and react using rational thinking.

This next week, write down what emotions you felt were harder for you to feel or the ones that you feel like you never felt. Emotions are tricky for us men, and it can take time to get comfortable with truly allowing ourselves to feel them. If you find that you are having trouble with a certain emotion (be that with feeling it or regulating it), then you should take a look at the people around you. Try your best to spot the emotion that you're having difficulty with them. If you manage to spot someone expressing the emotion, see how they react and write down what you thought about it.

This exercise is important, as it also helps you to begin noticing emotional displays in the people around you. Not only will you be more aware of the emotions of those that you interact with, but you will also be more in tune with your own emotions and have a deeper understanding of how they affect your choices and behavior.

You want to work with the mixed model as you go through this exercise. Remember that it is made of five components, and each of these components is important to have a full and comprehensive panel of abilities. You can also make use of the trait and ability models if you feel more comfortable with those, but you will have more of a complete picture if you look at the mixed model because it is also easy to take it to step by step and not overwhelm yourself.

## Day Fifteen

"There is only one corner of the universe you can be certain of improving, and that is your own self." - Aldous Huxley

Day fifteen is really a time where you need to take a look at all of your progress. I mean it, you need to sit down this morning and take some time to look at the week in your journal. See where your progress has improved, and how you are becoming more adept at regulating your emotions and being more aware of the emotions of those around you. You need to appreciate the progress that you are making. It can be hard when we do not take a moment to look at our progress. Sometimes, it can feel like you aren't getting anywhere, but that is mainly because you forget where you started and how far you have come.

As always, on the last day of an exercise week, I will share with you what my journal looked like. Your journal can look however best suits you, but you should be doing the work of keeping track of your emotional outputs and your responses to them.

"Today my goal is:

- to recognize my emotions

- to regulate my emotional responses with rational thinking
- to be slightly better than I was the day before
- to begin looking towards the emotions that other people feel and experience
- to try and model my responses to what will best fit the emotional climate of the person I am interacting with.

The emotions that I experienced today ranged from:

- happiness - I felt happy today when I interacted with my wife. She told me some good news about her job and then we went over our children's accomplishments at certain school events. The happiness feeling stayed with me for quite a while and I felt pretty light with my other interactions with people. The rational thought behind my actions was to let them see that I was happy with my interactions and to leave each person with a positive feeling from interacting with me. I smiled a lot, my tone was pleasant, and I maintained gentle eye contact with those around me.
- frustration - during the day I felt frustration rise up and I wanted to get really mad at a situation that I felt was out of my control. I wanted to take time off to go to my child's school event but my boss declined my time off. I had to stop and close my eyes, breathe in and out. Yes, at the moment I felt frustrated but deeper than that I was feeling sad at possibly disappointing my child. I thought about how to work out a solution and went back to my boss, asking them if I could come in earlier and just leave for a few hours to attend the event then come back to work. My boss agreed to the terms and everyone in the equation would be happy. I

felt better knowing that I hadn't acted out in frustration at first and stopped to think about what was really bothering me and then how to deal with it. My problem was disappointing my child, my child wanted me there and was excited about my presence, and my boss wanted me to put in my input and could not spare losing my work for the day. My solution worked out for everyone so that each person got what they wanted at a fair cost.

- relief - As soon as I had my work situation sorted out, relief flooded my body. I felt muscles that I had tensed up a release and my brow lines unfurrowed themselves. Soon, I was able to regulate my relief into happy emotional responses and interactions.

\*\*\* at this point you should be recognizing that emotions occur on a gradient, so you will be feeling more than just the six basic emotions that we covered in the first week of this journal. I bet that you will be feeling a lot of different emotions and you will be able to recognize each one. That definitely deserves a pat on the back! \*\*\*

Interactions that happened today:

- the most important interaction that I experienced today was with my boss. I applied for a day off and he denied me. He was not mean when he denied me and he was not trying to personally attack me, but he was firm that I could not take the day off. At first, I was upset then frustrated, but deep down I really felt disappointed that I could not attend my child's school event. I calmed down, rationalized my thinking and then approached my boss with a solution that could fit all of our needs. I realized that my boss's main problem was needing my staffing hours and research and so I made sure that my work would still output my regular workload. Everyone left this interaction happy.

So far in my journey, I have been able to recognize my own emotions and then regulate my responses. I have made sure to look at Goleman's mixed model so that I was able to stick to the basics that I have done and make sure that I am making progress towards my future steps in mastering my emotional intelligence."

# Days 16-21: Empathy

## Day Sixteen to Twenty

"Empathy is about finding echoes of another person in yourself." - Mohsin Hamid

You are halfway through your journey! This is a truly incredible time for you and your emotional intelligence. This next week you will be working on your empathy towards others. Basically, your main goal will be to feel what other people are feeling.

Everyone has emotions that affect them, and when you begin to understand these emotions you can cater to your responses so that the other party is more receptive to what you are trying to tell them, or to the message that you are trying to make. You want to understand why they feel the way that they do if it is a good or bad feeling, and then how you should respond to their emotions. Every single interaction that you have with a person is going to be emotionally charged, but if you put rationale in your decisions then your interactions will be far more successful than in the past.

You can analyze what a person is thinking and feeling, and then deduce why they are acting a certain way. For example, if you feel that your partner is angry and yelling at you, you should be able to get through to the real reason they are acting out, and instead of responding in anger you will work toward responding with rational thought to diffuse the situation.

You have an exercise in empathy for this week, and I want you to record every single day that you practice it. When you are interacting with someone, listen to their story and try to recognize the emotions that they are feeling. Place yourself in their shoes so that you have a better way to connect with them on an empathetic level. In every interaction that you have when you are practicing empathy, ask yourself this question: "What would I want to hear right now if I were feeling how they are?" This should be the question that guides your every response and reaction to others this week. Be present at the moment with the person, don't brush their feelings aside, don't brush them off, and more importantly sometimes all you have to do is listen. You don't have to offer a solution, but simply be there.

Practicing empathy is an important skill that adds to the social skills you need for emotional intelligence. The more empathetic you are, the easier it is to relate to others, form deeper connections, and have more positive interactions.

## Day Twenty-One

"If we share our story with someone who responds with empathy and understanding, shame can't survive." - Brene Brown

"My goals this week were to:

- demonstrate empathy by recognizing the emotions of others and responding with the best response that I would want to hear if I were in their shoes
- understand that being empathetic does not always require me to offer a solution, but to understand their emotion

Interactions I had in which I demonstrated empathy and focused on more than just my own feelings:

- My wife was expressing some concerns regarding one of our children's grades. She seemed frustrated and upset, but I was not sure what solution I could really offer her. I sat in silence for a minute and let her talk about what was eating at her regarding our child's school performance and I gathered that she was feeling like she was failing our child herself. This was about more than just his school performance, but her performance as a mother. At first, I listened to what my wife was saying and I let her vent. Then, when I realized that her feelings were internalized at herself I aimed to comfort her. I know that in this situation I would not want someone to ridicule my child's grades because that would make me feel like more of a failure. Instead, once she was calm I held her, reassured her that she was doing the best that she could and then I came up with a plan with her so that she and I could help our child raise their grades, or perhaps just find out the reason for the grades slipping."

# Days 22-30: Influence

"Leadership is an influence." - John C. Maxwell

You have made it almost a month into this incredible journey and I am so proud of how far your emotional intelligence has come. As a man, it takes big steps to even start trying to understand your emotions, accept your emotions, and then communicate these emotions to the people around you. If you have taken just one step towards trying to understand your emotions, then that deserves recognition.

Please remember that mastering your emotional intelligence is not a one day process; sometimes it is not even a one month process! It can take time, and you might have to spend more time on certain exercises before you feel completely ready to move onto the next one. That is completely okay, so do not feel like you have let yourself down, and do not be overly hard on yourself. This takes time. It is better to make sure you are being true to yourself versus rushing through this journey. There is also nothing stopping you from doing this journey again and again. Keep working it, keep improving on your ability to empathize and your ability to accept your own emotions, and then respond with rational thinking. There are endless possibilities in this world for you to practice on your emotional intelligence.

As you come into this last week of this journaling experience, our focus is going to shift into working on an entire and complete picture. Instead of working on just one area, you are going to work on recognizing your emotions, understanding your own emotions and where they are stemming from, as well as work on recognizing and empathizing with the emotions of the people that you interact with.

So, let us map this out in goals for our journal:

- Recognize my own emotions and handle them with rational thought
- Recognize the emotions of others and empathize with their feelings
- Navigate and use my emotional intelligence to create favorable social situations

There are two things that you will be working on during this week: your influence as well as your motivation.

Exercise one involves your influence during a social situation. When you are in any social interaction this week (remember to take it one day at a time), try using your influence on a social situation to your benefit. This means being honest and open about your own emotions and empathize with theirs. You will create an even playing field and the person you are interacting with will be more likely to hear your side of a story and agree to a course of action that you have planned.

Exercise two for the week (and yes, you will be working on each exercise each day of this week) involves your motivation. Without motivation, we get nowhere. As you work on understanding emotions this week, focus on why you want to increase your emotional intelligence. Focus on your goals. It helps if you have something that you are passionate about what you want to reach in order to motivate you to further analyze emotions. Keep track of your motivation. When you find yourself becoming unmotivated, pull out your journal and make a list of all the reasons that you should feel motivated. For example, I had a friend who was just starting this course out and they always struggled with feeling angry or sad. Their motivation came with the need to understand their emotions and strive to attain happier and more consistently healthy and positive emotions.

In your journal I also want you to write down about how you practiced listening each day. Remember, sometimes all the work you need to do is to listen to someone else and that meets all their needs. However, you do need to be an active listener. Take this excerpt from my journal on day twenty-five:

"Today I had the opportunity to really practice my listening skills when my daughter came up to me and wanted to discuss a situation at her school. Normally she goes to her mother with these things, but for some reason, she decided to entrust her story with me. This is a pivotal moment in our communication and if I handled it the right way then I know that I solidified a bond with my daughter. All I had to do was listen to her. Not just nod my head, or dismiss her story, but actively listen to what she had to tell me, what she wanted to say to me. When I was listening to her story I asked questions about her feelings, or questions that prompted her to go more in-depth with her story. Then, I repeated what she said back to me at certain intervals to show her that I was truly engaged in her story."

The outcome of that situation was that my daughter now comes to talk to me about a lot more things, and I treasure the foundation that we have built simply through active listening.

Listen to your emotions, don't shy away from them. Remember that negative emotions can be expressed positively. If you are angry at a work situation or even in your private family life, you do not have to express yourself in a negative manner. By now I am sure you have that point drilled into your head. I wish you luck as you continue through your journey and I hope this journal has helped you. I find that going through my journal every now and then helps cement the foundation that I have built my emotional intelligence on, so you might want to keep your journal around you even when you have finished this journey!

# Conclusion

Wow! This has surely been an incredible journey for you to go through. I want to start off by saying thank you for choosing this book and thank you for sticking through the guide and putting in the work to master your emotional intelligence. Mastering your emotional intelligence is no small feat, and you should be proud of yourself for coming this far.

I want you to remember that you can and should keep working on and practicing your emotional intelligence! It is like a muscle that you need to keep healthy and exercised. Don't make the mistake of becoming too cocky and self-assured and forgetting to control your own emotions or lose your ability to empathize with those around you.

My goal for you is that by now you have an understanding of your emotions. However, I really want more than just that for you. I want you to also understand the emotions of others and to be able to navigate their emotions so that you have successful social interactions. Emotional intelligence is an amazing ability to understand yourself and those around you. There is nothing else that will give you such insight into human behavior as understanding their emotions.

In chapter one, you learned all about what the basic emotions were. Remember that these are important emotions to understand, but that they do not make the emotional range. Emotions occur on a gradient, and they can vary from person to person based on cultural experiences as well. The most important part about experiencing our emotions is learning how to embrace them and fully embrace our feelings. Don't hide behind anger and pride because it is easier than confronting your other emotions.

As men, it can be easy to be fooled by our emotions. This is because most of the time we are not adjusted to understanding and handling our emotions the same way that women are. Our society has conditioned us to believe that anything more than anger or pride makes us less of a man. However, that is not the truth. You are not less of a man because you feel. Being in tune with your emotions makes it so that you are that much more of a man. You are complete when you have mastered your emotional intelligence because then you are at the top of your game. Every single decision that we make is based on emotion, not logic — as much as we try to convince ourselves otherwise. The goal is to understand your emotions and use rational reasoning to make your decisions.

In chapter two the EQ models were discussed, and while we learned that there were three different models, our area of focus was Daniel Goleman's mixed model. The mixed model is based on five components: your self-awareness, self-regulation, motivation, empathy, and social skills. All of these components are necessary to understand and implement in your reasoning so that you are able to be emotionally aware and emotionally mature. You can make use of all of the models, but study the mixed model the most because this is the most universal model when it comes to conquering your emotional intelligence.

As you have cycled through emotions, you have probably learned by now that being self-aware is the first step to truly getting anywhere when it comes to emotions. Learning how to be self-aware will help you learn how to evaluate what emotions you are feeling in each moment. When you recognize your emotions and feelings, then you stand a better chance at navigating your response to outside stimuli. It is also one of the first steps toward evaluating the emotions of others.

When you are self-aware, then you can self-regulate! This is an amazing step that shows you are making progress. Self-regulation means that you are able to manage your emotions. This means that simply because you are angry, that does not mean you act in inappropriate ways. You know how to navigate your emotions to make the right social choices. You are able to motivate yourself as well and keep yourself on track. Emotional intelligence is not a one-step solution to the world's problems, but it can certainly help alleviate the problems in your personal life.

Finally, you should also be able to interpret through social cues how people feel and go through emotions. Through your daily interactions, you and the people you are interacting with go through a hundred different feelings and emotions. Your interactions will go smoother when you are able to identify their emotions and rationalize your responses in accordance with what will best fit the social situation. It all ties in together, and it all needs to be there in order to work for your best benefit. You cannot have one quality without the other, otherwise, your emotional intelligence picture is not complete.

I hope that you enjoyed taking the thirty-day plan and making it work for you! I enjoyed making it, and it was designed to give you the best possible ability to succeed in this world. Remember that it does not have to only be thirty days. You can extend the program and work on it every single day for as long as you choose to. If you find that you are struggling in one particular area, then you should not hesitate to repeat the steps that you need some extra work in. There is never shame in making sure that you have all of your emotional intelligence skills sharpened and ready for use.

I have done my part. I have illustrated what emotional intelligence is, how it works, and how you can make it work to your best advantage. I have even included a thirty-day plan that is designed to help you boost your emotional intelligence further than where it currently sits. There is a solution to every problem that you encounter, and I am glad that I can offer up this solution to you. This does not have to be hard or trying on your patience. Simply take it one step at a time, and I am confident that by the end you will have mastered your emotions and raised your social awareness of others' emotions. In short, I know you've got this!

There will be an audiobook coming out soon that you should be on the lookout for. Like this book, it is geared toward men who are often overlooked in this market. The audiobook is based on affirmations and included guided meditation techniques and hypnosis that helps reprogram men who have a harder time being honest about their true emotions. There is a lot of fascinating information out in the world that will help you be your best and strongest self - both emotionally and mentally.

I want to give you a final thank you and good-bye as this book comes to a close, but this does not mean that your journey has to end here. I have faith and confidence in you.

# References

Ahearn, B. (2014). *The 7 most common persuasion mistakes.* Retrieved August 20, 2019, from https://www.influencepeople.biz/2014/09/the-7-most-common-persuasion-mistakes.html

All Mind Tools (2018). *Rational decision-making model.* Retrieved August 17, 2019, from https://allmindtools.com/rational-decision-making-model/

Andersen, R. (2014). *Elon Musk puts his case for a multi-planet civilization.* Retrieved August 20, 2019, from https://aeon.co/essays/elon-musk-puts-his-case-for-a-multi-planet-civilisation

BBC Worklife. (2014). *Why saying 'no' will boost your career.* Retrieved August 21, 2019, from https://www.bbc.com/worklife/article/20140314-just-say-no

Box, G. and Draper, N. (1987). *Empirical model-building and response surfaces.* Wiley; 1 edition (January 1987). ISBN-10: 0471810339

Brikman, Y. (2016). *A minimum viable product is not a product, it's a process.* Retrieved August 22, 2019, from https://blog.ycombinator.com/minimum-viable-product-process/

Bronner, S. J. (2012). Campus traditions: Folklore from the old-time college to the modern mega-university. University Press of Mississippi. ISBN 978-1-61703-617-0

BusinessDictionary.com. (n.d.) *Mental models.* Retrieved August 13, 2019, from http://www.businessdictionary.com/definition/mental-models.html

Cialdini, R. (2016). *Pre-suasion: A revolutionary way to influence and persuade.* Simon and Schuster, 1230 Avenue of the Americas, New York, NY 10020.

Clear, J. (n.d.). *All models are wrong: How to make decisions in an imperfect world.* Retrieved August 16, 2019, from https://jamesclear.com/all-models-are-wrong

Clear, J. (2019). *How to stop procrastinating and stick to good habits by using the "2-minute rule".* Retrieved August 16, 2019, from https://www.lifehack.org/articles/productivity/how-stop-procrastinating-and-stick-good-habits-using-the-2-minute-rule.html

Clear, J. (n.d.) *Warren Buffett's "2 lists" strategy: How to maximize your focus and master your priorities.* Retrieved August 22, 2019, from https://jamesclear.com/buffett-focus?source=post_page-----25c3724a5208---------------------

Cook, T. (2012). *Steve Jobs was an awesome flip-flopper, says Tim Cook (video).* Retrieved August 20, 2019, from http://allthingsd.com/20120529/steve-jobs-was-an-awesome-flip-flopper-says-tim-cook/

Covey, S. (1989). *7 habits of highly effective people.* Simon and Schuster (2013 edition), 1230 Avenue of the Americas, New York, NY 10020.

Dalio, R. (2017). *Principles.* Simon and Schuster, 1230 Avenue of the Americas, New York, NY 10020.

DuBroff, R. (2017). *Confirmation bias, conflicts of interest and cholesterol guidance: Can we trust expert opinions?* Retrieved August 17, 2019, from https://academic.oup.com/qjmed/article-abstract/111/10/687/4587483?redirectedFrom=fulltext

Dyson, J. (2003). *Against the odds: An autobiography.* Texere; 2 Edition (April 17, 2003). ISBN-13: 978-1587991707

Elon Musk Quotes. (n.d.). *BrainyQuote.com.* Retrieved August 20, 2019, from https://www.brainyquote.com/quotes/elon_musk_750652

Encyclopedia Britannica, (n.d.). *Information theory: Physiology.* Retrieved August 16, 2019, from https://www.britannica.com/science/information-theory/Physiology

Faletto, J. (2017). *The Seinfeld strategy can help you be productive and prolific.* Retrieved August 16, 2019, from https://curiosity.com/topics/the-seinfeld-strategy-can-help-you-be-productive-and-prolific-curiosity/

Farnam Street (2019). *A lesson on elementary worldly wisdom as it relates to investment management & business.* Retrieved August 21, 2019, from https://fs.blog/a-lesson-on-worldly-wisdom/

Farnam Street (2018). *First-principles: The building blocks of true knowledge.* Retrieved August 20, 2019, from https://fs.blog/2018/04/first-principles/

Farnam Street (2018). *The value of probabilistic thinking: Spies, crime, and lightning strikes*. Retrieved August 20, 2019, from https://fs.blog/2018/05/probabilistic-thinking/

Forbes (2017). *From Rockefeller to Ford, see Forbes' 1918 ranking of the richest people in America*. Retrieved August 22, 2019, from https://www.forbes.com/sites/chasewithorn/2017/09/19/the-first-forbes-list-see-who-the-richest-americans-were-in-1918/#4a81da3a4c0d

Forbes (2019). #303 James Dyson. Real-time net worth. Retrieved August 22, 2019, from https://www.forbes.com/profile/james-dyson/#77d6022f2b38

Forbes (2019). Ray Dalio. Retrieved August 20, 2019, from https://www.forbes.com/profile/ray-dalio/#73bd1374663a

Grant, A. (2014). 8 ways to say no without hurting your image. Retrieved August 21, 2019, from https://www.linkedin.com/pulse/20140311110227-69244073-8-ways-to-say-no-without-hurting-your-image

Groopman, J. (2007). How doctors think. Houghton Mifflin Harcourt. ISBN 0618610030

Haden, J. (2019). Billionaire Jeff Bezos: People who are 'right a lot' make decisions differently than everyone else—here's how. Retrieved August 20, 2019, from https://www.cnbc.com/2019/03/12/amazon-billionaire-jeff-bezos-explains-why-the-smartest-people-change-their-minds-often.html

Hyatt, M. (2016). 5 reasons why you should take a nap every day.

Retrieved August 21, 2019, from https://michaelhyatt.com/why-you-should-take-a-nap-every-day/

Indie Hacker (2018). Building a life-changing business with Austen Allred of Lambda school. Retrieved August 22, 2019, from https://www.indiehackers.com/podcast/046-austen-allred-of-lambda-school

Langer, Ellen & Blank, Arthur & Chanowitz, Benzion. (1978). The mindlessness of ostensibly thoughtful action: The role of "placebic" information in interpersonal interaction. Journal of Personality and Social Psychology. 36. 635-642. 10.1037/0022-3514.36.6.635. Retrieved August 21, 2019, from https://www.researchgate.net/publication/232505985_The_mindlessness_of_ostensibly_thoughtful_action_The_role_of_placebic_information_in_interpersonal_interaction

McVagh, A. (2018). Mental model summary: Redundancy. Retrieved August 22, 2019, from https://www.mymentalmodels.info/mms-redundancy/

McVagh, A. (2018). Mental model summary: Social proof. Retrieved August 20, 2019, from https://www.mymentalmodels.info/mms-social-proof/

Melnyck, R. (2019). Second-order thinking: This is how to make better decisions. Retrieved August 20, 2019, from https://primeyourpump.com/2019/03/04/second-order-thinking/

Munger, C. (2007). USC law commencement speech. Retrieved August 17, 2019, from https://genius.com/Charlie-munger-usc-law-commencement-speech-annotated

Munger, T. C. (2005). Poor Charlie's almanack: The wit and wisdom of Charles T Munger. Donning Co Pub; 2nd Expanded edition (December 30, 2005). ISBN-10: 157864366X

Poundstone, W. (2010). Priceless: The myth of fair value. Hill and Wang; First edition (January 5, 2010). SBN-13: 978-0809078813

Price, R. G. (2004). Division of labor, assembly line thought - the paradox of democratic capitalism. Retrieved August 22, 2019, from http://www.rationalrevolution.net/articles/division_of_labor.htm

Rampton, J. (2018). 6 common decision-making blunders that could kill your business. Retrieved August 20, 2019, from https://www.entrepreneur.com/article/313591

Scientific Thought: In Context. (2009). Physics: The Bohr model. Retrieved August 15, 2019, from https://www.encyclopedia.com/science/science-magazines/physics-bohr-model

Shapiro, J. (2018). Attorney general Shapiro announces a $575 million 50-state settlement with Wells Fargo Bank for opening unauthorized accounts and charging consumers for unnecessary auto insurance, mortgage fees. Retrieved August 22, 2019, from https://www.attorneygeneral.gov/taking-action/press-releases/attorney-general-shapiro-announces-575-million-50-state-settlement-with-wells-fargo-bank-for-opening-unauthorized-accounts-and-charging-consumers-for-unnecessary-auto-insurance-mortgage-fees/

Shelley, A. (2019). 10 tips to KISS your life. Retrieved August 22, 2019, from https://www.lifehack.org/articles/communication/10-420

tips-kiss-your-life.html

Simmons, M. (2015). What self-made billionaire Charlie Munger does differently. Retrieved August 16, 2019, from https://www.inc.com/michael-simmons/what-self-made-billionaire-charlie-munger-does-differently.html

Sparks, C. (2017). 104: Systems thinking — The essential mental models needed for growth. *Understanding bottlenecks, leverage, and feedback loops.* Retrieved August 22, 2019, from https://medium.com/@SparksRemarks/systems-thinking-the-essential-mental-models-needed-for-growth-5d3e7f93b420

Stillman, J. (2017). *3 Killer persuasion techniques you can learn from billionaire Warren Buffett.* Retrieved August 20, 2019, from https://www.inc.com/jessica-stillman/3-killer-persuasion-techniques-you-can-learn-from-billionaire-warren-buffett.html

The Guardian (2019). *Operation on wrong testicle leaves two-year-old boy 'castrated'.* Retrieved August 22, 2019, from https://www.theguardian.com/society/2018/dec/21/operation-on-wrong-testicle-two-year-old-boy-bristol

Toth, P. P. (2015). *Treatment of dyslipidemia in elderly patients with coronary heart disease: There are miles to go before we sleep.* Retrieved August 17, 2019, from https://www.sciencedirect.com/science/article/pii/S0735109715050032?via%3Dihub

Tracy, B. (2018). *The 80 20 rule explained.* Retrieved August 22, 2019, from https://www.briantracy.com/blog/personal-success/how-to-use-the-80-20-rule-pareto-principle/

Travis, C. and Aronson, E. (2007). *Mistakes were made (but not by me)*. Houghton Mifflin Harcourt; 1 edition (May 7, 2007)

Wikipedia (n.d). *KISS principle*. Retrieved August 22, 2019, from https://en.wikipedia.org/wiki/KISS_principle#Origin

Wikipedia (n.d). *Thomas J. Watson*. Retrieved August 21, 2019, from https://en.wikipedia.org/wiki/Thomas_J._Watson

http://idahoptv.org/sciencetrek/topics/brain/facts.cfm

https://lifehacker.com/the-science-behind-how-we-learn-new-skills-908488422

https://www.verywellmind.com/what-is-memory-2795006

https://www.verywellmind.com/explanations-for-forgetting-2795045

https://smallbiztrends.com/2014/11/reasons-we-forget-things.html

https://www.verywellmind.com/memory-retrieval-2795007

https://www.verywellmind.com/what-is-long-term-memory-2795347

http://www.breakthroughlearningcollege.com/memory/visual-memory/

https://study.com/academy/lesson/visual-memory-definition-skills.html

https://www.cognifit.com/science/cognitive-skills/auditory

http://www.breakthroughlearningcollege.com/memory/auditory-memory/

http://www.breakthroughlearningcollege.com/memory/kinesthetic-memory/

http://www.breakthroughlearningcollege.com/memory/mnemonics/

https://www.wikihow.com/Enter-Alpha-State-of-Mind

https://blog.mindvalley.com/accelerated-learning/

https://litemind.com/memory-palace/

http://www.skillstoolbox.com/career-and-education-skills/learning-skills/memory-skills/mnemonics/verbal-mnemonics/

https://www.healthline.com/nutrition/11-brain-foods#section1

https://draxe.com/15-brain-foods-to-boost-focus-and-memory/

https://www.menshealth.com.au/six-super-drinks-to-boost-your-brainpower

https://www.verywellmind.com/how-sugar-affects-the-brain-4065218

https://www.brainhq.com/brain-resources/everyday-brain-fitness/physical-exercise

https://www.health.harvard.edu/blog/regular-exercise-changes-brain-improve-memory-thinking-skills-201404097110

https://www.shape.com/lifestyle/mind-and-body/13-mental-health-benefits-exercise

https://www.maxworkouts.com/articles/entry/4-exercises-that-improve-brain-function

https://onfit.edu.au/health-fitness-blog/the-importance-of-resting-your-mind/

https://www.sleepassociation.org/about-sleep/sleep-hygiene-tips/

https://www.sleepscore.com/caffeine-effect-sleep/

https://www.verywellmind.com/does-caffeine-improve-memory-21846

https://www.neurocorecenters.com/blog/4-common-memory-myths

https://www.independent.co.uk/life-style/health-and-families/sleep-myths-debunked-coffee-tips-snoring-tired-dreams-a8240456.html

https://www.daniel-wong.com/2015/08/17/study-smart/

https://www.cbc.ca/news/technology/exams-studying-tips-brain-science-1.3864360

https://www.wikihow.com/Use-Your-Whole-Brain-While-Studying

http://workwell.unum.com/2018/05/7-ways-keep-mind-sharp-work/

https://www.huffingtonpost.in/entry/work-productivity-hacks_us_56659888e4b079b2818f1f79

https://bebrainfit.com/brain-exercises/

https://www.health.harvard.edu/mind-and-mood/6-simple-steps-to-keep-your-mind-sharp-at-any-age

https://www.psychologytoday.com/intl/articles/200803/pitfalls-perfectionism

https://www.forbes.com/sites/forbescoachescouncil/2018/01/02/why-being-a-perfectionist-can-hold-you-back/#216e0b95d1df

https://www.mindtools.com/pages/article/learn-from-mistakes.htm

Brogaard, B. (2018). Basic and Complex Emotions. Retrieved from https://www.psychologytoday.com/us/blog/the-superhuman-mind/201806/basic-and-complex-emotions

Burton, N. (2015). Empathy Vs Sympathy. Retrieved from https://www.psychologytoday.com/us/blog/hide-and-seek/201505/empathy-vs-sympathy

Chang, Ph.D., L. (2019). Retrieved from https://www.mindfulnessmuse.com/dialectical-behavior-therapy/recognize-your-emotions-in-6-steps

Cherry, K. (2019). How to Read Body Language and Facial Expressions. Retrieved from https://www.verywellmind.com/understand-body-language-and-facial-expressions-4147228

Cherry, K. (2019). The 6 Types of Basic Emotions and Their Effect on Human Behavior. Retrieved from https://www.verywellmind.com/an-overview-of-the-types-of-emotions-4163976

Cherry, K. (2019). 5 Key Components of Emotional Intelligence. Retrieved from https://www.verywellmind.com/components-of-emotional-intelligence-2795438

Deutschendorf, H. (2019). Why Emotionally Intelligent People Are More Successful. Retrieved from https://www.fastcompany.com/3047455/why-emotionally-intelligent-people-are-more-successful

Freedman, J. (2019). Emotional Intelligence and Your Career: EQ for Talent Infographic. Retrieved from https://www.6seconds.org/2014/04/12/emotional-intelligence-career/

Fitzgerald, V. (2016). HuffPost is now a part of Oath. Retrieved from https://www.huffpost.com/entry/2-phrases-men-are-afraid-to-say-to-our-partners_b_5790d103e4b0a86259d0d6a6

Goleman, D. (2019). Emotional Intelligence - Daniel Goleman. Retrieved from http://www.danielgoleman.info/topics/emotional-intelligence/

Harra, Dr, C. (2013). 6 Tips For Holding It Together. Retrieved from https://www.huffpost.com/entry/controlling-your-emotions_b_3654326?guce_referrer=aHR0cHM6Ly93d3cuZ29vZ2xlLm5sLw&guce_referrer_sig=AQAAAE2VJ5HpWx-6XCz0tiKcGOF2Nmx0wQ8A_tqN0asbtR9Ui7YwrlIVb1dKZfjBKyuzbR7grv0py4u90RH5WWWLhGiS3yGpTlmynhiI90-4UR_cDMZvEDLntivfN8ubrqZPVSHFJjz32FeUStcI32BDwiFWMe426

e_0RIyQqgmaDPd3TWY&guccounter=2

Helpful vs Harmful: Ways to Manage Emotions. (2019). Retrieved from http://www.mentalhealthamerica.net/conditions/helpful-vs-harmful-ways-manage-emotions

Krauss Whitbourne, S. (2015). 5 Ways to Get Your Unwanted Emotions Under Control. Retrieved from https://www.psychologytoday.com/intl/blog/fulfillment-any-age/201502/5-ways-get-your-unwanted-emotions-under-control

Managing Your Emotions at Work: Controlling Your Feelings... Before They Control You. (2019). Retrieved from https://www.mindtools.com/pages/article/newCDV_41.htm

Schmitz, T. (2016). Empathy - Responding to Others | The Conover Company. Retrieved from https://www.conovercompany.com/empathy-responding-to-others/

Simons, I. (2009). Why Do We Have Emotions?. Retrieved from https://www.psychologytoday.com/us/blog/the-literary-mind/200911/why-do-we-have-emotions

The 3 Models. (2019). Retrieved from http://theimportanceofemotionalintelligence.weebly.com/the-3-models.html

www.ingramcontent.com/pod-product-compliance
Lightning Source LLC
Chambersburg PA
CBHW071950110526
44592CB00012B/1049